MULTIMEDIA HISTORIES

From the Magic Lantern to the Internet

Multimedia Histories is an important new sourcebook for all those working on cinema, digital arts, photography, videogames, optical toys, television and the history of media and screen practice.

The first book to explore in detail the vital connections between today's digital culture and the history of screen entertainments and technologies, it moves from the magic lantern, the stereoscope and early film to the DVD and the internet.

The book shows how our assessment of what we see as new and innovative in contemporary multimedia culture needs to be re-evaluated in the light of a rich history of pioneering media practices that reaches back to the nineteenth century.

James Lyons is Senior Lecturer in Film Studies in the School of English at Exeter University; he is author of *Selling Seattle: Representing Contemporary Urban America* (2004) and co-editor of *Quality Popular Television* (2003).

John Plunkett is Senior Lecturer in Victorian Literature in the School of English at Exeter University; he is author of *Queen Victoria: First Media Monarch* (2003) and editor (with Andrew King) of *Popular Print Media 1820–1900* (2004) and *Victorian Print Media: A Reader* (2005).

Exeter Studies in Film History

Series Editors: **Richard Maltby**, Professor of Screen Studies, Flinders University, South Australia and **Steve Neale**, Professor of Film Studies and Academic Director of the Bill Douglas Centre for the History of Cinema and Popular Culture, University of Exeter.

Parallel Tracks: The Railroad and Silent Cinema
Lynne Kirby (1997)

The World According to Hollywood, 1918–1939
Ruth Vasey (1997)

'Film Europe' and 'Film America': Cinema, Commerce and Cultural Exchange 1920–1939
edited by Andrew Higson and Richard Maltby (1999)

A Paul Rotha Reader
edited by Duncan Petrie and Robert Kruger (1999)

A Chorus of Raspberries: British Film Comedy 1929–1939
David Sutton (2000)

The Great Art of Light and Shadow: Archaeology of the Cinema
Laurent Mannoni, translated by Richard Crangle (2000)

Popular Filmgoing in 1930s Britain: A Choice of Pleasures
John Sedgwick (2000)

Alternative Empires: European Modernist Cinemas and Cultures of Imperialism
Martin Stollery (2000)

Hollywood, Westerns and the 1930s: The Lost Trail
Peter Stanfield (2001)

Young and Innocent? The Cinema in Britain 1896–1930
edited by Andrew Higson (2002)

Legitimate Cinema: Theatre Stars in Silent British Films 1908–1918
Jon Burrows (2003)

The Big Show: British Cinema Culture in the Great War (1914–1918)
Michael Hammond (2006)

University of Exeter Press also publishes the celebrated five-volume series looking at the early years of English cinema, *The Beginnings of the Cinema in England*, by John Barnes.

MULTIMEDIA HISTORIES

From the Magic Lantern to the Internet

edited by
James Lyons and John Plunkett

UNIVERSITY
of
EXETER
PRESS

Paperback cover image: concept created by the authors using an image from the Bill Douglas Centre, University of Exeter.

First published 2007 by
University of Exeter Press
Reed Hall, Streatham Drive
Exeter, Devon EX4 4QR
UK
www.exeterpress.co.uk
Reprinted 2008

British Library Cataloguing in Publication Data
A catalogue record for this book is available from the British Library

Paperback ISBN 978 0 85989 773 0
Hardback ISBN 978 0 85989 772 3

Typeset in 11½/13½pt Adobe Caslon by
Kestrel Data, Exeter, Devon

Printed in Great Britain by
Athenæum Press Ltd, Gateshead, Tyne and Wear

Contents

Figures

Acknowledgements

This book is the culmination of a project, *Screen Practice Before Film*, undertaken under the auspices of the AHRB Centre for British Film and Television Studies. We are indebted to the AHRB Centre for supporting both this book and the 2003 conference that formed the springboard for it. We are especially grateful to the Directors of the Centre, Laura Mulvey and Ian Christie, and to Hester Higton and Duncan Petrie, for all their encouragement and advice.

We should also like to acknowledge the inspiration and challenge provided by the collection of the Bill Douglas Centre at the University of Exeter, and the efforts of Peter Jewell and Bill Douglas in creating such an archive over many years. Research can rarely be as enjoyable or diverting as when it consists of using a ninteenth-century stereoscope, reading an early film fanzine, or rummaging through seventy years of Disney merchandising.

All effort has been made to contact copyright holders but in some cases this has not been possible. Any copyright holder who believes that due acknowledgement has not been given should contact the publishers.

Notes on Contributors

Isobel Armstrong is Emeritus Professor of English at Birkbeck College, University of London. She has published widely on nineteenth-century literature, especially poetry, and contemporary literary theory. Her books include *The Radical Aesthetic* (Blackwell, 2000) and *Victorian Poetry: Poetry, Poetics and Politics* (Routledge, 1993). She is completing a study of glass in nineteenth-century culture.

Kaveh Askari received his PhD from the University of Chicago. He is a Mellon Postdoctoral Fellow at the University of California, Berkeley, where he is conducting research on pictorial aesthetics in early American film theory.

James Bennett is Senior Lecturer in Media Studies at London Metropolitan University. He is completing his PhD on digital television, interactivity and public-service broadcasting at the University of Warwick. He is the author of 'The public service value of interactive television', *New Review of Film & Television Studies*, 4.3 (2006), and a number of reviews in *Screen*.

William Boddy is Professor in the Department of Communication Studies, Baruch College, City University of New York. His publications include *Fifties Television: The Industry and Its Critics* (University of Illinois Press, 1990) and *New Media and Popular Imagination: Launching Radio, Television, and Digital Media in the United States* (Oxford University Press, 2004), as well as scores of articles and book chapters on media history, digital media and film studies.

Jonathan Bollen lectures in Drama at Flinders University, Australia. Previously he was research fellow in theatre at the University of New England, Australia. His research on social dancing, performativity and desire has been published in *TDR: The Journal of Performance Studies and Australasian Drama Studies*, and in the collections *Dancing Desires: Choreographing Sexualities on and off the Stage* (University of Wisconsin Press, 2001) and *Body Show/s: Australian Viewings of Live Performance* (Rodopi, 2000).

Ian Christie is Anniversary Professor of Film and Media History at Birkbeck College, and from 2003 to 2005 was Director of the AHRB Centre for British Film and Television Studies. He has published many books and articles on British and European cinema, including *Gilliam on Gilliam* (Faber, 1999), *The Cinema of Michael Powell: International Perspectives on an English Film-maker*, co-edited with Andrew Moor (BFI, 2005) and *The Last Machine: Early Cinema and the Birth of the Modern World* (BBC/BFI, 1994).

Patrizia Di Bello lectures on the history and theory of photography in the School of History of Art, Film and Visual Media at Birkbeck College, University of London. She is working on a book on Victorian women's albums, and researching the interactions between photography and tactility.

Charlie Gere is Reader in New Media Research at the Institute for Cultural Research, University of Lancaster. He is the author of *Digital Culture* (Reaktion, 2002), *Art, Time and Technology* (Berg, 2006), and many essays on digital culture and new media.

Richard Grusin is Professor and Chair in the Department of English at Wayne State University. He is the author of three books: *Transcendental Hermeneutics: Institutional Authority and the Higher Criticism of the Bible* (Duke University Press, 1991); *Remediation: Understanding New Media*, co-authored with Jay David Bolter (MIT, 1999); and *Culture, Technology, and the Creation of America's National Parks* (Cambridge University Press, 2004). He is working on the social, political and aesthetic relationships among affect, film and new media after 9/11.

Michelle Henning is Senior Lecturer in the Department of Culture and Media Studies at the University of the West of England in Bristol. She has worked as a visual artist and published essays on photography and new media. She is the author of *Museums, Media and Cultural Theory* (Open University Press, 2006).

James Lyons is Senior Lecturer in Film at the University of Exeter. He is co-editor (with Mark Jancovich) of *Quality Popular Television* (BFI, 2003) and author of *Selling Seattle: Representing Contemporary Urban America* (Wallflower Press and Columbia University Press, 2004).

Laura Mulvey is Professor of Film and Media Studies at Birkbeck College, University of London. She is the author of *Visual and Other Pleasures* (Macmillan, 1989), *Fetishism and Curiosity* (BFI, 1996), and *Citizen Kane* (BFI, 1996). Her latest book is *Death 24 Times a Second: Stillness and the Moving Image* (Reaktion, 2005).

Dan North is a Lecturer in Film at the University of Exeter. He is author of *Performing Illusions: Special Effects and the Coming of the Virtual Actor* (Wallflower Press, forthcoming) and is editing a collection of essays on unfinished films.

John Plunkett is Senior Lecturer in Victorian culture at the University of Exeter. He is author of *Queen Victoria—First Media Monarch* (Oxford University Press, 2003), and co-editor of *Popular Print Media 1820–1900* (Routledge, 2004) and *Victorian Print Media: A Reader* (Oxford University Press, 2005). He is working on a book concerning nineteenth-century optical recreations and early screen entertainment.

Andrew Shail is News International Research Fellow in Film at St Anne's College, Oxford University. In addition to articles on early British film culture, he has authored chapters in *Third Wave Feminism* (Palgrave, 2004) and *The Matrix Trilogy: Cyberpunk Reloaded* (Wallflower, 2005) and co-edited *Menstruation: A Cultural History* (Palgrave, 2005). His current work includes a monograph investigating the origins of the modern superhero.

Damian Sutton is Lecturer in the Department of Historical and Critical Studies at Glasgow School of Art. He has published pieces on cinema, photography, television and new media in several books and journals, and is the author of *Cinema, Photography, Time* (University of Minnesota Press, forthcoming).

Andrea Zapp is a media artist and theorist and Senior Lecturer and Media Arts (MA) Course Leader for the School of Art & Design/ MIRIAD at Manchester Metropolitan University. She has edited *Networked Narrative Environments as Imaginary Spaces of Being* (Manchester Metropolitan University/FACT Liverpool, 2004) and co-edited (with Martin Rieser) *New Screen Media, Cinema/Art/Narrative* (BFI and ZKM Karlsruhe, 2002). www.azapp.de.

Foreword

Laura Mulvey

The years leading up to the new millennium, which were also the years succeeding the centenary of cinema, have seen digital technology precipitate one of the great media revolutions of history. Technological change brings with it changes in human perception and understanding: the material cannot exist outside the conceptual. In this fascinating collection of essays, historians and theorists respond to both technological and perceptual aspects of the revolution. A period of transition could be seen as a one-way street, in which the past disappears from sight as the future appropriates the present. This book, however, takes as its point of departure that the shock of change should generate, rather, the idea of a threshold, on which the presence of the future demands also a look backwards at the past. An insistence on a consideration of the past, in the face of a rush to the future, implies that a pause on the threshold offers a principled, even political, opportunity for reflection.

In this book the backward look is revealed to have a further and particular relevance for understanding visual and audio media. Like the shifting patterns of a kaleidoscope, these relations between new and old technologies produce surprising new configurations in which the optical media of the nineteenth century link with the digital media of the twenty-first. In the first instance, these links emerge out of a changed perception of the history of cinema. While cinema was in command of the way forward, in technology, art and entertainment, all that came before it could be lumped together as 'pre-cinema'. Now, though, it exists as one technology among others, and one that is increasingly associated with its dominance throughout the twentieth century. The significance and status of cinema has shifted. In the era of 'post-cinema', the 'pre' era demands new approaches and analyses, and these are brilliantly articulated in the *Multimedia Histories* collection. To read these essays is to experience the field of new media scholarship in the exciting process of moving forward, engaging with the difficulty of understanding change, but through a crucial detour into history.

The case studies in the book bring out certain aesthetic lessons that may be well known in principle but should be reiterated in threshold moments such as this. For instance, the discourses in which technological change is realized tend to be anachronistic: familiar types of images and ideas continue to be produced by revolutionary technologies. In this sense, even the most commercial investments in the media of the future are seen to be hesitating on the threshold of the present. At the same time, as cinema's bold defining profile fades into a new alignment, the media that prefigured it are freed into their differentiated forms and histories to find affinities with the heterogeneity of contemporary media, challenging a linear, chronological concept of history. 'No fact that is a cause is for that very reason historical. It became historical posthumously, as it were, through events that may be separated from it by thousands of years. A historian who takes this as his point of departure stops telling the sequence of events like the beads of a rosary. Instead, he grasps the constellation which his own era has formed with an earlier one.'[1] Although, in this case, historians are not dealing with 'thousands of years', Walter Benjamin's image of the historian finding unexpected links across time seems most apposite for this book, especially as time itself seems to gather speed into the fast approaching future.

Introduction

The rapid evolution and expansion of multimedia culture has been one of the most profound and exciting developments of recent times. Advances in digital technology—the internet, mobile phones, DVDs, video games—are changing the way many of us live, work and play. The far-reaching impact of digital media, though, needs to be balanced against the fact that they are part of a long and fascinating genealogy of multimedia usage. Although this extended history is often acknowledged in scholarly work on contemporary new media, the actualities of its continuities and faultlines have only been cursorily elaborated. *Multimedia Histories* demonstrates the vital connections between digital culture and an absorbing history of screen and audio technologies. It explores the links between nineteenth-, twentieth- and twenty-first-century multimedia practices. In so doing, it aims to rethink past and present media through their relationship to each other.

From the early nineteenth century onwards, the proliferation of visual and audio technologies has been a key element of popular culture. The everyday presence of numerous media meant that their production and consumption was defined by their interrelationship. It is for this reason that, rather than simply focusing on the 'newness' of new media, we have chosen to examine the *multi*-media character of devices ranging from the stereoscope to television. New media do not remain new for very long: they soon become part of the constantly changing ensemble of forms that make up the media landscape. Moreover, as numerous critics have noted, new media invariably draw upon, refashion and attempt to improve existing aesthetics and technologies.[1] They are always already embedded in social and cultural contexts. Jay David Bolter and Richard Grusin have cogently noted that '[w]hat is new about new media comes from the particular ways in which they refashion older media and the way in which older media refashion themselves according to the challenge of new media'.[2] Their impact is thus always relationally-determined: claims of greater immediacy and interactivity for users, a more enhanced realism, or greater speed of communication are always dependent on the scope and limits of existing media.

It is argued frequently that contemporary digital media are characterized by their propensity towards convergence, remediation and intermediality.[3] These recently coined terms, which emphasize related phenomena, describe processes of fusion and crossover between discrete media. *Multimedia Histories* explores these concepts but extends them to the long history of screen practice. It thereby locates new media within an intermedial tradition of public and domestic forms of screen entertainment; however, it simultaneously calls into question the teleology sometimes evident in popular and scholarly accounts of contemporary media. As Mark Poster has argued, 'The conceptual problem is to enable a historical differentiation of old and new without initialising a totalising narrative.'[4] The essays, individually and collectively, attempt to address this question: their concerns are historiographic as well as historical.

Multimedia Histories proceeds necessarily from a broad and generous understanding of its subject. Essays include work on automata, digital art, wireless radio, curiosity cabinets and early film exhibition. The collection also points towards the diversity of the social, political and aesthetic ramifications of multimedia history: essays examine issues such as the boundaries of the human (Dan North's essay on the virtual actor), the political role of the military in designing new communications media (Charlie Gere's essay on John Cage), and the racial implications of moving-image technologies (Jonathan Bollen's essay on popular dancing). So open-ended is the field of multimedia history that this collection can only be a small contribution to a burgeoning area of enquiry. Strictly speaking, the number of *multi*-media phenomena is almost boundless. Nonetheless, despite the potential range of subject matter, the essays share a common aim in their desire to rethink the boundaries of film and media history.

Multimedia Histories is made up of sixteen short essays, a mixture of historical and theoretical case studies. The essays are grouped into four sections, each section dealing with a key concept that has emerged in recent work on new media. The collection demonstrates these concepts' applicability to the long history of screen practice, but also uses historical examples to critique some of their underlying assumptions. Section Two, for example, uses the idea of remediation to explore the links between 'old' and 'new' formats. The sections are organized conceptually rather than chronologically to emphasize the links between media from different periods. Rather than flattening historical differences so that 'new media' are prefigured or anticipated by 'old media', sections create unexpected constellations, to use Walter Benjamin's phrase, which cause us to rethink both past and present.

The proliferation of new media forms has invariably produced equal measures of excitement and anxiety concerning their influence. Whether it be the telegraph in the 1880s or the internet in the 1990s, they have almost by definition been ascribed an overdetermined social or technological agency. Section One engages with this central question of influence. The section has a double focus in that it demonstrates the impact of new media—the way they re-envision the world—while simultaneously addressing the problem of how to avoid teleological histories. Essays thus provide examples of the way cinema, radio and computing have affected conceptions of time, perception and social community, as registered through fields as diverse as enlightenment philosophy and avant-garde music. Conversely, however, the essays also call attention to the way these narratives of transition and innovation are often self-interested. They structurally repress the way new media are indebted to existing social contexts. Continuities exist because new media appropriate established formats or are assimilated into long-standing patterns of usage and consumption. Section One correspondingly suggests methods of recovering the longevity of many beliefs and practices relating to multimedia history.

Ian Christie's opening essay calls for a historical approach that pays more attention to the role of material artefacts, whether philosophical toys such as the kaleidoscope or the cinematograph itself. This approach quickly raises an important epistemological question: what is at stake in describing something as a device, toy, gadget, instrument or machine? Taxonomies have significant implications in how we understand artefacts because not only do terms such as 'toy' change their meaning over time, an artefact that starts off as a 'toy' can soon metamorphose into a 'machine'. It is both artefacts and the discursive paradigms from which they emerge that need to be rescued from the condescension of posterity.

Christie's essay is a salutary reminder of the way taxonomies are continuously repressing and rewriting aspects of the history of moving-image technology. His concern with teleological histories is furthered by

William Boddy's critique of the overstated claims concerning the convergence of contemporary digital media. Boddy traces a long genealogy of popular responses to new electronic media in the United States, from wireless radio in the 1920s to the internet in the 1990s, whereby their advent was used to bolster conservative ideas of rural identity and community.

Questions of teleology often go hand in hand with the issue of technological determinism. To what extent is aesthetic and social change driven by new technologies? What is the relationship between the material and perceptual? The remaining two essays in Section One are both concerned with the way that new imaging technology affects our understanding of the human sensorium. Damian Sutton traces the impact of the cinematograph upon the philosophy of perception developed by Henri Bergson at the end of the nineteenth century. Charlie Gere's essay is similarly concerned with the impact of new technology upon perceptions of time, speed and human attention, albeit in the very different context of 1950s Cold War America and the threat of nuclear war. Notably, both Boddy and Gere demonstrate that new media concern the reproduction of sound—the auditory imagination—as much as the visual illusion of movement. Gere focuses on the way computers, radar and cybernetics—as real-time military communications systems—fed into the performance of John Cage's famous silent piece, *4' 33"*.

Section Two draws together diverse examples of how new media have worked to refashion pre-existing artistic forms. Usefully conceptualized by Bolter and Grusin as *remediation*, this process reminds us not only that new media technologies are invariably introduced into aesthetic and social contexts that shape their contours, but that those new media appropriate and transform the facets of earlier arts. As these prior media forms are remediated, their place in our culture is inevitably refashioned, and in ways that often require us to rethink the experiential, institutional and ideological frameworks in which we encounter them. The essays in this section demonstrate the heterogeneous contexts in which the logic of remediation takes place. In so doing, they also enable us to identify significant continuities in the way media artefacts from different periods create the illusion of reality, address the viewer/user, and represent space, time and movement.

Patrizia Di Bello's essay opens the section with a consideration of one of our most familiar experiences of representational mediation across space and time, namely the photographs we take of the people we love.

Comparing the nineteenth-century family album with collections of digital photographs viewed and exchanged via the computer screen, Di Bello questions assumptions regarding the importance of the indexical trace of a beloved to the emotional investment in photographs. Pointing out the playful manipulation of the indexical in the construction of the nineteenth-century album, Di Bello illustrates the fact that photograph collections have always been multimedial. The loving care taken over the assemblage of albums, both nineteenth-century and digital, demonstrates that the popular social functions of photography are central to understanding its continuing appeal and significance.

Di Bello's essay also alerts us to an aspect of new media usage that is often neglected, namely the 'touch' and 'feel' of the objects we fashion, and considers whether such appeals to tactility are expunged in the realm of the virtual. Michelle Henning concerns herself with the survival of another, rather different, mode of engagement within computer-based delivery of information and images, and asks whether the World Wide Web might be seen to have re-ignited a return to a 'curiosity' culture first established in the curiosity cabinets of the sixteenth to eighteenth centuries, and which flourished in the popular curio museums of the nineteenth century. Henning situates the Web as a site for redeeming the chaotic, arbitrary character of curious looking suppressed by the schematized, rationalized ordering of the modern museum (and, ironically, the archiving techniques and military systems from which the internet emerged), while remaining wary of the potential for curiosity as a mode of attention to be manipulated for political ends.

Dan North exerts a similarly cautious fascination with another instance of digital remediation in his discussion of the myths that have accompanied the appearance of virtual actors on our cinema screens in recent years, and the confident claim that the 'synthespian' will one day replace human actors. North links such futurological myths with comparable stories that emerged during a period of interest in automata and androids in the eighteenth and nineteenth centuries. He alerts us to the recurring tropes of anthropomorphic masquerade and the fascination with the visualization of the scientific principles of performative human movement that characterize both of these periods, and serve to keep us enthralled. Jonathan Bollen's discussion of the relationship between moving-image technologies and the cultural politics of social dancing rounds off the section with another perspective on the dissemination of models of human movement, this time to meet the shifting kinaesthetic demands of the twentieth-century dance floor.

Anyone familiar with the perennial battles between the manufacturers of the video-game consoles that now generate more revenue than the Hollywood film industry will recognize claims for more immersive and embodied entertainment experiences as core to their competing appeals to potential consumers. Such appeals can be situated historically as one of the recurring features of our relationship with screen shows, toys and practices. Section Three explores the phenomenology of nineteenth- and twentieth-century screen entertainments, and outlines some of the diverse ways in which the desire to constitute interactive experiences has been reproduced. For example, John Plunkett's discussion of the stereo-scope, the nineteenth century's most popular optical toy, opens the section by situating it within a genealogy of prior and subsequent optical recreations seeking to create the embodied experience of immersive viewing, while Andrew Shail's essay on the popular discourses accompanying Britain's first cinema-building boom of 1908–14 underlines the complex negotiations with the class-based spectatorial practices associated with prior phases of entertainment, in particular that of the penny gaff.

Shail's essay reminds us that the 'sensational' nature of interactive entertainment, from the waxwork 'chamber of horrors' to *Grand Theft Auto*, often produces ideologically-fraught institutional and cultural anxieties regarding the social groups which consume them. These anxieties, moreover, afflict 'respectable' as well as populist media forms. James Bennett's examination of digital television provides an opportunity to consider the challenges interactive entertainment provides for what is arguably the most august of broadcasting institutions, namely the BBC. Looking at the corporation's launch of *Walking with Beasts*, one of its first forays into interactive television programmes, Bennett locates the show in the long history of natural-history display as a site of complex negotiation balancing the interests of education, spectacle and profit. As he points out, building interactivity into natural-history programming challenges the BBC to navigate the competing demands of edification and amusement in the context of discourses of public-service broad-casting in the digital era.

One of the most exciting ways in which the potentialities of digital interactivity have been examined in recent years is in the designing of works of art that explore the relationship between real and virtual spaces. Andrea Zapp's essay explains how her own artistic practice and research involve designing creative environments for user participation. Zapp's range of 'networked narrative environments', interactive for physical and

remote visitors, explores questions of creative participation and performance, and considers the moral and epistemological issues that physically
remote yet emotionally immersive virtual sites raise for artists and users
alike.

Along with 'interactivity', 'convergence' is probably the other term
most often used to characterize the impact of digital media. Where
Section Three called attention to the fuzziness of many rhetorical claims
for 'interactivity', Section Four encourages a similar type of reflection
through historical examples of different processes of media convergence.
In contemporary media practice, 'convergence' stands for the dominance
of fusion and transferability between different forms. As Henry Jenkins
has noted, we are in an era in which media are always used in relation to
each other:

> Our cell phones are not simply telecommunications devices; they
> also allow us to play games, download information from the internet
> and receive and send photographs or text messages. Any of these
> functions can also be performed through other media appliances.
> One can listen to The Dixie Chicks through a DVD player, car
> radio, walkman, computer MP3 files, a web radio station or a music
> cable channel . . . A teenager doing homework may juggle four or
> five windows, scanning the web, listening to and downloading MP3
> files, chatting with friends, wordprocessing a paper and responding
> to email, shifting rapidly between tasks.[5]

Convergence is usually thought of in relation to the impact of digital
technology. Yet against this contemporary focus, essays by Isobel
Armstrong and Kaveh Askari provide historical examples of the way
aesthetic forms circulate between different media. They also implicitly
challenge contemporary assertions of convergence, which often assume
that already-existing aesthetic and technological forms are distinct
and singular. Armstrong's opening essay, which can be related to the
questions of influence considered in Section One, concerns an unexpected crossover between literary and optical forms. Through a
detailed reading of the elaborate tropes of Alfred Tennyson's 'The Lady
of Shalott', Armstrong demonstrates the optical technologies immanent
to a poem she describes as 'one of the great lyrics of nineteenth-century
modernity'. In 'The Lady of Shalott', poetry takes upon itself the
aesthetics of the mirror, lens, magic lantern and camera obscura.

Askari reflects on multimedia historiography through the career of photographer and lanternist Alexander Black, whose 'picture plays' debuted in New York in 1894. The picture play combined the pictorialist tradition of privileged dramatic moments with the discontinuous instants created by photography and cinema. Black does not fit easily into an evolutionary version of cinema history, in part because, as Askari notes, he demonstrates that 'moments of convergence are shaped by discursive factors as much as by technical innovations.'

Two other aspects of media convergence come to the fore in the essays by Richard Grusin and James Lyons. The first is that of economic convergence, whereby—thanks to the increasingly horizontal integration of the entertainment industry—large international conglomerates have transmedia commercial interests including film, television, music, computer games and the internet. Inevitably related to this is the transmedia production and consumption of narratives, characters and brands. Convergence means that users move easily between different media while simultaneously engaging with the demands of each format. Jenkins has argued that this crossover is fostered as much by the creativity of individual users as by large entertainment conglomerates: access to multiple media 'fosters a new participatory folk culture by giving average people the tools to archive, annotate, appropriate and recirculate content'.[6]

Richard Grusin describes the aesthetic and technological convergence between cinema and digital technology. He poses the idea of contemporary cinema being a 'cinema of interactions', playing off Tom Gunning's well-known description of early film as a 'cinema of attractions'. Grusin's cinema of interactions describes the way DVDs, video games and the internet have impinged upon the aesthetics of cinema to a degree that determines the way films are conceived of, produced and consumed. Using examples ranging from blockbusters such as *Star Wars: Episode II – Attack of the Clones* to experimental work such as Mike Figgis's *Timecode*, Grusin argues that film as a distinctive medium is being superseded by film as a distributed form of mediation. Lyons' essay similarly focuses on transmedia production and consumption through the website accompanying FX Network's successful series 'Nip/Tuck' (FX Network being a subsidiary of Fox TV, itself part of News Corporation). Through considering users' engagement with the website's interactive cosmetic surgery 'games', Lyons reflects upon the congruence between the way screen and medical technologies remediate the body.

Taken together, the essays illustrate the fact that the plenitude of our current media landscape alerts us, paradoxically, to the material and phenomenological boundaries of the previously dominant visual media, cinema and television, as well as the plethora of nineteenth-century optical recreations. Contemporary intermediality often seems more akin to the creative melting-pot of early screen practices than to the formalized character of the Classical Hollywood studio system. It has now become customary to assert that panoramas, dioramas, magic lanterns, peepshows and stereoscopes were not inevitable forerunners of cinema; and a notable volume of recent work has begun to excavate the fullness of the nineteenth century's technological fascination with movement, optical illusion, sound, magic and the physiology of vision (and the popular devices and shows that fostered this attraction).[7] The impetus of such work, though, probably owes as much to contemporary media as to reinvigorated historical scholarship. Just as digital culture has unconsciously encouraged greater sensitivity towards the past, the examination of prior modes of screen practice has, in its turn, produced a standpoint to reflect upon recent mediamorphosis.[8] *Multimedia Histories* generates a creative friction between past and present, and reminds us that for all their propelling us forward into the world of the future, digital media also open up new genealogies, and allow hitherto unknown cultural formations to emerge.

James Lyons
John Plunkett

Section One

Culture, Aesthetics and the Influence
of New Media

1

Toys, Instruments, Machines
Why the Hardware Matters

Ian Christie

A machine was a thing made up of distinguishable 'parts', organised in imitation of some part of the human body. Machines were said to 'work'.

Hollis Frampton.[1]

For Peter Jewell

What were moving pictures *for*? I raise the question in order to explore a theme which is in danger of being obscured by the obvious fact that moving-picture apparatus quickly became the means to fulfil a number of purposes: to produce entertainment and to a lesser extent instruction. In this sense, it joined the ranks of machines—apparatuses with a 'definite function' (according to part of the *Oxford English Dictionary* definition, of which more later)—and became correspondingly invisible. Or, rather, the history of cameras, projectors and sound recorders became a matter for connoisseurship or for engineering history, rather than one likely to interest historians of the medium of cinema, whether aesthetic, social or ideological. What does it matter *how* the image is produced and delivered, once it has been sufficiently standardized to attract no interest in itself—except perhaps when it malfunctions?[2]

If we believe this, then collecting historic cinema apparatus or the various optical instruments, gadgets and toys that preceded and accompanied its rise to dominance is merely antiquarian. However curious or

3

valuable they may be as objects, they will not tell us anything about the experience of cinema. However, I want to argue against such an idealist position, and to assert a materialist history based on taking into account the machinery as well as its products; and on seeing cinema as part of a continuing tradition of spectacle and illusion, rather than as a separate art with a 'pre-history'. Part of my argument will take the kaleidoscope as an example of an instrument which appears, to us at least, to have no 'purpose'.

But let us return to the question of what moving pictures were 'for'. The simplest answer is that they demonstrated the successful achievement of animated photography. They were self-referential or reflexive, in the way that the phonograph or electrical lighting was primarily the demonstration of an achievement before it was a means to some end.[3] Such expectations are clear from the terms of press reports during the early months of projected film shows (terms are italicized for emphasis):

THE CINÉMATOGRAPHE, which is the invention of MM. A. and L. Lumière, is a *contrivance* belonging to the same family as Edison's Kinetoscope and the old 'Wheel of Life,' but in a rather higher state of development. The spectator no longer gazes through a narrow aperture at the changing picture, but has it presented to him full size on a large screen. The principle, however, is much the same, consisting simply of passing rapidly before the eye a series of pictures representing the successive stages of the action or the changing scene that has to be reproduced.[4]

Edison's beautiful optical *instrument*, the kinetoscope, has now become known to most people through its exhibition in various large towns.[5]

Animated lantern pictures are still the rage, for not only are there four different *machines* or projection *apparatus* being publicly exhibited at the present time in London, but these are being duplicated at the east and west ends, besides arrangements being in progress for provincial exhibitions.[6]

Another reason for paying close attention to such early reports is to note their terminology. The terms used by both the nonspecialist and professional press of 1896 range across 'invention', 'contrivance', 'instrument', 'machine', 'apparatus'. They are evocative of a period of intense development or 'perfecting' (a favourite Edison term) of basic mechanisms in order to fulfil their aim or potential.[7] There was indeed considerable contemporary amusement at the proliferation of pompous terminology, as evidenced in another 1896 press report that spoke of 'the new thing with the long name and the old thing with the name that isn't much shorter',[8] while the many variations on '. . . graph' already seemed absurd to the *British Journal of Photography* by the summer of that year. There would also be commercial considerations relating to proprietary names and legal ones relating to patented principles. But was there any significance in something being described as an 'instrument' or a 'machine' rather than a 'toy', as the *New York Times* called Edison's first projector in April 1896?

> The new thing at Koster and Bial's last night was Edison's vitascope, exhibited for the first time. The ingenious inventor's latest toy is a projection of his kinetoscope figures in stereopticon fashion, upon a white screen in a darkened hall.[9]

In the turn-of-the-century worldview, an instrument had a purpose. According to the 1910 edition of the *OED*, it is 'a material thing designed . . . for the accomplishment of some mechanical or other physical effect', which stands somewhere between a 'tool . . . used by a workman or artisan' and a machine, distinguished from this by 'having less mechanism', although, as the dictionary warned, 'the terms overlap'.[10] This ambiguity could equally apply to the status of moving picture devices in 1896. Lacking as yet any established use, these were exhibited for the entertainment and instruction of spectators, just as a long line of optical devices known as optical toys had been throughout the nineteenth century and earlier. However, by the end of the century, 'toy' was already restricted to the juvenile or trivial connotations we know today. Webster's definition in 1913 was 'a plaything for children . . . A thing for amusement, but of no real value';[11] while the 1910 *OED* offered within 'concrete senses': 'a material object for children or others to play with (often an imitation of some familiar object) . . . something contrived for amusement rather than practical use', noting that 'this is now the leading sense, to which others are referred'.[12]

It had not always been the leading sense; and the possibility of tracing shifts in the usage of this and other words was the result of another quintessentially Victorian enterprise, the study of the history of language, as part of a general preoccupation with classification which would serve

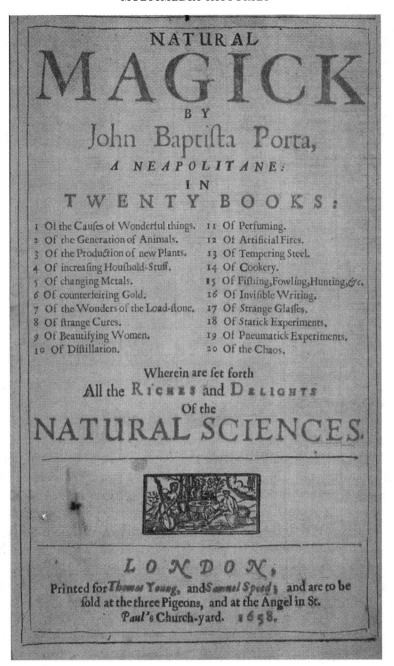

Fig. 1. John Baptista Porta (Giambattista della Porta), *Natural Magick in Twenty Books: Wherein are set forth All the Riches and Delights of the Natural Sciences* (London: Thomas Young and Samuel Speed, 1658), frontispiece. Courtesy of the Bill Douglas Centre, University of Exeter.

the new sciences of the era.[13] The 1910 *OED* history of the word 'toy' is revealing. Not only is the word's origin uncertain, but after a single recorded use in 1303, it seems to 'disappear for two centuries, and then . . . all at once burst into view with a wide sense-development'. This explosion of use in the sixteenth century ranges across 'fantastic acts and practices', jests and jokes, lively phrases of melody and odd conceits—all of which indicate how central concepts of fantasy and play were to Elizabethan culture.[14] Equally central, and related, was a fascination with magic; and the distinction between supernatural and natural forms of magic, although insisted on by such practitioners of the latter as Giambattista della Porta, was often hard to maintain. According to della Porta's bestseller, *Natural Magick*:

> There are two sorts of Magick; the one is infamous, and unhappy, because it has to do with foul Spirits, and consists of incantations and wicked curiosity; and this is called Sorcery; an art which all learned and good men detest; neither is it able to yield an truth of reason or nature, but stands merely upon fancies and imaginations . . . The other Magick is natural; which all excellent wise men do admit and embrace, and worship with great applause.[15]

Despite the protestations of della Porta and many other Renaissance scholars, such distinctions would remain hard to maintain, not least because of the fascination of the 'infamous' magic; and since the pioneering work of Frances Yates on the Elizabethan magus John Dee and on Giordano Bruno, it has become commonplace to acknowledge the continued co-habitation of magic and early science.[16] Something of this fascination was surely present in the following century's preoccupation with what became known as 'philosophical toys'. The most celebrated of these took the form of ingenious machines, initially imitating animals, as in the gardens of the Villa d'Este at Tivoli and the Villa Pratolino near Florence, where an early seventeenth-century English traveller described how

> the birds do sing, sitting upon twigs, so naturally, as one would verily think they were all quick and living birds . . . and, when they are in the midst of their best singing, then comes an owl flying: and the birds suddenly, all at once, are still.[17]

The birds' mechanical nature was dramatically revealed by their sudden immobility. Later mechanical marvels would aim at a more integral emulation of living behaviour, as in the celebrated excreting duck made by Jacques de Vaucanson and various humanoid automata such as Vaucanson's flautist, Pierre Jaquet-Droz's automatic writer and his son Henri-Louis's harpist, whose eyes 'followed' the music.[18] In Vienna, Wolfgang von Kempelen created two of the marvels of the age in his talking machine and chess player of 1783.

What gave this range of ingenious machines their scientific or 'philosophical' status was the speculation among such philosophers as Hume, Descartes and Bayle on whether animals, or even human bodies, could be regarded as machines, uniquely animated in the latter case by the possession of a soul. The ability of man-made automata to reproduce animal and human behaviour made this seem more likely, and helped to focus such debates around devices which were also entertaining and costly. Derek Price was one of the first scholars in the history of science and technology to argue that these mechanical marvels, like their ancestors in the ancient world, were not intended to be 'practical' or even strictly illusory.[19] Their appeal was rather aesthetic, or exemplary. They demonstrated principles and possibilities, such as those first proposed by the Greek philosopher and scientist Hero in his *Pneumatics*, which was widely studied as both a work of early physics and a guide to 'natural magic', which included phenomena relating to magnetism, change of state and optical illusion. Daniel Tiffany has summed up this complex of ideology and practice in his wide-ranging study of 'materialism and modern lyric', *Toy Medium*, arguing that the tradition of 'philosophical atomism' or materialism had long made use of 'a discourse of automated —and spectacular—"proofs"'.[20]

By the nineteenth century, such proofs had begun to assume more modest and didactic forms, and 'toy' was moving closer to its modern sense of something manual which is 'played with'. The sequence of specifically kinetic optical toys, as distinct from the static images of the magic lantern and the peep show, is usually traced from the launch of the thaumatrope and the phenakistoscope in the 1820s. Both of these were inspired, or at least explained, by Peter Mark Roget's 1824 paper, 'Explanation of an optical deception in the appearance of the spokes of a wheel seen through vertical apertures', and by Michael Faraday's subsequent demonstration of the consequences of afterimages, or the persistence of vision, with what became known as 'Faraday's wheel'.[21] All of these followed from the fundamental studies of vision initiated by Newton, Goethe and others, concerned with questions about how physiology conditions what we see. Human vision had become a form of 'apparatus', with specific limitations and properties, which were demonstrated by the paradoxes of the thaumatrope and phenakistoscope. Charles Wheatstone was the inventor of another such device, the kaleidophone, and defined the rationale of the modern philosophical toy in 1827:

> The application of the principles of science to ornamental and amusing purposes contributes, in a greater degree, to render them extensively popular; for the exhibition of striking experiments induces the observer to investigate their causes with additional interest, and enables him more permanently to remember their effects.[22]

Wheatstone's instrument or 'toy', which traced illuminated figures in space, was named after the recent and highly successful kaleidoscope; and I want to focus on this because it is something we now hardly think of as an instrument at all. If an instrument has by definition a purpose, a

Fig. 2. Tabletop kaleidoscope, c.1850.
Courtesy of the Bill Douglas Centre, University of Exeter.

use, then it is difficult to see what this could be in the case of the kaleidoscope with its display of ever-changing abstract patterns. Chronologically, it pre-dates the other nineteenth-century devices, having been invented in 1815 by the Scottish natural philosopher David Brewster. Brewster was working on optics and on crystallography, and his interest in angles of refraction and mirroring would lead him to anticipate the development of the Fresnel dioptric lens, which became standard equipment in lighthouses. As he noted in his 1819 treatise on the kaleidoscope, the device emerged by chance from his experimental practice: 'The first idea of this instrument presented itself to me in the year 1814, in the course of a series of experiments in the polarisation of light by successive reflections between plates of glass . . .' Brewster realized this could become a device that would produce an infinite range of symmetrical aesthetic patterns, and named it from a combination of the Greek words *kalos* (beautiful), *eidos* (form) and *scop* (to see). He proceeded to patent and develop it, while admitting that 'in its simplest form [it] could not be considered as a general philosophical instrument of universal application'. But it caused a sensation when marketed in 1816 and Brewster felt able to declare it a 'popular instrument for the purposes of rational amusement'.[23] He also argued that it had many practical applications, such as producing patterns for tiles, carpets and other forms of interior decoration.

> The Kaleidoscope will assume the character of the highest class of machinery, which improves at the same time as it abridges the exertions of individuals . . . it will create in an hour what a thousand artists could not create in a year.[24]

Here is a striking case of terminological slippage, from 'philosophical' to 'popular' instrument, and to 'machine'—all referring to the same device considered within different frames of reference. Yet the kaleidoscope is hardly a machine in the modern sense, lacking even the mechanism of the phenakistoscope or later, more complex, optical devices. It is strictly personal, activated by handling, and belongs to the object-type or instrument family that includes the telescope and the microscope.[25] Somewhat like the latter, the kaleidoscope reveals a microcosmic 'world' to the viewer, even if it is an artificial one.

Jonathan Crary has claimed, in his influential *Techniques of the Observer*, that Brewster's 'justification for making the kaleidoscope was productivity and efficiency', since it offered a 'mechanical means for the reformation of art according to an industrial paradigm'.[26] But a reading less influenced by Foucault's preoccupation with mechanisms of coercion and modernization might acknowledge Brewster's utilitarian rationalization, while noting his equal emphasis on 'amusement' and instruction. From his research in crystallography and physiology, Brewster was well aware of nature's underlying symmetry, as revealed by the microscope and now simulated by the kaleidoscope. Brewster stood on the threshold of the era when machinery was expected to be labour-saving and profitable. And as a Scot his hopes for the kaleidoscope as a pattern generator reflect the importance of textile weaving and carpet making in Scotland in the early nineteenth century, the recent innovation of the Jacquard loom making pattern variety both possible and commercially vital.[27] But Brewster also had his roots in the tradition of the philosophical toy as a precision instrument designed to impress with its craftsmanship and ingenuity, while demonstrating some basic principles which might be scientific but also moral.

Helen Weston has shown how another key optical device, the magic lantern, could signify either illusion or illumination, depending on the political context, and how it stood for both during the French Revolution.[28] The kaleidoscope similarly became a polemical figure for Marx and Engels, in their critique of Saint-Simon in *The German Ideology*, as 'a kaleidoscopic display . . . composed entirely of reflections of itself'.[29] For the poet Charles Baudelaire, however, it offered an emblem of modernity, a trope for the dandy's experience of urban life.

> [the dandy] moves into the crowd as though into an enormous reservoir of electricity. He, the lover of life, may also be compared to a mirror as vast as this crowd; to a kaleidoscope endowed with consciousness, with which every one of its movements presents a pattern of life, in all its multiplicity . . .[30]

Not only did Baudelaire link the kaleidoscope with the newer technology of electricity, but he postulated a purposeful 'conscious' instrument which might represent a 'pattern of life'. The temptation is strong to read this as an anticipation of the cinema's ability to represent the crowd; and yet it is equally important to resist this if we want to understand the *mentalité* of the mid-century and the place of optical toys within it.[31] In a slightly earlier essay, Baudelaire described at length the effect produced by the phenakistoscope with its decomposed images of a dancer or juggler which unite into one moving figure.[32] Such 'scientific toys', he observes, can develop in the child's brain 'a taste for marvellous and surprising effects'.

In spite of Brewster's hopes for the kaleidoscope as an aid to industry, there is little evidence that it became so. However, it did not disappear —despite Crary's assumption to the contrary—but joined the stereoscope, which enjoyed an even greater popular success in the 1850s, as a staple 'toy' continuing to be produced in a vast range of variations up to

Fig. 3.   Foldout stereoscope, *c.*1870.
Courtesy of the Bill Douglas Centre, University of Exeter.

the present day.[33] But if Crary is clearly right that we cannot 'know what the stereoscope looked like to a nineteenth-century viewer', can we still recover the fascination that remains in diluted form today in our very different sensory world? In part, we may be able to do so when the conjunction of apparatus and image is sufficiently unusual to short-circuit the sense of condescension that often accompanies such exercises. I can vividly recall seeing a series of stereo views of Western Front trenches in a Somme battlefield museum which made me feel 'closer' to the experience than anything I have seen in any other medium. In the absence of such personal experience, we may have to resort to collecting written evidence. One such account of the kaleidoscope is particularly valuable in challenging our sense that it offers only fleeting diversion. In his autobiography, André Gide recalled his fascination with 'that worker of marvels called a kaleidoscope', which would have been in the 1870s (Gide was born in 1869). He describes how the shifting of the patterns 'filled me with unspeakable delight', and lists the colours and shapes, before drawing a distinction between how his girl cousins used the toy, shaking and turning it 'to get a complete change', while he preferred to turn it slowly and savour the process of change. Gide also recounts how his fascination led to his taking the kaleidoscope apart, removing some of the pieces of glass, and replacing them with objects such as a nib, a fly's wing and a blade of grass, which produced a duller picture but one that still had some 'geometrical interest'.[34]

Gide's recollection of passing 'hours and days over this amusement' valuably restores a temporal as well as a haptic or experimental dimension to the enjoyment of the kaleidoscope. Reading his account, written nearly fifty years after the experience and in an era already saturated with photography and film, we can understand the kind of response evoked by Brewster and Baudelaire. Harder to appreciate is the spatial, material *contextual* dimension, when we know these devices only in museum collections. How did kaleidoscopes, stereoscopes and the other optical toys fit into the drawing rooms, smoking rooms, studies and nurseries that were their natural habitats? While there is some evidence that can be deduced from the elaborate panoply of 'optical' allusions in Proust and Joyce, it must be admitted that the detailed contextualization of nineteenth-century optical devices still awaits serious study.[35] A model for the kind of exploration required might be Dolf Sternberger's chapter 'The Domestic Interior' in his *Panorama of the Nineteenth Century*, which traces the theme of light gradually entering this originally dark and densely cluttered space.[36] The brightly coloured vignettes offered by the kaleidoscope and the stereoscope need to be imagined against contemporary wall-coverings and furnishings, and mediated by the transition from candles to gas lamps and finally electricity.

We can find a wider frame of reference for the consideration of instructive illusion in another of Brewster's texts, his *Letters on Natural Magic*, addressed to his famous fellow-countryman Sir Walter Scott in 1832. Here Brewster, who was also a pious churchman, set out to expose

how corrupt governments throughout history had 'maintained their
influence over the human mind' by cynically exploiting natural
phenomena as 'magic'. An example of this from Brewster's own era was
the mission undertaken by the magician Robert-Houdin in 1856 at the
request of the French state, to help suppress an uprising in Algeria by
demonstrating superior European magic.[37] Another important theme
of much later nineteenth-century illusionism was the performance of
magic as an 'antidote' to superstition and especially the growing
Victorian fascination with spiritualism. By showing that furniture
could mysteriously move and apparitions appear at the behest of skilled
magicians, it was claimed, the credulous would realize how they were
deceived by fraudulent mediums. In his dramatic monologue 'Mr Sludge,
"The Medium"', Robert Browning would lay bare the tricks of the
medium's trade, while allowing his subject, Mr Sludge, to indict the
'curious gentlefolk' who have encouraged him to make a living by
satisfying their desire for 'signs and wonders'.[38] In a similar vein, J.N.
Maskelyne's avowed intention in his Egyptian Hall magic shows was to
unmask fraudulent spiritualists such as the Davenports by replicating
their effects. Behind such conspicuous professions of rationality and
responsibility, we may suspect some form of over-compensation at
work, perhaps related to the apparent self-deception in responses to the
eighteenth-century automata. We might further suspect—although there
is no space to explore this further here—a connection with the source
material of Freud's essay 'The Uncanny': namely the suggestion that
'uncertainty over whether a figure in a story is a human being or an
automaton' induces the feeling of uncanniness.[39]

Many early-modern media proposed what may seem today to be either
fraudulent or at best utopian fantasies of empowerment. Others claimed
seemingly practical, instrument-like, capabilities which also seem like
fantasies within the technological capability of the time—such as the
idea of a phonograph to take messages at the front door, or to fill an
opera house; or a moving image so 'real' that it compels viewers to dive
for cover, or to doubt their spouses' fidelity. Here instrument history may
help to explain how these conform to a general historical pattern. Derek
Price's study of *parerga*, or ancient ornamental devices, led him to
conclude that

> [t]he most ingenious mechanical devices of antiquity were not useful
> machines but trivial toys. Only slowly do the machines of every-day
> life take up the scientific advances and principles used long before in

despicable playthings and overly-ingenious, impracticable scientific models and instruments.[40]

Moving pictures emerged from the flux of optical toys and devices to become 'machines of everyday life'; and in doing so their apparatus became invisible, while this institutionalization perhaps served to 'infantilize' their forerunners, making them imperfect approximations to the achieved illusion of cinema.

However, this repression of the instrumental is worth probing further. The first successful manufacturers of moving-picture apparatus were necessarily precision engineers and instrument makers, such as Jules Carpentier, responsible for fabricating the Lumières' first cinématographes, and Robert Paul, who produced replica kinetoscopes for the British market before producing his own camera and projector. Paul was an instrument maker when he entered the moving-picture business in 1894, to become Britain's leading producer and leader of the film industry over the next fifteen years, before concentrating solely on instrument making after 1910. These have sometimes seemed to be incompatible careers, as if Paul were distracted or seduced into becoming a purveyor of risqué jokes, ghost stories and travelogues, before returning to his 'true' vocation. But within the perspective outlined here,

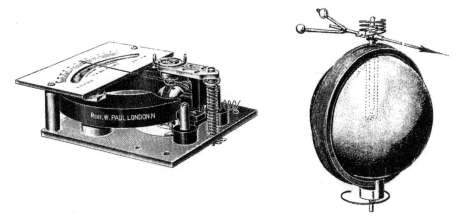

Fig. 4. R.W. Paul's unipivot galvanometer (1913): 'an ideal instrument'. Paul's patent of 1902 for a portable sensitive galvanometer formed the basis of a successful range of instruments produced by his company over many decades. Illustration from *Unipivot Galvanometers and Measuring Instruments for Continuous Current and for Alternating Current of High and Low Frequency* (London: Robt. W. Paul, 1913).

instrument makers had long been in the business of illusion and demonstration. When Paul branched out from electrical instruments in 1894, he became central to a new conjunction of engineering, electricity and chemistry in moving pictures. But he never abandoned instrument making; and his kinetoscopes, cameras, projectors and other related machines were in the tradition of the philosophical toy, later adapted to the growing demand for science teaching.[41] Initially, they had no immediate *function* except to satisfy curiosity—while certainly covering their costs—and they could also serve to demonstrate new principles and discoveries, as when Paul produced animated illustrations of magnetic fields for lectures by the director of the Royal Institution, Professor Sylvanus Thompson, in the early 1900s.[42] By the same token, he continued to work on other types of instrument. In 1902, at the height of his moving-picture success, he patented the 'unipivot' galvanometer, as a portable, accurate means of measuring current. Earlier, Carpentier had produced a pioneering extended-scale galvanometer in 1889, in response to the demand for such new instruments that had been stimulated by new developments in telegraphy after the laying of the first transatlantic cable in 1858, and by the rise of electrical power distribution in the 1880s.[43]

Classical film theory fetishized an idealized institution that functioned between approximately 1939 and 1959, neglecting the burgeoning process of technological development which long preceded (and followed) the hallowed threshold of 1894–96. It was helped in doing so by a largely uncritical acceptance of André Bazin's 'myth of total cinema', which claimed that the pioneers of cinema were aiming at an 'integral illusion' which was more or less achieved at an early stage even in advance of incremental improvements through the addition of synchronized sound, colour and stereoscopy.[44] The fundamental axiom of this paradigm became the 'impression of reality' regarded as cinema's distinctive feature, distinguishing it from all other forms of artistic representation and releasing automatically, as Christian Metz describes it, 'a mechanism of affective and perceptual participation in the spectator'.[45] Yet moving-image media have always been hybrid, and relentlessly engaged in the 'spectacular demonstration' of their own premises, as evidenced in the cinema industry's relentless marketing of innovation.

The argument against Bazin's myth has been put most persuasively by Laurent Mannoni, outlining the scope of what he calls 'deceptive art'. According to Mannoni, it is thanks to collectors such as Werner Nekes —and we might add Bill Douglas and Peter Jewell, as well as William and John Barnes—that the 'vastness, beauty and complexity' of the history of deceptive art is beginning to be realized. However, we are enjoined not just to admire, but to recognize that cinema remains an art of illusion, 'not merely a mechanical transfer of the exterior world onto the screen', and that deceptive art should be treated 'as an autonomous current of aesthetic and technical questing', of which cinema is just one strand. Instead of seeing the kaleidoscope as merely a decorative digression in the history of toys, or the stereoscope as (teleologically) an anticipation of cinema's immersive effect, we would do better to regard these as having their own identity, albeit within a constantly shifting and evolving tradition of 'illusion' wherein today's 'plaything' or 'overly ingenious instrument' may indeed become tomorrow's 'machine of every-day life'.[46]

2

'The suppleness of everyday life'
CGI, the Lumières, and Perception after Photography

Damian Sutton

The Virtualization of Cinema

One of the most famous stories surrounding the birth of cinema in 1895 is that of Georges Méliès who, upon seeing the Lumières' projection of *Le Repas de bébé*, remarked at the film's astounding depiction of movement.[1] What impressed Méliès so much was not the movement of the Lumière family at dinner, but instead the incidental detail of the rustling leaves of the trees in the background, a random detailing that even the most sophisticated magic-lantern slide could not reproduce. This fascination with the ability to capture such details continues to be a central theme of photographic theory and discussion, not least since the development of digital photography. Photography's apparent indexical link with reality, seemingly under threat from digitization, is partly reliant upon its ability to capture the momentary, the fleeting, and the aleatory that life throws in its way. Whereas painting, and now digitization, provides the opportunity to erase elements of an image, or add in others, a photograph's unique relation to reality is that it is trapped in the moment of unpredictability in which the shutter is activated: whatever is in front of the lens when this happens is recorded by it. For years this has meant that photography's measure of the lifelike has been made via the 'privileged link to the contingent', as Mary Ann Doane describes it. Photography's relationship with cinema did nothing to diminish this,

Fig. 5.   Still from Louis Lumière, *Le Repas de bébé* (1895).
Copyright Association frères Lumière.

and filmmaking spent its early years 'preoccupied with the minute examination of the realm of the contingent, persistently displaying the camera's aptitude for recording.'[2]

Whilst this privileged link might seem unremarkable to contemporary cinema audiences, it is taken for granted rather less in the development of animation techniques, whether they are employed in 'pure' animation or, as is increasingly the case, used to supplement and even replace corporeal production design, acting extras and even, in some cases, principal actors. The 'virtualization' of the film-production line (now often referred to as a 'pipeline' after the ways in which software used by film personnel draws off data from the project reservoir) has led to a renewed concern for the appearance of the lifelike since the process itself has become more and more remote from the act of recording 'live' action. Digital convergence has ultimately led to a homogeneous cinema image made up of many separate parts individually and differently captured, and which can be made to appear photographed as live action or drawn on two dimensions. At its heart is a unifying conception of cinema as the creation of a virtual world which is then 'filmed', and in which objects, creatures and people are made to look as if they existed before the filming process in the same way that we know 'real' actors, objects and places to have done.

The idea of a unifying conception of cinematic creation might seem tailor-made for new media, not least since new media are routinely expected to change the way we think about old media, like cinema. Yet whilst it seems that, for the first time in recent memory, pure animation and live action cinema are thought of and conceptualized in the same way, this is not the first time in its history that the process of cinema has been regarded as an 'animation' of individual elements to create a coherent, lifelike whole. Indeed, such a proposal had a crucial role in one of the first theories of cinema, when cinema was itself an example of 'new media'. When cinema first made a public appearance in the 1890s, the philosopher Henri Bergson, who would be an influence on Walter Benjamin, Gilles Deleuze and others in the twentieth century, saw in the cinématographe a paradigm of perception and imagination. Bergson, for example, described his idea of human perception as a kind of 'cinematographic' recording and projecting of mental images, whilst human imagination, on the other hand, was seen as an incremental process of *animating* discrete objects as they appear in the mind. Whilst much of Bergson's writing on cinema was put aside as cinema theory developed, it is his somewhat whimsical appreciation of an imagining mind that comes back to provide a method of understanding the virtualization of filmmaking. This essay will demonstrate how some of Bergson's original ideas, first published when the Lumière films were at their most spectacular, can help create an understanding of the modelling and animation in filmmaking of discrete elements and objects, as they correspond to our experiences of life, to create a complete world view.

Optical Convergence

For much of the first ten years of digital cinema, critical debate focused on the perceived 'threat' that digitization posed to the chemical photograph's indexical link with reality.[3] Yet the imaginative hold of the photographing camera as an 'indicator' of reality has never been stronger, particularly in recent photography and mainstream cinema. Computer-Generated Imagery (CGI), particularly that used to create fantastic worlds of science fiction or historical worlds of the romantic past, constantly relies upon the appearance of these as having been filmed. For example, a notable 'trick' available in some software platforms, such as Adobe Photoshop or AfterEffects, for both still and moving images is achieved by mimicking optical defects to suggest the presence of a 'camera'. One of the most spectacular of these is the addition of lens flare—seen as a tunnel or vortex of octagonal translucent discs—as would normally be seen when the camera is pointed too close to the incident light of the sun. Whilst this effect can be added to any image, whether the 'original' was a photograph or not, the principle of optics is used here to simulate or appropriate the technology of photography as it was once practised. This commonly used effect is seen in television shows, advertisements and films, even when, as in shows such as *Battlefield Britain* (BBC, 2004), the use of CGI is itself an 'open' spectacle. The special effect in such images can be called a digital *trompe l'oeil*. An example of optical 'reliability' without the addition of effects—but here using combination images—occurs in photographer Paul M. Smith's 'snapshots' from a night out on the town. In the *Make My Night* series (1998) it is barely noticeable that all the people in the photographs

Fig. 6.   Paul M. Smith, Untitled [kebab shop], *Make My Night* series, 1998.
Copyright Paul M. Smith, 2005.

are Smith himself. His acid commentary on 'lad' culture is sharpened by the appearance of the signs of photography, in particular flash glare, which serves to 'guarantee' that all these moments existed in the same homogeneous instant that the photograph was apparently 'taken'.

Whilst Smith's photographs are examples of the combination of individual photographic images, the most common use of combination in cinema is that of 'live' and 'virtual' elements. In the period film *The Aviator* (Martin Scorcese, Warner Bros./Miramax, 2004) CGI was used to 'place' actor Leonardo DiCaprio in the digitally constructed gunner's seat of a Vickers Vimy for the spectacular scenes depicting Howard Hughes's own filming of the aerial sequences of *Hell's Angels*. The conceit of this production/plot hinged on Hughes's obsession with filming *Hell's Angels* in the air rather than from the ground, in order to record multiple aircraft flying against and through stationary cloud—all of which were digitally rendered in the final sequence of *The Aviator*.[4] Lighting effects were added in this rendering process, whose manipulation also included the simulation of the two-strip Technicolor process of the early 1930s.

In both of the above examples, the photographer or filmmaker is required to render a two-dimensional image that has been approached, planned and staged in three dimensions, with separate elements combined in the final image. Behind the post-production special effect of rendering lies the conceptual special effect of the original synthesis of elements carried out virtually, either through modelling and animation or the use of actors playing to empty space.

Such promises inherent in the capabilities of CGI in cinema obviously encourage directors to attempt grand vistas or complex action in a manner never previously attempted. On the other hand, CGI artists like Thad Beier see things differently: 'It's much easier to hand off the sequence to the effects department and say "OK, this is all we have. Make it perfect".'[5] Not for nothing, therefore, has CGI been called a 'digital band-aid for live-action shots'.[6] For Beier, whose work at this time was on the Sci-Fi Channel's ambitious adaptation of Frank Herbert's *Dune* (Evision/New Amsterdam, 2000), the often onerous task of the digital animator was to create whole battle sequences, including the setting, soldiers and effects, from scratch—mostly because the pre-production budget had already been spent. Then, as had been developed on blockbuster films such as *Titanic* (James Cameron, Fox/Paramount, 1997) and *Gladiator* (Ridley Scott, Universal/Scott Free, 2000), the technology involved the modelling and rendering of individual soldiers and civilians, created and animated in an artificial world and then virtually 'filmed'.[7] In all of these examples, the ultimate goal is the appearance of lifelike reality or, as Walter Benjamin famously described, of 'the tiny spark of chance, of the here and now, with which reality has, as it were, seared the character in the picture'.[8] This is what makes it appear that these scenes consisted of real places and people photographed with real cameras. Where the 'appearance' of the camera in the action reproduces the indexicality of photography, the independent movement of animated actors recreates the contingency of movement and time in front of the cinematic camera, whose unified point-of-view acts as the audience's own and makes it appear that the events were photographed.

The rendering process which involves the addition of lens flare, film scratches, motion blur and other telltale signs of the use of film and camera, as well as general clothing and lighting effects, is the most intensive part of contemporary film animation, both for feature-length films and in combination with live action. In a production pipeline for a major animated feature, the 'farm' of computer processors can run to several thousands of units. The earlier stages of production, the modelling and the animation process itself, although separately managed, are comparatively simple, and yet, as suggested above, they are perhaps more fundamental to the illusion of reality than are the two-dimensional effects of Photoshop or AfterEffects. The software used to create a homogeneous, Newtonian world in which virtual actors can perform (as in *The Aviator*) is essential for many of the spectacular effects of CGI in cinema. The central value of industry products such as Alias Wavefront Maya is in the creation of real-world physics, and the triumph of such efforts often becomes the headline act of a full-animation feature. When, for instance, competing companies Pacific Data Images and Pixar were 2004 box-office rivals with, respectively, *Shrek 2* (Andrew Adamson/ Kelly Asbury/Conrad Vernon, DreamWorks SKG/PDI, 2004) and *The Incredibles* (Brad Bird, Disney/Pixar, 2004), each film represented groundbreaking modelling effects, in particular those relating to hair. This meant that, for *The Incredibles*, the major characters' otherwise cartoonish bodies were topped with seemingly real hair, with showcase sequences of hair getting wet, or of various characters with appropriately dry, greasy or luxurious hair. Animators on *Shrek 2* went a step further by developing the physics of hair and hats, and by making one particularly vain character, Prince Charming, continually refer to his coiffure. Where skin effects are largely two-dimensional and can be added in rendering,

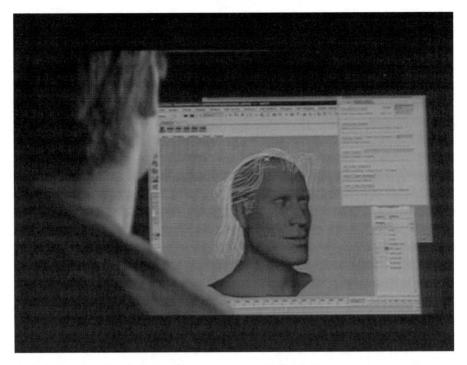

Fig. 7. Animating Prince Charming's coiffure in *The Tech of Shrek 2*.
Copyright DreamWorks SKG/Pacific Data Images, 2004.

physical elements such as hair and clothing have to be thought through in three dimensions, as if they were real objects to begin with, especially in terms of perfecting their movement and in their lighting.

Projects such as *The Aviator*, *Shrek 2* and *The Incredibles* do more, however, than simply add the telltale signs of photography or combine photographed actors. The technology of the production is specifically geared to disassemble the world into discrete objects and parts which can be modelled and animated independently of the filmmaking process itself. Indeed, one of the other applications of packages such as Alias Wavefront Maya is in the creation of computer games. With its application of new media and its seemingly radical transformation of the filmmaking experience, the virtualization of film production in this manner suggests a conceptual approach that is totally new, or at the very least uncinematic. Yet such a process of imagining cinema, of bringing images about, is echoed in Bergson's writing from cinema's first few years.

Cinematographic Perception

Bergson's *Creative Evolution* of 1907, in which he uses the ciné-matographe machine as an example to illustrate the process of perception, came at a time of widespread critical and philosophical discourse on the nature of modern experience.[9] Changing perceptions of temporality were often seen as key to the 'modern' character of contemporary life. Leo Charney has described the *fin de siècle* and the decades surrounding it as characterized by an intense philosophical debate around the idea of the moment; it was a period in which the *ephemeral*, or the momentary, was taking shape as the defining concept of the modern industrial experience.[10] This widespread philosophical concern reached beyond its own time to include the work of Walter Benjamin. Benjamin had been influenced by Bergson's earlier *Matter and Memory* (1896), in which it is suggested that perception apprehended the world in the ephemeral manner of photography.[11] Taking up the idea later in *Creative Evolution*, Bergson surmised that perception is a process in which images as states are joined together to create an impression or apprehension of reality. In fact, thought Bergson, underlying our appreciation of time, so often understood as the sensation of these discrete passing moments, lies the true, indivisible ongoing time of duration. This is the world coming into being—becoming—and it is this sense of coming into being that perception tries to recreate from the passing moments. The invention of cinema in this period must, for Bergson, have seemed fortuitously 'timed' to perfection:

> We take snapshots, as it were, of the passing reality, and, as these are characteristic of the reality, we have only to string them on a becoming . . . Perception, intellection, language so proceed in general. Whether we would think becoming, or express it, or even perceive it, we hardly do anything else that set going a kind of cinematograph inside us.[12]

The question for Bergson was thus: why should we adopt this process when another seems more logical? Famously, whilst musing over perception towards the end of *Creative Evolution*, Bergson imagined the process by which perception might recreate the movement of objects for the screen—he chose the passing of a regiment along a street. For him, an *imagination* would automatically try to build such an image of movement by combining the movements of individual bodies: '. . . to

25

give each of them the movement of marching, a movement varying from individual to individual although common to the human species, and to throw the whole lot on the screen.'[13] Such an undertaking would be overwhelming in its totality, and would not begin to express the movement of objects independent of the regiment: 'How could it, at best, reproduce the suppleness of everyday life?'[14] The answer, for Bergson, is to 'think the unstable by means of the stable'.[15] The mind imagines itself as an organ of perception, separate to but yet 'in' the world, apprehending momentary glances as 'snapshots of the passing reality': 'Instead of attaching ourselves to the inner becoming of things, we place ourselves outside them in order to recompose their becoming artificially.'[16] For Bergson, perception that is not 'cinematographic' could never reproduce any scene or visual impression that was initially appreciated, since the whole cannot be adequately subdivided or individuated adequately enough. The mind adopts this 'stringing together' to make sense of the human environment. Crucially, this is not a 'true' appreciation of the world's movement and time, its *becoming*, but it can reproduce the impression of becoming. Thus Bergson sees the cinema as an obvious parallel to this apprehension, or grasping, of the world.

The historical context of Bergson's writing (roughly 1895–1907) is revealing. Edison had been experimenting with the kinetoscope for at least five years; moving photographic images had been the subject of scientific debate for anything up to forty years, and the Lumière brothers had perfected and demonstrated their cinématographe as recently as March 1895. By the time of writing *Creative Evolution*, Bergson's model of perception had become predicated on the reversibility of the Lumière cinématographe machine, which was both camera and projector.

Tom Gunning has famously described the period of cinema from 1895 to 1906–7 as that of a 'cinema of attractions' (after Sergei Eisenstein), a cinema that exploited a population eager for visual excitement and heightened stimulus and who desired its particular 'accent on direct stimulation'. At this time, cinema was seen 'less as a way of telling stories than as a way of presenting a series of views to an audience, fascinating because of their illusory power, and exoticism'.[17] As Gunning argues, in the first decade or so of cinema the apparatus was itself an attraction for the patron, and the cinématographe provides the archetypal example of the explosion in popular interest.[18] Is it surprising, then, that Bergson used this invention, whether the Lumières' machine or cinema in general, as a paradigm or metaphor for perception? He could hardly have failed to notice the worldwide public fanfare that arose shortly after the

Lumières' invention, and when Bergson leapt upon the example of the passing regiment he was not imagining some event that might one day be of sufficient interest—instead he was describing actual footage from widely distributed films of a popular public spectacle. According to Jacques Aumont, such procession films made up almost half of all films produced directly or indirectly by the Lumières, suggesting that it was a favourite topic of early patrons, and that Bergson's experience of the cinema therefore included an understanding of not only its actual working but also its popular appeal.[19] The fact that Bergson uses a real example suggests that his illustration of cinema as a powerful metaphor for perception relies upon its ability to record, validate and, ultimately, as Doane suggests, to 'corroborate' events.[20]

The Seductive Metaphor

Bergson used cinema as a method of explaining the manner in which perception is forced to apprehend reality, in order for memory to make sense of it. Cinema was convenient; the notion of the mind grasping the world in discrete elements, of parcelling the world up into individual objects, images and memories, is illustrated just as easily through the comic strip or painted tableaux. These others, however, were not to have such a profound influence as did cinema on the cultural notions of memory, narrative and even of time itself. Cinematographic perception turns out to be highly appropriate as a model for the mind in twentieth-century modernity. If Bergson's use of cinema as an illustration of perception is accurate, its efficiency is not hindered by the extension of the model into mainstream cinema. For example, much of Deleuze's understanding of time, expressed in his hugely influential *Cinema* books, relies heavily on Bergson's often-quoted principles of photographic and cinematographic perception.[21] Deleuze's proposal of the movement-image describes a dominant cinema narration in which all expression of time relies on the sequencing of shots, which are themselves reliant on the logical depiction of movement. At the very core of this process is the strip of still images that run through the projector's gate (once again reversing, or mirroring, the film running through the camera's mechanism). The binding together of these immobile images into a mobile image became the mechanism for the logic of cinema narration: shots are the stringing together of frames; editing is the stringing together of shots. It is easy to see how the correlation of narration to perception itself provides a strong foundation for identification in cinema.

But whither Bergson's wistful example of the imagining mind? Does cinematographic perception completely replace the mind that seeks to create, assemble and articulate the world in a manner so unlike cinema? As the new processes of digital production suggest, Bergson's initial musings seem more relevant now than the cinematographic method tied to the photographic 'apprehension' of reality. Paul Douglass points to an early 1990s bottled-water advertisement, made by Industrial Light and Magic and featuring marching CGI soldiers, suggesting it as a return to this type of *imagining* creativity. Douglass's conclusion is that, to Bergson, such an animation would have seemed impossible for the mind to conceive in its totality. Therefore Bergson suggested that perception that apprehends reality is more likely. Similarly, whilst a practical act of an animation (such as in theatre or puppetry) could, at that time, never achieve the contingent complexity of the experience of the 'real' world, cinema appeared to return reality to us on the screen as if reality itself assisted in its own representation. The ease with which cinema itself adopted the paradigm of perception in its own system of frame-shot-edit does indeed suggest that perception has always been a kind of cinema. After all, everyone is familiar with the commonsense connection between the snapshot and memory. But, suggests Douglass, '[t]he cinematic experience usually ends in adjusting people to its functions, not vice versa', and it is not difficult to see why cinema was so seductive a metaphor.[22] Early cinema must have seemed a revelation to patrons and thinkers immersed in a fascinating and bewildering culture of spectacle, thrill and entertainment, a culture whose sensitivity to 'the moment' had been sharpened. The spectacular sights and stimuli of the modern were experienced as ephemera, with attention paid to the sensation of that experience as something about to be lost. The proximity of the instant is counteracted by an awareness of the creation of history, and the passing moment is experienced both as the instant that passes and the instant that will pass; thus creating a sense of immediate loss that has been characterized by Miriam Hansen as a 'dialectic of remembering and forgetting'.[23] Photography revealed and took part in this sensation: it had an unquestionable link with reality, and when reconstituted as cinema it captured reality's unpredictable charm and terror and replayed it for eager audiences. The Lumière films still possess a charm because they depict the random event becoming a precious moment. The fleeting and incidental details of accident, un-remarkable to our contemporary eyes, were captured by cinématographe as a guarantee of the everyday life that would ordinarily have slipped past the sensational experiences of that modern moment.

The fact that a concept of virtual cinema has its roots in the birth of cinema and its popular reception means that the films of the Lumières and others, with their details of movement that fascinated so many, like Méliès, are significant in understanding the capacity for cinema to display lifelike movement and time. Also, it is not insignificant that the index of photography, represented by the camera's flaws, should be used to signify its veracity. The first few years of its invention are responsible, materially and philosophically, for certain ideas of cinema as well as wider ideas of perception. Encompassing all of this was a more general historical and social trajectory of industrial modernity, reflected in cinema's capacity for representing movement and time through the experience of the everyday—of which there are perhaps no better examples than the actuality films of the Lumières and others. Despite representing one of the most popular forms of early cinema, these films are routinely passed over as having little philosophical or critical value. This is surprising when one considers the crucial role they play in the development of the cinematic metaphor of perception, particularly that developed by Bergson and taken up by Benjamin, Gilles Deleuze and others.

The reversibility of cinema embodied in the cinématographe, as Sean Cubitt has noted, 'opposes the presumption of a "natural" vision that sees the "real" world as an assemblage of objects: it proposes another, synthetic vision'.[24] Cinematographic perception is synthetic because it is not natural imagination, but, as Bergson suggests, a kind of easy manipulation of perception and memory. Yet within the cinematographic process and within cinematographic perception, at the back of our field of vision, rather like the leaves rustling behind Louis Lumière and his young family, is a reminder of that other model of the imagining mind. Inconsequential, incidental movement of the world is the desired result of this imagination, to recreate the 'suppleness of everyday life'. It is this 'guarantee' of the lifelike that is one of the desired effects in contemporary mainstream effects cinema. The virtual camera of this new form corroborates the events created in the three-dimensional world of the computer in the same way that the old form of the cinématographe replayed the events of the street. Contemporary effects animators seek to create characteristic and recognizable moments whilst giving them the impression of contingency. These need only adhere to the cinematographic perception to guarantee their realistic effect. Ironically, Bergson's whimsical depiction of our perception attempting to recreate movement reveals itself in the methods used to mimic reality on film.

The creation and deployment of digital film extras to replace crowds and, more recently, the combination of wholly 'animated' elements in a coherent virtual world have demonstrated an uncanny resemblance to Bergson's 'animation' of reality. The virtualization of cinema can easily be recognized as an attempt to give virtual actors 'movement varying from individual to individual although common to the human species, and to throw the whole lot on the screen'.[25]

3

'Wouldn't you rather be at home?'
Electronic Media and the Anti-Urban Impulse

William Boddy

One inescapable task for contemporary media scholars is to place into critical context the ubiquitous and frequently self-serving claims of technological convergence which pervade current industry discourses on digital media. Indeed, I would nominate the term 'convergence', alongside that of 'interactivity' (described in 1990 by one critic as 'already the soggy buzzword of the '90s'[1]), as one of the longest-surviving rhetorical figures of that decade's spectacular dotcom boom and bust. Against the teleological assumptions of the term 'convergence', it is appropriate to ask precisely how the putatively merging media were historically constructed as institutionally and aesthetically autonomous in the first place and who stands to profit from their realignment. It may also be productive to ask how the differing institutional and commercial forms of cinema and electronic media have inflected their distinct academic institutionalization and historiographies. Recent critical scholarship on new media has challenged both the widespread claims for the unprecedented novelty of contemporary multimedia and the historical amnesia and theoretical naivete evident in much of the trade- and popular-press writing of the past fifteen years. In this context, media historians might profit not only from a closer look at privileged historical moments of media convergence and hybridity past and present, but also from a broader examination of the assumptions and stakes of such definitions and recombinations. In the face of the prevailing characterization of the current transition in moving-image culture from

31

analog to digital as novel and unprecedented, it may be worthwhile to consider the longevity of some of the wider popular assumptions about the social implications of electronic media. As a modest step in this larger project, this essay will examine the persistence of anti-urbanism as a theme running through a century of popular discourses on electronic media.

The association of electronic media with anti-urbanism stands in contrast to the historical association of cinema with urban life. Despite the shared roots of early cinema and electronic media in nineteenth-century world's fairs and popular science, and their mutual association with the wider cultural fascination with the mysterious and disquieting fluidity of natural phenomena and the human mind, there is one seemingly irreconcilable distinction in the social topography of early cinema and wireless, one that continues to shape the social position of both media.[2] It is an opposition founded on that between the publicness of cinema's site of reception and the domestic context of wireless fabrication and reception. Indeed, it was cinema's evocation of a new type of public sphere that provoked both the exhilaration of Walter Benjamin about film's liberating potential and the deep anxiety about film-going among many early twentieth-century conservative social critics. The popular press of the period frequently contrasted the social hazards of cinema attendance (associated with the city, the street, the dance hall and the amusement park) with the domestic, therapeutic and family-affirming qualities of radio as a hobby, especially for male adolescents. A typical expression of paternalistic concern over the threatening implications of the cinema as public leisure are the comments of the 'employment and service superintendent' of an American textile firm writing in the *Annals of the American Academy of Political and Social Science* in 1916:

> Beginning with the young girl, there is the growing independence, the impatience with parental restraint, the cheap amusements which are slowly but surely vitiating her taste and lowering her standards . . . How can a girl develop into a good worker when her parents permit her to frequent cheap dance halls and movies any and every day of the week?[3]

On the other hand, in one of the first of many published testimonies to the moral efficacy of the radio hobby for young men, Hugo Gernsback, pioneer radio retailer, amateur-electronics publisher and science-fiction writer, praised radio as a socially beneficial hobby in a 1912 letter to the *New York Times*: 'This new art does much toward keeping the boy at home, where other diversions usually, sooner or later, lead him to questionable resorts; and for this reason well-informed parents are only too willing to allow their sons to become interested in wireless.'[4]

However, despite the apparent opposition between the public and private contexts of cinema and wireless as leisure activities, it is important to note that the late nineteenth century witnessed a prolonged crisis in the wider cultural definitions of private and public space, exemplified by a number of contradictory spaces which conflate the domestic and public realms, which, as Tom Gunning has pointed out, include the public railway carriage appointed in the deeply upholstered style of the bourgeois living room, the urban arcade presenting the street as furnished interior, and the domestic parlour penetrated by the new industrial artefacts of the telephone, stereoscope and magic lantern.[5]

Likewise, while early radio participated in a well-established anti-urban vision of demographic dispersal and domestic self-sufficiency going back to the introduction of electric power in nineteenth-century factories, the nature of domesticity that wireless helped to bring about was itself deeply contradictory. A Maine newspaper article in 1898, foreseeing the electrical transmission of live public events into the home, predicted that 'We may hope to have the movements, the actual happenings of the world, as they are transpiring, brought to our firesides in the form of pictures.'[6] As Carolyn Marvin notes, 'one's own family and neighbourhood would then be the stable center of the universe—beyond it would be margin and chaos'.[7] At the same time, broadcasting also represented an unprecedented integration of the home with the time values and economic imperatives of an ascendant consumer economy.[8] Thus the prominent claims for a new, technologically achieved domesticity in the early twentieth century begin to seem less like observations about the empirical role of wireless in the home and more like another example of a reaction to modernity's assault on subjectivity, which film scholars and social historians have been writing about for decades. Although as early as 1930, Bertold Brecht was pointing to what he saw as the hopelessness of radio's project of 'bringing back coziness to the home and making family life bearable again', the persistence of such reactionary appeals to an imagined domesticity restored by electronic communication is apparent in the promotion of contemporary digital media in our post-cinema and post-broadcasting era.[9]

The recurrent twentieth-century visions of a recovered rural hegemony brought about by the electronic media were anticipated in earlier predictions that the provision of electric power and lighting in the late nineteenth century would disperse the prevailing geographical concentration of industry organized around earlier water and steam power.[10] Similarly, the telephone was also hailed as a saviour of rural life; *Telephony* magazine in 1905 predicted that 'with a telephone in the house, a buggy in the barn, and a rural mail box at the gate, the problem of how to keep the boys and the girls on the farm is solved'.[11] Such conservative hopes for a reinvigorated rural hegemony were widely echoed in discussions of early radio. A 1922 article entitled 'Removing the Last Objection to Living in the Country', in London's *Country Life* magazine noted that the US radio boom coincided with the results of the 1920 census, which had recorded that nation's urban population as larger than its rural population for the first time, and its author looked hopefully for radio's help in 'solving the problem of keeping the youngster on the farm'. Indeed, the challenge of preserving endangered rural life was frequently posed as the physical containment of rural youth, although the so-called 'servant problem' of the early twentieth century sometimes provoked similar imagery. 'Removing the Last Objection to Living in the Country', for example, concluded with a rosy scenario depicting the hostess of a country estate entertaining guests with a radio comedy programme in the parlour, 'while below-stairs the servants are enjoying the same entertainment on special extensions, with never a thought of the city and its glaring attractions'.[12]

Similar arguments for the efficacy of new electronic media for maintaining or restoring rural primacy were offered in the early marketing texts of postwar American television. The 1944 trade book *Get Ready Now to Sell Television: A Guidebook for Merchants Who Recognize an Extraordinary Opportunity* argued that

> in one sense the farmer is a better television prospect than the city dweller. For in our congested towns and cities, television programs are forced to compete with movies, legitimate playhouses, concerts and other attractions. But the isolated farmer cannot easily or readily get to town to enjoy these entertainments . . . as his urban brother . . .[13]

Making a similar demographic distinction among early TV audiences, radio pioneer Lee DeForest's 1945 book, *Television Today and Tomorrow*, lamented what the author saw as the tendency within the new

TV industry to use experimental telecasts in New York City as the national laboratory for the medium's commercial development. He worried that the city's 'theatre and cinema-fed population seems to be more immune than elsewhere to modern magic . . . Perhaps these folks are too sophisticated to become television-minded'.[14] At the same time, taking a longer and more optimistic view, DeForest predicted that among the nascent medium's eventual social effects, 'foremost in significance will be the strengthening of the home ties, especially of the younger set. If the program directors of television do well their part it will no longer be difficult for parents to induce their children to spend evening hours in the family circle.'[15] DeForest concluded with a vision of technologically revivified and geographically dispersed domesticity:

> The heyday of the cloud-scraping towers in the city has passed its meridian. Henceforth you will note a gradual razing of these ridiculous structures, no more to be proudly exploited. Those aggressive skylines must eventually subside . . . A population which once more centers its interest in the home will inherit the earth and find it good. It will be a maturer population, with hours for leisure in small homes, away from today's crowded apartments. Into such a picture, ideally adapted to the benefits and physical limitations of television, this new magic art will enter and become a vital element of the daily life.[16]

It is perhaps not surprising to find these early and historically disparate scenarios of anti-urban domesticity associated with the new media of the telephone, radio and television echoed by some prominent tycoons and pundits of the 1990s dotcom era. For example, Microsoft CEO Bill Gates's 1995 book *The Road Ahead* argued that digital multimedia would make communication less dependent on location: 'In the long run, as the information highway makes physical proximity to urban service less important, many businesses will decentralize and disperse their activities, and cities, like companies, may be downsized'.[17] Gates elaborated:

> Many of today's social problems have arisen because the population has been crowded into urban areas. The drawbacks of city life are obvious and substantial—traffic, cost of living, crime, and limited access to the outdoors, among others.[18]

Gates analogized the 1990s information superhighway with the US interstate highway system, which helped to segregate and depopulate American cities in the 1950s and 1960s, as 'the information highway also encourages people to move away from city centers'.[19] He suggested: 'If the population of a city were reduced by even 10 percent, the result would be a major difference in property values and wear and tear on transportation and other urban systems.' Admitting that a technologically enabled exodus of affluent information workers might leave city populations even poorer, Gates noted optimistically that this might also lead to cheaper urban rents.[20] Echoing the 1898 Maine newspaper image of the networked home as the stable centre of the universe surrounded by margin and chaos, Gates's book a century later offered rhapsodic descriptions of a computer-assisted dream house 'that tracks its occupants in order to meet their particular needs [and] combines two traditions. The first is the tradition of unobtrusive service, and the other is that an object we carry entitles us to be treated in a certain way.'[21] The electronic-talisman-equipped master of Gates's smart-house, sovereign in the stable centre of the universe, might be reassured by the Microsoft CEO's scenario of the technologically perfected video surveillance of the 'margin and chaos' of the abandoned public spaces occupied by the restive and unwired inhabitants of his downsized urban centres. Gates explained:

> Every city streetlight represents a substantial investment by a community in public safety. In a few years it will require only a relatively modest additional sum to add and operate cameras with connections to the information highway. Within a decade, computers will be able to scan video records very inexpensively looking for a particular person or activity. I can easily imagine proposals that every pole supporting a streetlight should also have one or more cameras.[22]

According to Gates, almost everyone would be willing to accept some restrictions upon personal privacy in exchange for a sense of heightened domestic security.[23]

Notwithstanding Gates's rosy scenarios of networked domesticity, by the time of the putative digital revolution of the 1990s, some conservative techno-critics had to admit the manifest failure of previous electronic media to restore the perennial vision of an idealized anti-urban domesticity. Indeed, among some technological pundits of the 1990s, commercial television had become the chief instrument of a despised common culture. After citing Jose Ortega y Gasset's 1930 *Revolt of the Masses*, conservative writer George Gilder explained in 1994:

> What do we have in common? . . . our prurient interests, our morbid fears and anxieties, our ambivalent dread of violence and suppressed longings for it, our hunger for sexual images and fantasies, all the undertow of lusts and rages and derangements that it is the prime goal and glory of civilization to overcome. This means commercial television is necessarily the enemy of civilization . . . To reach an adequate market, mass broadcasts almost necessarily must pander to prurient interests and morbid fears and anxieties.[24]

Gilder lauded Bill Gates, the 'Microsoft liberator', 'a man without a television in his home', who had stormed off a recent live TV interview when displeased with an interviewer's question.[25] Calling Gates's 'defiance . . . an omen of an America free of TV within the next five years', Gilder argued that 'the personal computer championed by Bill Gates . . . [promises] to revitalize capitalism and culture in the U.S. and around the globe and to retrieve the hopes of a conservative era in politics'.[26] Offering one version of the politics of convergence and implicitly invoking earlier hopes associated with previous electronic eras, Gilder argued that 'the teleputer—a revolutionary PC of the next decade —will give every household hacker the productive potential of a factory czar of the industrial era and the communications power of a broadcast tycoon of the television age'.[27] He concluded with a quasi-survivalist vision of the technological future, when 'great cities will hollow out, as the best and brightest in them retreat to rural redoubts and reach out to global markets and communities . . . Families will regroup around the evolving silicon hearths of a new cottage economy.'[28] Gilder's contradictory gestures toward domestic self-sufficiency and market penetration lie at the heart of a century of conservative responses to electronic communication.

The anti-metropolitan impulses and the embrace of a mythologized domestic self-sufficiency found in the public comments of dotcom industry leaders and pundits were concretized in a number of prominent television ad campaigns of the late 1990s, at a time when the US computer industry faced a unique set of challenges. With this context in mind, I would like to examine Packard Bell computers' so-called 'Home' campaign, launched in autumn 1996 and Microsoft's autumn 1998 'Lusk, Wyoming' TV advertisement. Facing unprecedented declines in the growth rate of personal computer sales (then seeming to reach a stubborn plateau after reaching about 40 per cent of US homes) and a shift from a technology-driven market of early adopters to a yet-unknown mass market, PC makers in the US more than doubled their advertising spending between 1995 and 1997 in order to reach general consumers, especially through TV ads.[29] 'This year's buzzword for buyers is "multimedia",' wrote *USA Today* in November 1994: 'That's high-tech talk for computers with audio and video wizardry right on their screens. They'll play compact discs, show clips from a favorite film or let you watch TV on-screen. They'll also answer the telephone and send faxes. At least, that's what the ads say.'[30]

Furthermore, by the late 1990s, industry leaders and ad executives recognized the need to 'brand' their technically nearly-identical products in an increasingly price-sensitive market. These efforts were amplified when chip-maker Intel began its unprecedented drive to brand its new Pentium processor in its massive 'Intel Inside' campaign launched in 1996; Intel paid 50 per cent of the cost of PC manufacturers' broadcast ads if they included the 'Intel Inside' logo and the accompanying four musical bongs; Intel spent $750 million in such advertising support that year alone.[31]

PC maker Packard Bell, which by the mid-90s had captured 40 percent of the US PC market through aggressive price-cutting of under-$1000 desktop PCs through over 15,000 mass retailers, had produced no broadcast advertising before 1996, despite never-realized plans for national campaigns announced in the fourth quarters of 1994 and 1995.[32] Notwithstanding its formidable market share, Packard Bell was hobbled by low profit margins in the fiercely competitive home-PC market and was the target of a March 1995 lawsuit from competitor Compaq alleging that Packard Bell was installing used parts as new in its computers; in June 1996 Japan-based NEC acquired 40 per cent of the cash-starved Packard Bell.[33] Meanwhile, the recently opened New York office of the M&S Saatchi advertising agency acquired the $40 million Packard Bell account in May 1996, its first major US client. An agency executive explained at the time: 'We're obviously coming into the branding game late, and we want to move the needle as fast as we can . . . If they don't build a stronger brand image, Packard Bell is going to be relegated to a price game, and it's going to be impossible to survive.' According to the Saatchi executive, the advertising campaign 'dramatizes how harsh the big bad world can be, and how peaceful it is at home'.[34] The campaign, launched in October 1996, consisted of one 60-second 'spectacular' and three 30-second commercials; Packard Bell spent $13 million in national TV air time in the fourth quarter of 1996 alone.[35] In the US, the ads appeared in everything from the daytime soap opera *The Young and Restless* to prime time professional football broadcasts, and the commercials also aired in the UK, Ireland, France, Italy, Spain and South Africa, in what a London trade journal described as Packard Bell's use of 'blockbuster advertising tactics to muscle its way into Europe's burgeoning home-PC market'.[36] Saatchi executives boasted that the ad was the most expensive TV commercial ever filmed at the Universal Studios in Los Angeles, and it featured a cast of 150 actors and extremely elaborate post-production effects.[37] *Adweek*, including the commercial in its list of best spots for the month of October 1996, described the ad in this way: 'It's a cruel world out there: Rain falls, cars don't run, and talking is prohibited. Inside, where a Packard Bell home computer sits on a desk, it's much nicer.'[38] Jeremy Pemberton, writing in the British advertising journal *Campaign* in December 1996 pointed to the ad's depiction of a 'futuristic world you might experience if you went to sleep having spent a week at the NFT then ate far too much cheese'.[39]

As an anti-urban polemic, the Packard Bell advertisement from 1996 is striking in its fluid, dreamlike treatment of space, heightened by off-centre framing and the use of match cuts and dissolves that serve to magically remove obstacles to the camera's eye. After forty seconds exploring the dreary and rain-soaked monochrome urban landscapes of endless bank queues and public libraries patrolled by goose-stepping soldiers, the camera spirals away from the oppressive cityscape to settle in front of a tidy detached single-family home on a patch of green lawn; the closing (and only) narration asks: 'Wouldn't you rather be at home?' The ad's visual stylization also includes the liberal use of oblique lighting, fog and soft focus, the direct visual address of actors to the camera, the non-realist combination of monochrome and colour palettes within a single frame, and the magical morphing into old age of the Pre-Raphaelite face of a young woman in a bank queue. Likewise, the Lynchean soundtrack, eschewing both voice-over and synchronized sound for the most part, features assorted sighs, laughter, thunder and discordant choral music. The ad's urban landscape plays off the iconography of Cold War America's visualization of life behind the Iron Curtain, and the monochromatic, monumental architecture of massive stone and grotesque ornamentation (including gargoyles of severed female heads on rooftop precipices) evokes a long tradition of cinematic dystopian urban worlds, from *Metropolis* to *Blade Runner* (as well as

Ridley Scott's celebrated 1984 Apple Macintosh ad). For its part, the 30-second commercial's narrative offers an inverted echo of *The Wizard of Oz*, in this case leaving the monochrome city for an emerald Kansas at the end of a yellow brick road. Urban space here is depersonalized, emiserated and repressive, permeated with the imagery of the abject, including the grotesquely ageing young woman and a close-up of a spider crawling across a human hand.

The commercial's transition from monochrome to colour coincides with the magical movement from city to country via the use of gliding camera, fog and dissolves, delivering viewers to an equally stylized isolated single-family house. The house lacks any spatial context beyond a featureless lawn (evoking the placelessness of a literal utopia). The interior of the commercial's modest house, furnished in the minimalist good taste and abstraction of an Ikea display window, is saturated with the visual tropes of domesticity, including a purple armchair, coffee cup and billowing sunlit curtains.

At the same time, however, the commercial is tellingly vague about the precise nature of the consumer's activity in front of the computer, offering little more than an extreme close-up of a disembodied finger on the keyboard, and minimal text and animation on a computer screen, including 'Pay to the order of . . .' and symbols for pounds and dollars. Despite Saatchi's claims for the ad's effectiveness in increased consumer recall rates and intended-purchase reports, as Jeremy Pemberton concludes, 'It is always hard to show the positives of something like a computer, and it is easier to find dramatic potential in demonstrating the negative before introducing the product, but it's hard bolting the two bits together successfully and avoiding a let-down at the end.'[40] Indeed, it is hard to believe that the Packard Bell ads could have been terribly effective, since the first three-quarters of the commercial is so obscure and visually compelling that it overpowers the brief concluding voice-over slogan and happy product take-up. The non-realist depiction of the house and sketchy representation of interaction with the computer fail to leave viewers with a strong sense of the precise utility of the home computer; instead, the effect is one of generalized city-bashing and cinematic aestheticism. Indeed, despite Saatchi's expensive attempts to brand the Packard Bell product by linking it to a new high-tech domesticity, within a few years the company had succumbed to new direct-to-consumer PC manufacturers like Dell and to the dwindling profits of the stagnant home-PC market. Packard Bell went out of business completely in 1999.[41]

The market position of software monopolist Microsoft in the second half of the 1990s was certainly quite different from that of companies in the fiercely competitive home-PC market who faced minimal barriers to entry and little room for product differentiation. However, the television ad campaigns of Packard Bell and Microsoft from the late 1990s share some of the same anti-urban animus and imagery. Microsoft's 1998 'Lusk, Wyoming' campaign followed close on the heels of it's unprecedented marketing of the Windows 95 operating system from its ad agency Wieden and Kennedy. However, while the Windows 95 launch was considered a major success for the software giant, it is important to note Microsoft's failed marketing efforts on behalf of the software shell Microsoft Bob and the company's AOL-clone MSN around the same time.

The Lusk campaign by Wieden and Kennedy is in stark contrast to the earlier Rolling Stones-backed 'Start me up' campaign for Windows 95; in place of that campaign's fast-moving, highly edited and edgy urban imagery (accompanied by the slogan 'Where do you want to go today?'), the Lusk Wyoming ad's leisurely sixty seconds, avuncular narrator, college-radio friendly score, and relentless iconography of rural Americana seems to reflect Microsoft's attempt to reintroduce itself as corporate all-American in the context of escalating anti-trust complaints. The 2,500-person former gold-mining, cattle and oil town of Lusk is located in the most sparsely settled county of the nation's most sparsely settled state (Lusk residents faced a 57-mile journey to the nearest movie theatre). The small community gained national press attention in the mid-90s after its mayor, inspired by *Megatrends*, John Nesbitt's 1980s bestseller on the promise of the information economy to revive the economic prospects for rural areas, successfully applied for state and federal grants to install seventeen miles of fibre-optic cable in the town. The town's efforts to promote its place on America's much-ballyhooed information superhighway was the subject of a 1995 CBS *Sunday Morning* news broadcast, which included an interview with John Battelle, the executive managing editor of *Wired* magazine, who argued that the Internet promised a path to rural revival across the US.

However, as print media delighted in pointing out, years after the Microsoft Lusk ad began running, the town had yet to devise how to financially support the connection of its fibre-optic system to the outside world. One local resident commented on Microsoft's choice to celebrate Lusk as the wired rural future in a 1999 *Denver Post* article: 'You wonder who checked it out, because it's been obvious . . . to the local community for some time that it really hasn't provided a tangible benefit. It's kind of a joke, but it just keeps popping its head up and people keep giving the town kudos for it. It's the story that won't die.'[42] Indeed, as the reporter noted, even the local school's 56k dial-up Internet access was cut off by school officials in early 1999 after students used Microsoft's Hotmail service to send pornographic messages. A 2001 front-page article in the same newspaper on Microsoft's Lusk campaign concluded by analogizing Microsoft's marketing exploitation of the town to the itinerant clients of its once-famous whorehouse: 'Like the roughnecks who frequented Dell's bordello, Microsoft got what it wanted from Lusk and left . . . Such are the rhythms of prosperity in Wyoming: Life is good when somebody somewhere else wants something Wyoming has. Grass, land, gold, oil or just a good backdrop for ads.'[43]

This brief tour of some of the technophilic punditry and marketing images from the fevered dotcom era of the 1990s suggests some that some caution is appropriate in approaching conventional accounts of the social impact of media technologies. The track record of a century of optimistic predictions from conservative commentators about the power of electronic media to reverse the forces of urbanization is not impressive. Electric power and the telephone, for example, fueled both the growth of streetcar suburbs and the modern skyscraper, enabling both unprecedented sprawl and concentration. However, despite their dubious predictive value, the implications for media historians of these failed, if persistent, traditions of wishful thinking remain worth considering. Beyond pointing to the value of the close examination of specific historical moments of media hybridity, the perennial appeal to anti-urban sentiments in historically distinct debates regarding the electronic media suggests the value of examining the role of long-standing, if often implicit, ideas which enjoy genuine historical agency in shaping the reception and uses of new media technologies. The widely predicted disruptive effects of a range of currently emerging public and domestic moving-image platforms suggest the usefulness of a historical reconsideration both of earlier periods of technological innovation and of the lingering effects of modes of thought in unravelling the meaning of our own era's prospects and choices.

4

Breaking the Time Barrier
with John Cage

Charlie Gere

The plane may have been going to Montreal, or just to upstate New York. Or it could have been coming the other way, flying towards one of the recently opened airports surrounding New York City, LaGuardia, Newark or Idlewild. It might have been a B52 Bomber, production of which started in that year. Perhaps its contrail was spotted by a member of the Ground Observer Corp, inaugurated that year by President Truman under the name 'Operation Skywatch', to watch the skies for Soviet nuclear bombers. It is unlikely the crew or passengers would have realized they were being so surveyed, or that they would have appreciated the role they would play in one of the most important events in postwar art. Just as they passed over Woodstock, a town then best known for its artists' colony and later to become a metonym for sex, drugs and rock and roll, the pianist David Tudor was starting to play the last piece in a concert of works for piano being held at the Maverick Hall in Woodstock. Before the plane passed over Woodstock, Tudor had already sat down and raised the piano lid, but to the audience's consternation he had not touched the keys. This went on for thirty seconds. He then lowered the lid, raised it again, and again did nothing, this time for two minutes and twenty-three seconds, during which time the noise of the plane passing over was clearly audible. He then lowered the lid a second time, raised it again, and played nothing for one minute and forty seconds.[1]

The audience in the concert hall were bemused, confused and in some cases angry, and the reverberations of the performance were felt far

43

beyond Woodstock. What they had just heard was, of course, the first performance of John Cage's *4' 33"*, the so-called 'silent piece'. Despite being referred to as such, not least by Cage himself, it is not actually about silence. According to Cage it was inspired, in part at least, by his experience in Harvard University's anechoic chamber, where he failed to hear the silence he expected.[2] What he heard instead, according to his own account, was the noise of his nervous system. This experience taught him that silence as such was not possible, or at least it is impossible to hear silence.[3] Thus *4' 33"* is about dismantling the boundaries between noise and music and between the performer(s), the audience and the environment. The noise in this case was that of wind in the trees outside, of the confused and even angry murmurs of the audience, of cars driving past the concert hall and, of course, of the solitary plane.[4]

4' 33" was an extraordinary achievement. It was a kind of ground zero of the postwar avant-garde, clearing the ground for subsequent developments in one apocalyptic gesture. It was and indeed remains controversial and has generated a great deal of critical noise. It succeeded partly because of Cage's patent sincerity and engagement, though as a number of commentators have pointed out, this did not prevent him from editing and embroidering the story of its creation. Nevertheless, along with Cage's other famous work of 1952, the 'untitled event' performed at Black Mountain College in Asheville, North Carolina, *4' 33"* expressed, in artistic form, ideas about radical changes in our conceptions of history, time, speed and attention brought about by technological developments and made evident by the Cold War and the threat of nuclear conflict, ideas which found different kinds of expression in the development of real-time information and communications technologies, and in concomitant later developments such as interactive, real-time multimedia systems.

The Cold War, which began even as the Second World War was ending, made it necessary to develop new forms of attention and observation and new means of interpreting what was observed. At first, through the 1940s and 1950s, the public, in the United States at least, was comparatively unperturbed by the dangers of nuclear war. Though there was clearly some anxiety, there was also a general belief in the nation's military and industrial power, particularly in the light of the unprecedented postwar prosperity and the accompanying rise of the consumer culture. This in turn led to a generally conformist and conservative society: Margot Henriksen has described America's 'unnerving and unnatural' placidity in this period.[5] Yet each Cold War flare-up, each statement by figures such as John Foster Dulles (best known as President Eisenhower's Secretary of State) about 'brinkmanship' or 'more bang for the buck', as his massive retaliation policy became known as, brought Americans face to face with the stark facts of nuclear conflict, and made their serenity seem 'nothing less than an insane denial of reality'.[6] Gradually the reality of the situation became too overwhelming to be repressed and Americans woke up to the need to properly consider civil defence. Throughout the 1950s numerous plans were proposed and debated. These plans interestingly led to ever-greater popularity for the suburbs, residence in which was seen as more likely to enable survival.[7]

Norbert Wiener, the developer of cybernetics, even advocated encouraging the building of out-of-town supermarkets as useful in the context of possible social infrastructures.[8] One of the most widely taken pieces of advice was to build a bomb shelter. In the early '60s Americans in their millions built shelters in a kind of frenzy.[9] Despite such action and the increasingly available government advice on what to do in the event of a nuclear attack, it had already become fairly obvious that the chances of surviving one were minimal, and such life as might be lived in the aftermath might not be worth it. Mental health problems proliferated in the United States.[10] A generation of schoolchildren were made intensely aware of the fragility of their existence through constant drilling in how to behave in the event of air raids.[11] What distinguished the fears kindled in the Cold War was the hopelessness and utter destructiveness promised by the Bomb as well as the pervasive paranoia, in which being able to identify whether a film actor was a communist intent on subtly undermining American morale and whether an object in the sky was a Soviet bomber were both urgent matters of national security.

The Ground Observer Corps, mentioned at the beginning of this essay, was an early and desperate response to the latter question. Originally founded in the Second World War and revived by Truman in 1952 for 'Operation Skywatch', it consisted of some 300,000 volunteers whose job was to supplement inadequate radar defences. The volunteers sat in wooden huts positioned at strategic points in the United States and Canada. Their job was to watch and listen for airplanes, paying particular attention to their contrails and shapes. With the help of a booklet issued by the Air Force they had to identify passing planes. Any sighting had to be reported immediately to the local 'Filter Center' with the words 'Aircraft Flash Aircraft Flash'. In the Filter Center the report would be interpreted, and compared with other reports and with radar data. In theory any sighting could have been of Soviet bombers, at which point the apparatus of military defence and retaliation and civil defence would have been put into motion, with schoolchildren presumably 'ducking and covering' under their desks, as they had been taught to in their drills. In fact no Soviet bomber was ever spotted by the GOC.[12]

While John Cage's work was rarely explicitly political, and it would be simplistic to suggest that *4' 33"* was in any direct sense a comment on questions of nuclear paranoia and defence, at a deeper level it can be read as symptomatic of a context in which new forms of attention and new understandings of time were necessary. The bemused audience at the first performance of *4' 33"* and the members of the Ground Observer Corps were both new kinds of observers, necessitated by a context in which the time available to pay attention was radically attenuated. Cage was also inspired to compose *4' 33"* by the all-white paintings of his friend Robert Rauschenberg, which were immediately preceded by his extraordinary early collage 'Mother of God', which took its title from the Catholic prayer 'Hail Mary' ('Holy Mary, Mother of God, pray for us sinners, now and at the hour of our death') and which consists of a number of black and white city maps over which a white circle has been crudely painted, invoking both diagrams of blast areas, with which the American public were probably familiar, and the round screen of the radar. The words 'Mother of God' may be taken both as a prayer that might be uttered at the moment of nuclear apocalypse and as a vernacular epithet of horror and outrage. The theme of nuclear annihilation lends additional irony to the collaged caption at lower right that reads: 'An invaluable spiritual road map. As simple and fundamental as life itself.—Catholic Review.'

It is hard not to read the nihilism of 'Mother of God' in Rauschenberg's subsequent white series. Yet Cage famously refused to see these works as empty, describing them instead as environments or surfaces in which events may take place. He even describes them as 'landing-grounds' for dust.[13] Thus Cage repudiated the implicit nihilism of Rauschenberg's use of white, by suggesting that empty spaces, whether visual or aural, can become the space in which something happens, something goes on happening. Art can thus cease to be about objects and become the space in which things happen, anything happens, and people communicate. In a sense Cage invents interactivity and multimedia. Or rather he anticipates the development of the technologies that would make them possible and opens up another space for thinking about their use.

In fact Cage himself was in a good position to appreciate such scientific and technical concepts. His father was an occasionally successful inventor[14] and Cage himself had been incorporating communication devices such as radios and gramophones in his work since the 1930s.[15] Cage was also exempted from military service during the Second World War, on the grounds that he was assisting his father's research on radar.[16] Though it is hard to know how much research he actually did, and what it involved, this is intriguing. Radar, one of the most important inventions of the War, has had a far greater influence on our contemporary culture than is usually acknowledged,[17] and was more important than the original digital computer in the development of contemporary real-time interactive technologies and multimedia. It was only when the computer was combined with radar in the 1950s as part of nuclear defence that the current understanding of the computer as a real-time technology began to form. The radar also embodied many of the issues concerning feedback and communication that drove research into information and communication systems. Above all it was the first instantiation of the apparatus of real-time attention and response, allowing instant calculation and communication and the handling of different types of data, whose further development in the Cold War would consequently enable the restructuring of capital and finance in the seventies and eighties. Radar is also particularly relevant to Cage's notions of noise and silence, in that it uses sound to map the surrounding environment. Even more appropriate, given the close relationship between the aural and the visual in Cage's work and his interest in the theatrical, is that the information that is generated by the sound is rendered visually. Cage's *4' 3"* highlighted the need to pay attention to the immediate environment and to be able to interpret the noise it produced as signal. Thus the piece is a kind of anticipation of real-time technologies of attention that were beginning to emerge as a result of the Cold War.

The development of digital and other information-communication technologies was greatly facilitated by the work of engineers such as Claude Shannon, whose information theory presents some interesting parallels to Cage's work of the same period. Shannon's concerns were how to find the most efficient way of encoding what he called information in a particular coding system in a noiseless environment and how to deal with the problem of noise when it occurred.[18] 'Noise' was

Shannon's term for the elements of a signal that are extraneous to the message being transmitted.[19] Through these means Shannon developed a successful general theory for mathematically calculating the efficiency of a communications system that was applicable to both analog and digital systems. After the War, Shannon's theory was of great use in the burgeoning development of binary digital computers, in the expansion and technological advance of telecommunications, telegraphy, radio and television, as well as in servomechanical devices using feedback signals, and in computers, for which his emphasis on binary logic made the application of his ideas particularly appropriate. He also developed the concept of redundancy, which showed that messages often contained extraneous and repetitive elements to ensure transmission despite the presence of noise.[20] In a sense Shannon's concept of communication is the exact inverse of Cage's strategy in *4' 33"*, in that Cage seeks to show that, in Shannonian terms, noise *is* signal.

Shannon adopted the term 'entropy' from thermodynamics to refer to the measure of a communication system's efficiency in transmitting a signal, which was computed on the basis of the statistical properties of the message source.[21] For Shannon the greater the disorder, or higher the entropy, of a message, the more choices are available and therefore the more information that message contains. Though this formulation works for Shannon's purposes in thinking about communication, it remains controversial in terms of the uncertain relation between information and the physical sciences. For some the problem is simply one of semantics and there is no connection between the concerns of physics and those of information.[22] For others, particularly those involved with chaos theory and complexity theory, the conflation of thermodynamics and information shows that randomness, understood as maximum information, is 'the source of all that is new in the world'.[23] This idea was crucial for theorists concerned with the application of information theory to the creative arts.

In his book *The Coming of the Golden Age: A View of the End of Progress* the biologist Gunther Stent used Shannon's information theory to show how Cage represented 'the end of art'. Stent follows the work of musicologist Leonard Meyer, whom he quotes as arguing that 'musical meaning arises when an antecedent situation [of tone sequences], requiring an estimate [by the listener] of probable modes of pattern continuation, produces uncertainty about the temporal nature of the expected consequent'.[24] This definition derives from information theory, in which, as Stent puts it, the 'amount of information embodied in any event is the higher the greater the number of alternative events which the percipient would expect to occur given the antecedent situation'.[25] For an event to have meaning 'it's occurrence must not only have been uncertain, but it must be capable also of modifying the probabilistic appreciation of the consequences of the earlier antecedent situation. Thus as a meaningful piece of music unfolds the listener is constantly modifying what he expects to hear on the basis of what he has already heard . . .'[26]

From this, Stent extrapolates the idea that music must evolve towards greater freedom, as listeners develop their sophistication through the accumulated capital of previously created significant structures.[27] Thus for Stent the history of music is a process of the achievement of successive freedoms in which styles emerge and their possibilities are exhausted, necessitating the development of new styles with greater degrees of unpredictability. In the course of this history this process of stylistic evolution has accelerated, particularly because of the parallel progress in the technological means of securing 'the accumulation of musical capital against the vagaries of human memory'.[28] This starts with musical notation but gathers speed with printing and then the advent of the phonograph, radio, the LP and tape. 'Thus listener sophistication could rise at an ever greater rate, allowing in turn for an ever-faster stylistic evolution.'[29] Stent suggests that:

> as artistic evolution unfolds, the artist is being freed more and more from strict canons governing the method of working his medium of creative expression. The end result of this evolution has been that, finally, in our time, the artist's liberation has been almost total. However, the artist's succession to near-total freedom of expression now presents very great difficulties for the appreciation of his work: the absence of recognisable canons reduces his act of creation to near randomness for the perceiver. In other words, artistic evolution along the one-way street to freedom embodies an element of self-limitation. The greater the freedom already attained and hence the closer the approach to the random of any artistic style for the percipient, the less possible for any successor style to seem significantly different from its predecessor.[30]

For Stent, the serial music of Arnold Schönberg, though radically evolved towards almost total freedom, still has rules; but the final stages of this evolutionary process have been reached with the work of John

Cage, which relies for its effects either on pure chance or on the eschewal of any predetermined goal. 'For here almost all rules that would allow communication to the listener of a musical structure have been abandoned . . . Thus, with this development, music as an art which endeavours to communicate truths about the world *has* reached the end of the line.'[31]

Stent suggests that in order to understand what composers such as Cage are attempting it is necessary to understand their view of the world, which is radically different to that associated with rationality. Stent quotes Meyer's notion of 'transcendentalism', which 'shows strong affinities to the precepts of Zen Buddhism':

> . . . [T]he transcendentalist believes that concrete, particular sense experiences are the only truths to be found in the world. Any attempt to construct a reality by inferring imaginary causal relations between or among these sense experiences obscures rather than reveals the essential truth of existence, namely that every fact of the universe is unique. It becomes apparent at once to anyone holding such a belief that the very idea is anathema that the meaning of a piece of music for the listener devolves from the structure he perceives in the probabilistic connections of its temporal–tonal sequence. Instead, for a transcendentalist the music is just *there*, and any analytical cerebrations only interfere with its experience as primary fact.[32]

For Meyer the transcendentalist mode entails a rejection of what he describes as goal orientation or teleology in music, and more generally of the notion of progress. He quotes the composer Christian Wolff (from Cage's book *Silence*) as saying that:

> The music has a static character. It goes in no particular direction. There is no necessary concern with time as a measure of distance from a point in the past to a point in the future . . . It is not a question of getting anywhere, of making progress, or having come from anywhere in particular.[33]

Thus the end of time in music and the threatened end of human existence through nuclear annihilation converge in *4' 33"*, to effect what Ernst Jünger described as the 'breaking of the time barrier', the point where technology overhauls human progress.[34] The threat of annihilation in a few hours or, eventually, minutes meant that previous linear models of development and progress, whether at a personal or societal level, were no longer tenable. *4' 33"* was about paying attention to the now, in a time when time itself appeared radically foreshortened. *4' 33"* seems intent on forestalling the very acts of protention and retention through which consciousness synthesizes time (and for which the ordered experience of music is a privileged instance), and replacing them with the inchoate experience of the now, or what Christian Wolff called 'Zero Time'.

In 1969 Cage featured in a special edition of Marshall McLuhan's *Dew-Line Newsletter*, which McLuhan began as a comparatively immediate way of presenting his ideas and those of his collaborators.[35] Part of this edition is in the form of a pack of cards, the 'Distant Early Warning Deck'. (In keeping with McLuhan's interest in the forms of media, many of the newsletters took unusual and experimental form). Each card has a quote from a different thinker or artist. The five of diamonds is dedicated to Cage, and bears the following quote: '[s]ilence is all the sounds of the environment at once.' Developing Ezra Pound's idea that artists are the antennae of the human race, McLuhan had earlier suggested that '*[art] at its most significant is a distant early warning system that can always be relied on to tell the old culture what is beginning to happen to it.*'[36] 'Distant early warning system' and the newsletter's title are references to the DEW (distant early warning) Line, the air-defence system manned by the GOC as described above. Much of the DEW Line was sited in McLuhan's native Canada, and it is possibly this connection that gave it particular meaning for him, beyond its obvious Cold War resonance. As he had spent much of his early career in the United States, relations between one of the world's two superpowers and its northern neighbour would have been an interest and a concern. When understood in relation to the system that inspired it, the McLuhan quotation takes on a different and more sinister meaning than at first might appear. Far from being a system for warning about distant events, art must respond to what is happening right now, to events and situations that have potentially apocalyptic meanings and consequences, and which, like the nuclear catastrophes the DEW Line was supposed to anticipate, radically alter our relationship with time and history.

Systems such as the DEW Line were first constructed at almost exactly the same time as the first performance of *4' 33"*, when the inadequacies of Cold War defence systems such as the GOC began to be addressed. In 1951 installation of the 'Pinetree' Line of thirty or so early-warning radar stations along the 50th parallel was started. Three years later the Mid-Canada Line with ninety-eight sites along the 54th and 55th parallels was instigated. In 1955 work on the DEW Line was started. This was a chain of over sixty radar and communications stations stretching 3,000 miles from the northwest coast of Alaska to the eastern shore of Baffin Island opposite Greenland. It was designed to detect and discourage any attack by the Soviet Union taking place by way of the North Pole. There is a fascinating connection between Cage and the DEW Line, in that the radar arrays were housed in geodesic 'radomes' designed by Cage's mentor and friend R(ichard) Buckminster Fuller.[37] The increasingly complex task of coordinating data from these networks led to the development of centralized computer control systems, such as the Strategic Air-Ground Environment, or SAGE.

The idea was to build a national perimeter radar air defence, controlled by computers, which would not only detect incoming planes, but also issue flight vectors to intercepting aircraft. This would involve not just thousands of radar stations but also the development of extremely powerful and reliable computers, incorporating many innovative technologies. Though, in the end, SAGE did not contribute much in practical terms to air defence, it was of enormous importance in the development of computers. In practical terms it enabled the development of almost all of the technology we now take for granted as part of computing and multimedia. Among specific technologies it made possible or helped develop are magnetic memory, video displays, effective computer languages, graphic display techniques, simulation techniques, analog-to-digital and digital-to-analog conversion techniques, multiprocessing and networking. This list comprises some, if not the majority, of the most important developments in computing. It might be said that Whirlwind and SAGE were in effect the beginning of computing, as we now understand it, as a 'real-time' technology, as well as making possible computer multimedia (Whirlwind was the computer developed at MIT that was later adopted by SAGE). They were the means by which the computer ceased to be regarded as simply a number cruncher and became instead something more like radar, a real-time symbolic representation and manipulation machine.[38]

The rise of publicly available computer multimedia is, arguably, an epiphenomenon of this process of transformation, in which we apprehend and engage with the world using the technologies of nuclear paranoia. McLuhan clearly regarded Cage as a kind of artistic early warning system. This is what John Cage perhaps foresaw on his own radar screen, and about which *4' 33"* constitutes a warning: a world of blank screens and empty spaces in which events can happen, without warning, and in which it may no longer be possible or even necessary to distinguish noise from signal, a world demanding new understandings of time, speed and history and requiring new forms of attention. It is a tribute to Cage's optimism that he could embrace such emptiness as an opportunity for the new and the unexpected. Confronted with the abyss of nuclear destruction few would have felt so positive about such technologies. And perhaps confronted now with the speed and reach of globalized capitalism made possible by the technologies of nuclear paranoia his optimism may still seem misplaced, even if we have, so far, avoided nuclear apocalypse. It is worth noting that, exactly a decade after *4' 3"* , Cage produced an even more radical sequel *0' 00" (4' 33" no. 2)*, which consisted of the instructions 'in a situation provided with maximum amplification (no feedback), perform a disciplined action'. The title suggests perhaps that in the ten years between the two pieces time had become even more attenuated.

Section Two

Exploring Remediation:
Old Formats into New

5

From the Album Page to the Computer Screen
Collecting Photographs at Home

Patrizia Di Bello

The development of photography in the nineteenth century is often discussed in terms of theories of vision and the gaze.[1] This is partly a response to the way photographs are made. The image is set up by the photographer, who frames it spatially and temporally, but unlike a draughtsman, who has to use his hands to record on paper the image formed by the camera obscura, the photographer stands back and lets technology do the job. As Walter Benjamin noted in 'The Work of Art in the Age of Mechanical Reproduction', 'photography freed the hand of the most important artistic function which henceforth devolved only upon the eye looking into the lens'.[2]

Photographic prints, however, are used in ways and social contexts that often involve not only gazing but also holding and touching. The photograph is 'accessible to handling in a way that painting, for example, is not'.[3] Writing about 'Photographs as Objects of Memory', Elizabeth Edwards emphasizes the importance of the tactile experience of photographic prints, in their role as privileged conduits of memory.[4] Making wider claims for the importance of considering photographs as tactile visual objects, Geoffrey Batchen argues that 'photography is privileged within modern culture because, unlike other systems of representation, the camera does more than just see the world: it is also touched by it'.[5] Drawing on Roland Barthes identification of the '*noeme*' of photography as the way in which the photograph's sensitive surface is touched by the same rays of light that had touched the world, Batchen argues that objects integrating photographic images with handmade arrangements, reciprocate not the visual but the tactile gift of the photograph.[6] In this essay, I compare the dynamics of vision and touch in nineteenth-century albums with those in the contemporary album, mediated by digital technologies.

1) Albums, digital and non

Much of the literature on digital photography, or photography in the digital age, emphasizes a drastic break in the nature of the medium. Photography is dead, or at least not itself anymore. As Hubertus van Amelunxen writes in the catalogue of the exhibition *Photography after Photography*, an 'existential doubt' has 'crept into our understanding of these images', caused by 'a digital world which would no longer permit a distinction . . . between the real impression . . . and a "representation" generated in the darkness of the computer'.[7] In Victor Burgin's contribution to the same catalogue, he points out how 'the largely unquestioned assumption that the intrinsic and essential nature of the photographic apparatus is to record factual reality has been completely over-turned with the arrival of digital photography'.[8] In 'analog' photography, as Laura Marks explains:

> it is possible to trace a physical path from the object represented, to the light that reflects off it, to the photographic emulsion . . . that the light hits, to the resulting image. In digital imaging this path is not traceable, for an additional step is added: converting the image into data, and thereby breaking the link between image and physical referent. Any iteration of the image may be altered, and there is no 'generational' difference to alert us to the stage at which the change occurred.[9]

Narratives about the death of photography as we know it tend to focus on its uses as evidence, particularly in documentary or legal contexts. The view from home seems less troubled by the introduction of digital technologies. As Mary Warner Marien argues:

> Perhaps the best example of the persistence of photography as an idea issues from the willingness of cyberspace-dwelling vernacular

images of births, parties, and vacation trips, taken with digital cameras or made chemically, printed, and then scanned into computers. These images are widely understood by their makers and viewers to be historically continuous with chemically-based photographs, regardless of their electronic means of recording and dissemination.[10]

Personal albums in the age of digital media seem comfortable with multimediality and hybridity, happy to mix photographs with computer manipulations, and to deploy the latest developments in scanners and digicams to create nostalgic photographic objects embroidered with 'Victorian' designs, following instructions and templates downloaded from the plethora of amateur and commercial websites dedicated to album making, 'scrapbooking', and 'Victorian Albums'.[11]

We might of course consider this to be simply a case of naivete. Don Slater, for example, argues that the family album has not been as affected as it should have been by digital culture, nor by postmodern critiques of the transparency and realism of the photograph.[12] For Lev Manovich, 'any photographic image also connotes memory and nostalgia, nostalgia for . . . the era of the pre-digital, pre-post-modern'.[13] I would suggest that if the makers of cyberalbums do not 'panic about the loss of the real' (to paraphrase a comment by Sarah Kember) it is because album makers have always known, even in the nineteenth century, that 'the real is always already lost in representation'.[14]

In a circa 2002 television ad for the Nokia 'Imaging Phone' (as Nokia used to call camera phones) we see a young couple at a fair. The boy wins a ring on one of the stalls, and gives it to the girl. She puts it on, and then, in a casual parody of 'share a moment, share a life', sends a picture of her ringed finger to a friend, accompanied by the caption 'can you keep a secret?' As the image bounces across mobile phones and computers, girlfriends and sisters, it is not clear if the excited response of the recipients is make-believe, going along with the joke, or a sign of having been taken in by the prank ('winding your mates up' is an important function of camera phones, if ads are anything to go by). When the couple arrives back at her home they are totally puzzled by the ecstatic reception they get from her parents, who think they really got engaged. The ad neatly makes the point that most photographs are likely to be ambiguous, their meaning unclear even when straight and un-manipulated. Writers on photography such as Martha Rosler, Allan Sekula and John Tagg have been arguing since the 1970s that the meaning of photographs is context-determined, open to different and conflicting readings, their 'realism' a cultural construction.[15] The most insidious manipulation of photographs can be in captions and texts, even if—especially if—they are not actually lying. Can you keep a secret? But, in the social interactions described by the ad, these ambiguities are accepted, celebrated and played with; they are not a cause of anxiety, but a source of fun.

These social interactions, at once acknowledging and sending up the idea of photography's correspondence to reality, are rooted in those engendered by photographic exchanges in the mid-nineteenth century, when photographs first became widespread in the West, in the form of the *carte-de-visite* portrait. As I have argued elsewhere, the reason for its success lay not in its correspondence with some truth about the inner or social qualities of the portrayed, but in participating in a social sphere—at once real and imaginary—of drawing-room albums and photographic studios.[16] As these studios also sold to the general public the *carte* portraits of famous, fashionable or simply beautiful people who had happened to patronize them, the same *carte* could be exchanged as a gift from the portrayed to family, friends and acquaintances while also being available to anyone. As 'cartomania' spread, photographic albums became all the rage, mixing bestowed or commissioned *cartes* of people one really knew with bought *cartes* of people one wanted to fantasize about knowing.

First used to describe publicly available lists of people, for example, those who had matriculated in a university, the word 'album' (from the Latin '*albus*', 'white') was used from the mid-seventeenth century for the blank books in which visitors, for example to a country house, were invited to contribute signatures or short pieces of writing, in a practice not unlike that of contemporary websites. In general terms, to be included in an album was a sign of participating in or belonging to a community defined by intellectual, social or sentimental connections. By the early nineteenth century, albums were used to collect music, poetry, watercolours and prints, as well as any other flat and light-weight souvenir. Images and texts could be handmade or mechanically reproduced, original or copied. Albums were an important part of drawing-room entertainment, providing scope for solitary visual perusal and something to talk about with superficial acquaintances, as well as a basis for intimate chats and occasion for flirting. The skills involved in making them were valued female accomplishments, particularly in fashionable upper-class society, or in political circles, where albums could

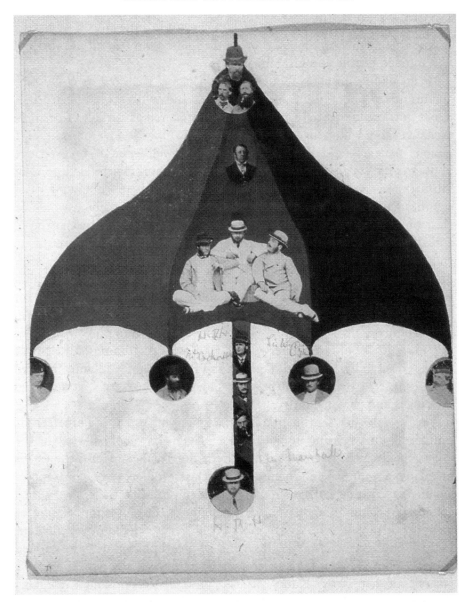

Fig. 8.   Page from Lady Mary Filmer's album, 1860s. Cut-out albumen prints of photographs of HRH The Prince of Wales and other men, on a watercolour and gold-paint umbrella. Courtesy of Musée d'Orsay. Photo: RMN—© Hervé Lewandowski.

also function as public-relations tools. Displayed to the stream of visitors to important drawing rooms, they defined and consolidated networks of like-minded people and fashionable sets.

As do albums on many contemporary personal websites, carte-de-visite albums mixed photographs of family and friends with those of celebrities —but how could one tell which had been procured as a result of personal exchange and which had been bought? Owning a carte portrait of a famous person could imply knowing them well enough to exchange photographs, a gesture that remained associated with a degree of intimacy, or it might simply imply knowing where to buy it. The significance of including a celebrity photograph in one's album would be clear only in the context of the relative social statuses of the portrayed and the owner of the album, and the likelihood of their being intimate enough to exchange photographs. In a society preoccupied with nuances of status, and with suggesting, demonstrating, or even exaggerating social connections, assessing this likelihood was part of the fun of looking at these albums. Conversely, the fantasy of being seen 'in good company' in someone else's album, or even mingling with other celebrities in the photographer's shop window, was an important element in the desirability of studio portraits. Photographic albums blurred distinctions between private persons and public characters, commercial exchanges and personal gifts.

The social and sentimental connections suggested by nineteenth-century albums became at once more playful and sophisticated in the mixed-media albums created throughout the 1860s and into the 1870s by many accomplished, mainly upper-class women, who customized albums by creating collages mixing photographs with their own water-colours. A common motif of these albums is the insertion of photo-graphic portraits into images of everyday objects rendered in watercolour. Lady Filmer seemed to like inserting photographs of men in painted parasols—both crucial female accessories, perhaps. Lady Milles pasted a portrait of her sister Fanny Stracey onto a teacup, and Georgiana Berkeley pasted photographs of family and friends on a whole range of objects, from jewellery and luggage to the posters and sandwich boards crowding a London street scene.[17] Another recurring strategy is the use of small portrait 'heads'(usually sold to be mounted in lockets) as postage stamps on drawings of envelopes or to personalize the Kings, Queens and Knaves of painted playing cards. Even when the watercolour sections are painted in a realistic style, the two orders of representation— the pictorial and the photographic—remain obviously in conflict. The

Fig. 9.   Page from Lady Charlotte Milles's album, *c*.1868. Cut-out
albumen print of a photograph of her sister Fanny Stracey, on
a watercolour and ink teacup.
Courtesy of Harry Ransom Humanities Research Center,
University of Texas at Austin.

different spatial orders—the photograph, the object depicted, and the flat page—seem to pull and deform even the most accomplished collage, undermining any semblance of actuality that might have come from the detailed realism of either the photographs or the watercolours on their own.

What these mixed-media albums seem to emphasize is not only the collector's skills in customizing the usually stereotyped portrait photographs according to different, desirable styles of femininity (fashionable flirt, twirling men around her fingers like parasols; devoted sister; or girl-about-town, busy on the social circuit), but also the gap between reality and representation present in all photographs. This gap opens up a space for the collector to fill with fantasies, jokes, melancholic longings (nonetheless pleasurable for being so), and above all her or his own touch.

2) Fingers and Digits

Lewis Carroll, in the 1870s, recorded in his diary that he spent 'four hours over family album' and that 'mounting photos (including finding and cutting out the print) takes about 9 min. apiece'.[18] Less painstaking collectors had been able to use, since the 1860s, 'slip-in' albums, conveniently pre-cut with window mounts in which standard-sized *cartes-de-visite* and cabinet prints could be inserted easily. By the late 1870s, printers were also selling ready-customized albums, imitating the look of earlier upper-class albums, decorated with printed borders, floral motifs and landscapes, not unlike the templates available today for digital albums. As these became widespread, the fashion for hand-decorated albums started to wane amongst upper-class women.

Albums, like photography itself, can be seen as operating according to the logic of fashion and commodification. Commercial culture follows the cultural practices of elite groups, making them available to wider sections of society, until they begin to lose their connotations of exclusivity and desirability. At the same time, complex, time-consuming skilled labour is reduced to the operation of a machine.

By the late twentieth century the sheer quantity of snapshot prints arriving in most Western homes, meant that they largely remained in the wallets provided by the processing services, with the exception of those displayed in wedding albums, baby books or other photo collections documenting important life events. At the same time, personal computers and the internet were beginning to be used to digitize and manipulate photographs, and create personal websites. Now, easy-to-use software and digital services turn photos into digital collections to be viewed on the computer or television screen, made into a website or kept as customized or customized-looking collections of paper pages.

Digital technologies promise to make Carroll's painstaking task of mounting photos in the album 'quick, easy and interesting', as one website selling family-album software says—just 'Click Here to Order This Product!' The speed at which something amazing happens at the click of a button is a staple of ads for computers and software. Labelling, sorting and finding are no longer mediated by the thick carnality of bodies and hands, looking through endless envelopes, sorting piles ever getting mixed up again, struggling with scissors, glues and inks, which never behave as smoothly as they should. In the thin medium of cyberspace, snapshots fly into place like toys in Mary Poppins' nursery. At the click of a button we can copy and send pictures to our sister, our family, to everyone in our address book, in an exhilarating gesture a bit like the last move in a game of FreeCell, that most addictive click which screams 'again, again' like a Teletubby. And we don't need to worry about the album's being spoiled by too many visitors, children's sticky hands and drinkers' carelessness with their glasses. The digital album is always shiny and brand new, untouched by domestic dirt and finger-prints.

3) Visual and Tactile Traces

Charles Sander Peirce was, at the turn of the century, the first to write explicitly about the photograph's affinity with other signs, such as footprints or mirror images, which denote objects by physically being caused by them.[19] These are signs that point to their material cause as their meaning, like an index finger. An icon is a sign which looks the same as the object signified, for example a portrait; and a symbol is a sign related to its meaning only by social conventions. In the photograph, iconic and indexical features come together; a photographic portrait refers to the portrayed because it looks like him or her, but it is also an index of that person, physically caused by his or her presence in front of the camera. Unlike a painted or digitally simulated portrait, a photo-graph cannot be made from memory or the imagination.

Roland Barthes' *Camera Lucida* is perhaps the most cited formulation of the power of photographic portraits to affect us. Influenced by phenomenology and Lacanian psychoanalysis, Barthes' reflections are framed as a search for the common element in his, and by extension his culture's, fascination with photographs, beyond their individual historical or aesthetic significance. He finds this common element in their capacity to point to something 'that has been', their power as 'an emanation of the referent': 'from a real body, which was there, proceed radiations which ultimately touch me, who am here'.[20] This becomes apparent to him only when he turns to a photograph of his own mother. She was there, and the light reflected off her body has been captured and 'cast' into precious silver by the photographic process, creating an image of luminosity.

The indexical characteristics of photography were not unnoticed in the nineteenth century. They were probably first theorized by David Brewster, in an article published in 1843, discussing the special values of photography—historical, mystical and sentimental—as an image caused by the same light reflected off the world. In the sphere of the affections, he wrote, photographs are interesting not only for 'their minute accuracy as works of art' but also because they are

> instinct with associations . . . vivid and endearing. The picture is connected with its prototype by sensibilities peculiarly touching. It was the very light which radiated from its brow—the identical gleam which lighted up his eye—. . . that pencilled the cherished image, and fixed themselves forever there.[21]

It is worth noting his subtle distinction between the 'minute accuracy' of photographs and their 'peculiarly touching' connection to the proto-type—between, in Peirce's terms, icon and index.

Indexical traces were valued in Western culture before the develop-ment of photography, for example as signatures, used ribbons, and hair jewellery. The last two were often combined with icons, in the form of miniatures, the most established form of small portraiture before photography. From the 1840s, the availability of photographic portraits almost wiped out miniature painting as a commercial activity, as is well documented in histories of photography. Interestingly, the diffusion of photography also adversely affected the demand for jewellery made with human hair. Hair jewellery was often made at home, to avoid commer-cial jewellery-makers mixing the hair provided by the customer with extraneous, traded human hair.[22]

Photography owed its success to more than just its relative cheapness, or its superior realism compared with miniatures. In the press of the period, photographic portraits were often criticized for their stiff and contrived nature, and their rendition of the human features as ghostly and unrecognizable in their black and white tones.[23] Their success was based on their ability to combine the mnemonic functions of the portrait with the fetishistic charge of the lock of hair, fulfilling at once the job of the miniature and of its hair-jewellery frame. Unlike a miniature, which has to be touched by the hand of the painter, or hair jewellery, which might be contaminated by other people's hair, the photographic image has an aura of untouched purity. It is a trace that bypasses the hand of the image maker and goes directly from the sitter to the hand holding the photograph.

Elizabeth Barrett Browning wrote of daguerreotypes:

> It is not merely the likeness which is precious in some cases—but the association, and the sense of nearness involved in the thing . . . I would rather have such a memorial of one I dearly loved, than the noblest Artist's work ever produced. I do not say so in . . . disrespect to Art, But for Love's sake.[24]

Photographic portraits were precious because 'the sense of nearness involved in the thing' would allow the bonds of love to make up for any artistic or technical limitations. While 'the noblest Artist's work' would produce a likeness that might be good, but would remain above all a representation by some (other) body, the photograph seemed to have been produced directly by the body of the loved one.

This sentiment is echoed in Elizabeth Eastlake's article 'Photography' of 1857:

> What indeed are nine tenths of those facial maps called photographic portraits, but accurate landmarks and measurements for loving eyes and memories to deck with beauty and animate with expression, in perfect certainty, that the ground-plan is founded upon fact?[25]

The implication seems to be that a painted portrait is animated with beauty and truth by the valuable skill and vision of the artist, while a photographic portrait, animated by the viewer's loving eyes, has value as a map to retrace the experience of the beloved person through the landscape of memory.

Digital photography records light as light—pixels—substituting the blackened silver stage with the less tangible medium of data, sequences of zeros and ones. But the 'Look, no hands' effect is still there. Like all photographs, digital photographs *can* be manipulated, mixed with other photographs or with material generated by the operations of the computer rather than by the light passing through the lens. But they don't *have* to be. As sound images become ever easier to obtain, and as digital cameras enable the capture of numerous poses from which to choose the perfect one, 'loving eyes' are still being used to make up, not for technical deficiencies, but for any weakening of the indexical certainty of photographs, now understood to be an indexical probability.

In his influential essay 'Photography and Fetish', Christian Metz considers the photograph's closeness 'to the pure index, stubbornly pointing to the print of what was, but no longer is' as the key to its role in the realm of personal images. He argues for the fetishistic qualities of photography above those of film, listing the features that make it so: it is small and portable; can be touched, handled and kept in a private container; it makes the spectator master of the gaze, allowing the possibility of a lingering look; it is closer to the 'pure index', notwithstanding its iconic and symbolic aspects.[26]

Metz's essay remains open on the issue of indexicality—photographs are 'closer to the pure index' but not identical to it. However, his introduction of the concept of fetishism opens up the possibility of reading the belief in photography's indexicality as one founded upon fetishistic structures of disavowal. I know (that the photograph is a construction), but . . . (my 'loving' eyes will disavow this knowledge). As John Tagg argues, to understand what makes the photographic image meaningful 'we must look to . . . the conscious and unconscious processes, the practices and institutions through which the photograph can incite a phantasy, take on a meaning, and exercise an effect'.[27] Indexicality itself can be seen as one of the fantasies incited by photography, whether digital or silver-based, needed to fill any gaps in the technical or ontological structure of the medium. In darkroom-based photography, this fantasy is based on matter that tangibly shapes itself in relation to the body in front of the camera, as thicker and thinner layers of silver on a negative, just about visible to the naked eye, felt by a sensitive finger, vulnerable to being scratched by clumsy handling, or falsified by careful retouching. The indexical fantasy of digital photography has to rely on a more intangible medium, encoded data not readily available to any of our senses. 'Digital media are indeed indexical, if we keep in mind what level of materiality they are indexing.'[28]

In the personal sphere, we can further overcome any indexical uncertainty brought about by digital technologies by making and manipulating the images ourselves, like the nineteenth-century women who made hair jewellery at home. Not because we want the image to be unmanipulated, but because we want any manipulations to be a trace of our own emotional investment in the image, rather than the commercial convenience of a stranger. In her analysis of the mixed-media album pages by Lady Milles, Lindsay Smith interprets the elaborate borders around the photographic images as a tactile trace, not of the beloved but of the lover. This substitute tactile trace is understood as a compensation for the extravagant promise of photography—total presence—always broken by its actuality, total absence.[29]

Yet, in many of the mixed-media albums of the period, the indeterminacy of many of the relationships implied, as well as the more playful references—holding parasols, licking stamps, playing cards and socializing in fashionable circles—seems to give the tactile trace of the hand-painted sections a different function. Touch does not aim to compensate for the shortcomings of the photograph as a keepsake, or to anchor its indeterminate meaning, but is a more casual caress, enjoying *and* brushing aside questions of photographic and social meaning. In these images the photographic ambiguity between presence and absence, and the album's 'oscillation between fullness and emptiness',[30] are all part of the fun. As is the case with many personal albums, scrapbooks and websites today, not to mention the exchanges of picture messages via mobile phones, the fetishistic potency of the index is treated lightly, with a playful physicality that defies the melancholia usually associated with collecting photographs, or with a flirtatious, ambiguous attitude, refusing to take photographs and their meaning seriously.

I do not want to suggest, however, that there are no discontinuities or losses in the passage from traditional to digital photographic processing and printing. But I think these are of a tactile rather than visual nature. The richness of nineteenth-century albums is not only visual but also gestural. Collage at once cuts and repairs, fragments and makes whole again. In these albums, unlike in combination printing or in Photoshop, these cuts and wounds are never fully resolved, never fully 'healed' into a smooth continuous surface, neither physically nor conceptually. Computers place photographs in the reduced tactility of virtual space—CD-ROMs or the internet—and on screens where physical contact is reduced to the repetitive clicking of a plastic button. At the same time, album-making software is mechanizing the accomplished

Fig. 10. My office mug, with a digital transfer print
of a photograph of my daughter, Judith.
Private Collection.

touch of the nineteenth-century collector, enabling everyone to make
complex customized albums: handicraft transformed into 'digital' craft.
'Restless and unstill', the mouse might, at times, become 'an extension of
the pointing finger',[31] but it is no substitute for tactile perception. The

70

touch of the maker, reduced to clicking and dragging—no cuts, tears or three-dimensional joins—is no longer registered as a tangible trace on the final image (whether this is on screen or printed on paper). And yet, computer-based printing technologies have also made it possible to print photographs on any number of objects—mugs, t-shirts and computer mouse mats—leading to a resurgence of the one-off object decorated with photographs, as parodied in nineteenth-century women's albums. We might not look very carefully at the photographs, but these objects seem to testify to how strong the desire still is to hold photographs of our loved ones in our hands, and to mingle the photograph as a visual trace of the there and then with the tactile trace of our emotions here and now.

6

The Return of Curiosity
The World Wide Web as Curiosity Museum

Michelle Henning

I dream of a new age of curiosity. We have the technical means for
it; the desire is there; the things to be known are infinite; the people
who can employ themselves at this task exist. Why do we suffer?
From too little: from channels that are too narrow, skimpy, quasi-
monopolistic, insufficient. There is no point in adopting a
protectionist attitude, to prevent 'bad' information from invading
and suffocating the 'good'. Rather, we must multiply the paths and
the possibility of comings and goings.[1]

This statement by Michel Foucault predates the expansion of the
internet and the widespread availability of e-mail in the 1990s, yet we
might speculate that these could well be the 'technical means' by which
the new age of curiosity would be achieved. It raises the question of how
forms of attention and emotions or appetites, such as curiosity, are
facilitated by technologies once those technologies become a part of
everyday life, absorbed into the mundane, even if only for certain social
groups. In the sixteenth to eighteenth centuries the curiosity cabinet, or
Wunderkammer, was one such technology, which enabled curiosity, an
appetite historically classified as a vice, to flourish amongst a narrow
group of aristocrats, scholars and virtuosos.[2] The return to curiosity, as
Foucault characterizes it, is something different: no longer elite, perhaps,
and dependent on proliferating, uncensored, two- (and more) way communication. In this essay I want to use this notion of a return to curiosity

to think about the internet, and especially the Web. Using Walter Benjamin's work on Baroque allegory, I want to examine the question of what a modern culture of curiosity might be, and what might constitute 'bad' and 'good' information in such circumstances.

It has now become commonplace to associate the curiosity museum with the internet, to draw parallels between the *Wunderkammer* and the World Wide Web, or to link the period of the Baroque with the information society.[3] This is best understood as a productive juxtaposition rather than a metapheric or historical connection. We are used to describing the internet through metaphor, in particular the pervasive travel metaphors used in relation to it—surfing, home pages, Netscape Navigator, Internet Explorer. These situate us in a drama of exploration: they work to lend greater weight to the everyday, while at the same time giving a familiar gloss to the new. Attempts to trace the ancestry of present developments in different historical moments are similarly conservative insofar as they attempt to demonstrate that nothing is really new, but, more significantly, because they reproduce an ideology of progress in which the relationship between past and present is understood as a linear evolution.

If the internet is to be thought of in terms of Foucault's 'new age of curiosity' it should also be thought of in terms of his own critique of false continuity. Some of the most compelling media histories confirm Foucault's assertion that '[w]hat is found at the historical beginning of things is not the inviolable identity of their origin; it is the dissention of other things. It is disparity.'[4] The influence of this view is felt in the work of the Berlins school of 'media archaeologists', which includes Friedrich Kittler and Wolfgang Ernst, and in the writing of American media theorists, including Jonathan Crary and Geoffrey Batchen.[5] In these approaches to new media, historical beginnings work to defamiliarize the present moment, and the past is told in such a way that its otherness is maintained at the same time as it casts new light on the present. In this respect, this work has something in common with Walter Benjamin's historical methodology. Benjamin was an early critic of the construction of history as teleology, and of illusory continuity. For Benjamin, the task of the historical materialist was to 'blast open the continuum of history'.[6] The practice of writing history should be, according to Benjamin, not sequential, but based on the establishing of constellations, a collage-like process in which past moments and historical material operate as a denaturalizing 'shock' to the present.

Benjamin envisaged the social historian as a collector or, perhaps more precisely, a ragpicker, picking through the detritus of modernity, finding all that has been left over or rendered obsolete. Against the version of history told by the historical victors, we have another version told through its leftovers.

However, for Benjamin the task of such discontinuous history was determined by the historical circumstances in which the social historian finds him or herself, that is, at a time when the production of junk and waste is accelerating. Benjamin characterized modernity partly in terms of the continual accumulation and discarding of commodities, and its impact on the individual in terms of sensory bombardment.[7] The sociologist Georg Simmel (who was Benjamin's tutor) saw modernity in similar terms, and as having direct effects on the psychological make-up of the modern individual, who is unable to process the wealth of information, goods and sensations on offer. Like Benjamin, Simmel turned his attention to collections and displays to think through this aspect of modernity. In an essay on the Berlin Trade Exhibition of 1896, he argued that world's fairs drew together diverse material to give an illusory impression of coherence:

> Nowhere else is such a richness of different impressions brought together so that overall there seems to be an outward unity, whereas underneath a vigorous interaction produces mutual contrasts, in-tensification and lack of relatedness . . . It is a particular attraction of world fairs that they form a momentary centre of world civilization, assembling the products of the entire world in a confined space as if in a single picture.[8]

By putting together such diverse material under one roof, the world's fairs constructed an illusion of continuity amongst disparate and fragmentary historical material. Museum dioramas and new techniques in museum lighting and department store displays worked similarly, placing objects in imaginary worlds and interlinking them in an illusory space. The internet is not a material collection as such—for, as Wolfgang Ernst has pointed out, nothing is stored on the internet, but only dynamically retrieved through the search engine.[9] Nevertheless, it too might be seen as a vast accumulation of sounds, images, data, over-whelming in its scale and diversity. It too presents us with the problem of how to make sense of an overaccumulation of 'stuff', how to examine it, translate it into something communicable and meaningful. Following Benjamin, we might see the detritus it accumulates as both poison and cure—as symptomatic of our historical moment but also the means by which we may make sense of it.

The tendency of the internet not to add up, and to expose the disparate, unassimilable nature of the material found on it, is more suggestive of a *Wunderkammer* or curiosity cabinet than of a modern museum. The *Wunderkammers* could be small and ornate cabinets (such as the Uppsala Kunstschrank) or whole rooms. We are able to imagine these rooms primarily through engravings made at the time; most commonly reproduced are the cabinets of Olaus Worm, Ferdinand Cospi and Francesco Imperato. These engravings depict rooms absolutely full of objects in cupboards, on shelves, mounted on walls and on ceilings. The cabinets include *naturalia* and *artificialia*, natural and man-made objects, and, as in the case of the faked 'monsters' they often included, objects that were both.

The curiosity cabinet collections were displayed without any apparent order other than a decorative one. Indeed, by the late nineteenth century they had gained a reputation for being disorderly, irrational and based on superstition. This reputation allowed the *Wunderkammer* to be in-corporated into a teleological history of the museum as the progress from disorderly private collections to order, scientific rationality and democracy. Objects inherited by the Victorian public museum from curiosity cabinets were marshalled into their place in the new scientific and chronological classificatory systems, and the museum now defined itself against this antecedent as well as against the popular diplays of its own time. For the display of anomalies, oddities and the atypical had become the specialism of popular commercial sites, of fairgrounds and circuses, freak shows and curio museums, including places such as Bullock's Egyptian Hall in Piccadilly, London, and P.T. Barnum's American Museum in New York.

Recent historians have distanced the curiosity cabinet from its *déclassé* descendents, emphasizing its rigorous, philosophical character. Writers such as Eilean Hooper-Greenhill have argued that in fact the com-bination of objects in curiosity cabinets followed strict rules based on thoroughgoing philosophical understandings. Hooper-Greenhill shows that their systems derived from Guido Camillo's memory theatre, developed in the early sixteenth century, the encyclopaedic work of Quiccheberg in the 1560s, the Hermeticism of Giordano Bruno, and the magical and religious theories of Robert Fludd.[10] These systems stressed symmetry, correspondences and dissimilarity. The choice of objects was based on rarity and curiosity value, and on the relationship between the microcosm and the macrocosm. According to such arguments (which also share a Foucauldian emphasis on historical discontinuities and ruptures), the problem is that the curiosity cabinets are entirely 'other' to a modern way of thinking which is accustomed to seeing systematicity in similarity, and typological or evolutionary arrangement.

The curiosity cabinets existed when science and magic were siblings, when paganism survived in allegorical form within a Christian framework, when numbers had occult significance, and rare objects could unlock the secrets of the universe. Certainly we can account for the modern misunderstanding of them in terms of the rupture between Renaissance and Baroque systems of knowledge and modern ones (Foucault characterized the classical and the modern as distinct 'epistemes'). We can also explain it through the history of the denigration of curiosity and curiosity collecting. The undeserved reputation of the curiosity cabinets, as the primitive ancestor of the modern museum, emerged out of the class struggle between the bourgeoisie and the aristocracy in the seventeenth and eighteenth centuries. While the aristocracy constructed their own legitimacy through their practices of collecting and display, such practices were read against the grain and satirized by the bourgeoisie, who saw the attachment to the rare, the useless and the monstrous as evidence of superficiality, dissimulation and suspect sexual practices.[11] By the mid nineteenth century curiosity as an emotion had lost the privileged status it had in the late sixteenth and early seventeenth centuries: now it was associated with gawping and gawking, the prurient looking of the sensation-seeking working classes and the naivety of the country bumpkin. From the nineteenth century to the present day, curious looking has been policed through the reproduction of worth, of acceptable behaviour, as parents teach their children to avert their eyes from the misfortunes of others. Current arguments regarding the policing of the Web are related to the scapegoating of curiosity, whilst at the same time, our curiosity is courted by sensationalist media. This denigration of curiosity as a mode of attention produces a separation of good objects (the typical, the instructive) from bad objects (the anomalous, the sensational), which feeds into exactly the 'protectionist' attitude Foucault mentions.

Nevertheless, to restore to the curiosity cabinets their philosophical significance, as Hooper-Greenhill does, is also to distance them from the curio and dime museums (as well as fair sideshows and other popular curiosity displays). The side-effect is that material and historical relationships between the different forms are occluded and the question of how such complex systems collapse into an apparently chaotic accumulation of stuff is sidestepped. This is a question I will address in more detail further on, but first it is worth noting that recent recognition of the connections between curiosity collections and the Web have seen something redeeming in this chaotic, arbitrary character. This is noticeable in several recent artists' projects that have engaged with the idea of the Web as a curiosity museum or *Wunderkammer*. These have encouraged people to see the process of searching the Web as a practice of curious looking and/or curious collecting. They are interested in how we collate and make sense of this vast accumulation or dispersal of stuff—how it offers itself up as a totality, or just as fragments, how it becomes compiled into a unity.

Wonderwalker, a project by Marek Walczak and Martin Wattenberg for the Walker Art Gallery in Minneapolis (2000), is basically a shared library of links: users draw icons to represent the link they want to make, and place the icon where they want to in the space provided by the artists, and as the icons accumulate, an arbitrary image or 'map' of the web grows.[12] *Information Tsunami Wunderkammer* by the Australian Shiralee Saul (1998) is text-based and works straightforwardly through hypertext links, which reveal some interesting connections. Saul represents the Internet as a Hokusai tidal wave carrying detritus to our shores. She uses the much-used navigation metaphor to understand the Web in relation to the *Wunderkammer* of objects brought back from the New World in the sixteenth century, and to the flotsam and jetsam that gets washed up on Australian beaches. The Internet turns us into curiosity collectors and ragpickers; in her words, 'You become an electronic beachcomber.'[13] In his installation *Encyclopaedia Mundi* (2003), British artist Tony Kemplen takes tourist souvenirs found in charity shops and photographs them using security cameras he has connected to computers.[14] Using software designed for the blind, the images are translated into sounds, and then these sounds are put through speech recognition software and turned into words. These words are then entered as search terms into a Web Image search, and turned back into images, which have only this very arbitrary connection with the original object. As Kemplen says:

> Once the *Encyclopaedia Mundi* starts you can't stop it. It's constantly trying to wring meaning out of these objects, which they don't inherently have. But it's so desperate to try and make sense of its surroundings that it's throwing up images and texts which

don't visually seem to have anything to do with the objects. The *Encyclopaedia Mundi* is highlighting this human need to find meaning in everything, and constantly refers back to the internet as a vast library to be grazed or browsed.[15]

Both Saul and Kemplen see Web searching, like Benjamin's ragpicking, as attentive to the significance of the obsolescent and the accidental find. All three projects highlight its lack of coherence, its arbitrariness and, simultaneously, its utopian potential for the construction of new constellations of experience. They see the internet as propagating chaotic overaccumulation and fragmentation of experience, but also operating as the means for new aesthetic practices which might enable us to better negotiate the present.

For Benjamin, too, the technological world which assaults our senses and produces increasingly fragmentary, alienated experience also offers us the means to analyse experience and to counter alienation.[16] The problem of experience in modernity was something which needed to be addressed through formal, aesthetic invention. Benjamin saw film montage as offering one possible aesthetic.[17] Montage produces coherence without recourse to illusion, through the friction it sets up between its disparate elements, and it allows for gaps in understanding. Neither classical symbolism nor the faithful reproduction of external appearances may adequately capture a world shaped by commodity fetishism and alienation. However, a representation built around the resonances produced through the juxtaposition of disparate material can allow for the impact of capitalist modernity and industrialization on experience.

Benjamin's theory of montage, and his analysis of the mid-nineteenth-century lyric poetry of Charles Baudelaire as modern allegory, is related to his earlier work on the Baroque.[18] Many recent writers have drawn parallels between Baroque culture and contemporary culture: Baroque art offers an immersive model of space that has been compared to everything from Virtual Reality technologies, to film special effects, to immersive theme-park exhibits. For Benjamin, though, what links his present moment and the Baroque period is an aesthetic based around the accumulation of fragments, and the unstable relationship between form and meaning.

Benjamin contrasted Baroque allegory with the classical symbol. Classicism expressed the timelessness of nature, divine presence in nature, and emphasized a harmonious unity of form and meaning.

However, allegory 'extinguishes', in Benjamin's words, 'the false appearance of totality'.[19] In allegory, the relationship between form and meaning is unstable, patched together. Examples can be found in the books of 'Emblems', both graphic and poetic, which circulated throughout Europe from the sixteenth to the eighteenth century, in the same period that the *Wunderkammer* flourished. In Baroque allegory, the gods of antiquity which had survived in a Christian culture only as 'dead figures' were appropriated as emblems, since they had become part of the corporeal and the earthly. Losing her divinity, Aphrodite, for instance, becomes the allegorical emblem of profane love or lust.[20] Baroque allegories, preoccupied with the inevitability of death and the transience of nature, drew on ancient Greek and Egyptian symbolism because these were associated with the discovery of divine meaning in nature.[21] However, Benjamin notes that this dependence on a mishmash of different traditions has the reverse effect of destroying the tight relationship between form and meaning and loosening the chains of ritual and tradition in favour of arbitrary and subjective meanings. The compilers of these books drew on so many different symbolic traditions and overinvested each emblem with such moral and political messages, that the accumulation of imagery constantly threatens to collapse, to become scattered ('Zerstreuung') rather than coherent. Ultimately Baroque emblem books became increasingly complicated, so overendowed with meaning that they were virtually untranslatable, unable to signify anything at all.

Perhaps it is possible to see through this the connection between the curiosity cabinet in its complex Baroque form and its more arbitrary, illegible manifestations. Benjamin's argument about Baroque allegory suggests that what begins as a complex system rooted in the search for divine meaning in nature ends up as an arbitrary accumulation of objects, which can be combined in endless different ways and attributed multiple, contradictory symbolic meanings. For Benjamin, the radical possibilities of Baroque allegory lie in the way it exposes the arbitrary relationship between an object and its attributed meaning, and thus undermines the very notion of an underlying natural order it was intended to support. Similarly, it may be that in its descent into overaccumulation and disorder, the curiosity collection threatened the notion of divinity in nature which it was originally intended to express. The resemblance of the internet, and especially the Web, to a curiosity collection, is based on its character as a vast accumulation of data that coheres and collapses into meaninglessness, but which has the potential to expose the arbitrariness of the present order of things. (Like the curio and dime museums, the Web is often seen as a commercialized and debased form, especially in comparison to the early internet, which seemed to promise the possibility of a new virtual public sphere and a space where identities could be reinvented from scratch).[22]

In the allegorical culture of curiosity, in Baudelaire's poetry, and in film and photographic montage, Benjamin finds aesthetic forms which are anti-auratic, that is, which contribute to the revolutionary and liberatory destruction of a mythic and ritualistic relation to the past and to the world of things. Baudelaire's *Les Fleurs du Mal*, published in 1857, combined a new modern aesthetic with a revival of symbolism drawn from antiquity, and references to sin and evil which had also preoccupied the Christian, Baroque tradition. Benjamin concluded that Baudelaire gave this tradition an entirely new purpose: to express the modern condition in which things had been emptied of their original meaning and turned into ciphers of subjective desire in the form of commodities.[23] In Baroque allegory, the arbitrary superfluity of meanings that can be attached to material things comes to signify a fallen state of nature— earthliness is associated with evil, and matter is represented as transient, debased, lifeless—but the allegorists also display a 'loyalty to things', to the very nature that they simultaneously represent as ruined.[24] Baudelaire's modern allegories display a deep attachment to the urban phantasmagoria of nineteenth-century Paris, to the new and ephemeral material of mass production, but he did not succumb to the phantasmagoric appearance of modernity.[25] Instead, he is intoxicated by a world stripped of aura, empathizing with the inorganic and the commodified, while his allegory tore down 'the harmonious façade of the world that surrounded him'.[26]

The anti-auratic and destructive aspect of allegory, and the paradox of its tenderness toward the raw nature it demystifies, can be seen in the work of an idiosyncratic Baroque allegorist, the Dutch anatomist Frederik Ruysch (1638–1731). Ruysch's work combined the modern anatomical interrogation of bodies with the allegorical and aestheticized representation of human transience which belonged to the Baroque. He produced allegorical arrangements out of immaculately embalmed anatomical specimens, often the body parts of infants found drowned in the harbour at Amsterdam, and with the help of his daughter, the painter Rachel Ruysch, arranged them in glass jars adorned with delicate lace collars and cuffs. Ruysch also made miniature tableaux which used skeletons in much the same way as the emblem books did. In his

Fig. 11. Frederick Ruysch, Etching with Engraving of Skeleton Tableau,
from *Alle de ontleed—genees—en heelkundige werken*, vol. 3
(Amsterdam, Janssons von Waesberge 1744).
Courtesy of the United States National Library of Medicine.

tableaux, the skeletons used are foetus skeletons, and landscape-like
settings are constructed out of preserved human and animal body parts.
These curiosities may seem unusually macabre now, but that is perhaps
only a marker of the distance between seventeenth- and eighteenth-
century Dutch society and present Western society, which has emptied
ordinary death and dying of ritual content and isolated it from the rest of

life. Rosamond Wolff Purcell and Stephen Jay Gould have cautioned against judging Ruysch's compositions by the standards of our own culture. His tableaux are memento mori, reminders not just of the transience of life, but also of the paradox of preservation, as expressed in the written emblem texts which are inscribed on them, which contain such phrases as 'Vita quid est?' ('What is life?') and 'Tempus Volat' ('Time flies').[27]

Ruysch's remarkable preserving technique allows us to see seventeenth-century bodies as if they had only just died. Purcell, who has photographed Ruysch's work, writes: 'I for one had never seen the eyes of a person who lived in the seventeenth century until I saw the girl with the lace collar.'[28] Purcell is arguing for the value and emotive power of Ruysch's work today. Yet what she says also indicates one of the ways in which it can be understood as anti-auratic. Benjamin associated 'aura' with the ability of things seemingly to transport us to an earlier moment.[29] Yet, while Purcell is commenting on the ability of the girl with the lace collar to connect her directly to an earlier historical moment, what she describes is not an auratic experience. Purcell is precise when she says that she 'saw' (as opposed to 'looked into') the perfectly preserved eyes: for the dead, however perfectly preserved, cannot look back. The 'windows of the soul' become object-like. The preserved corpse is both immediate and distant. Benjamin specifically defined aura in relation to the gaze that is returned. In 'On Some Motifs in Baudelaire' he discusses how aura exists where we attribute to inanimate objects the ability to look back:

> Experience of the aura thus rests on the transposition of a response common in human relationships to the relationship between the inanimate or natural object and man. The person we look at, or who feels he is being looked at, looks at us in turn. To perceive the aura of an object we look at means to invest it with the ability to look at us in return.[30]

By extension, the decline of aura is related to a remote gaze. Benjamin finds this remote gaze in Baudelaire's modern allegorical poetry. There, the classic notion of love (as a communion of souls expressed in lovers gazing deep into one another's eyes), is replaced by a modern desire for the remote and distant, for the blank and protective stare.[31] Urbanization, the city crowd and modern transportation all combine to produce this protective gaze. But Baudelaire is drawn to it, to eyes that are not the windows to an inner self, but are instead 'lit up like shop windows', so that looking into them is to look into an advertisement.[32] The parallel between the modern gaze which Baudelaire describes and the perfectly preserved but unseeing eyes of Ruysch's girl with a lace collar is suggested in Benjamin's statement that 'Baudelaire describes eyes of which one is inclined to say that they have lost their ability to look'.[33]

The perfect preservation of seventeenth-century eyes gives them a kind of immortality, but what is lost is the life which gives those eyes the ability to look back. The paradox of Ruysch's preservation is also the paradox of modern media. Each new medium, at its inception, attempts to preserve and render immortal, and in the process expands 'the realm of the dead'—this is as true of the internet as it is of photography and the phonograph.[34] Modern media and Baroque allegory are heavily destructive of aura almost despite themselves. They are also destructive and violent in a wider sense. In the Baroque, the breakdown of the tight relationship between form and meaning and the loosening of the chains of ritual and tradition correspond to an increasingly alienated representation of the world. A central figure in the emblem books, and a literal presence in Ruysch's work, is the skeleton, sometimes just shown as a skull, which represents more than simply 'death': it stands for the way all earthly things decay, and mocks human vanity, since all human achievement, all history, must end in death.[35] However, this figure is endlessly repeated in Baroque emblem books, its shock value drained.

By overinvesting objects with meaning, Baroque allegory succeeds only in making them become banal once more: 'The overbearing ostentation with which the banal object seems to rise up from the depths of allegory may soon give way to its dismal everyday countenance.'[36] Allegorists had to keep finding fresh and more shocking ways to represent the death's-head and the skeleton. In his writing on film, Benjamin pointed to how, under Fascism and Nazism, this became a means of turning destruction and genocide into an aestheticized spectacle. Likewise, Baroque allegory, born of an age 'drunk with atrocities both real and imagined', descends into a hideous frenzy of destruction.[37]

Paradoxically, then, the very aesthetic techniques and technologies which promise to counter alienation can also be deployed for the opposite purpose. The price of the destruction of aura is a heavy one, and it includes a sense of the equivalence between people and things which can result in people's becoming little more than objects. In the curiosity cabinet this objectification is brought about not just by the processes of collecting and preservation, but by the harnessing of these to expressions of political power. Ruysch's work came to form part of a politically significant collection when it was bought by Peter the Great and incorporated into his curiosity cabinet in St Petersburg. This collection contained the taxidermied freaks and anomalous wonders that were the staple of curiosity museums. It also contained human teeth, which Peter liked to personally extract—he 'would often demand this sacrifice of a member of his retinue, or even of an idle passer-by'—and living humans exhibited as freaks, such as the boy Foma, who was also preserved and placed on display after his death.[38]

Peter the Great's incorporation of Ruysch's work into his collection marked the merging of socio-political power and wealth with scientific and technical knowledge. We can learn something from this for the purposes of thinking about the distinction between 'good' and 'bad' information on the internet. In the Web, as in the Baroque, the high value given to curiosity, and the progressive potential of this, is offset by the high price of increased alienation, and aestheticized destruction. Compare, finally, the Visible Human Project, in which the body of Joseph Jerrigan, executed by the State of Texas, was physically sliced up, photographed, digitized and circulated via the Web, made available for corporate and medical use, and offered up for 'virtual tours'. This is one spectacular demonstration of how combined technological, corporate and governmental power produces an aestheticized spectacle of destruction. In place of the usual definitions of bad information as untrustworthy, not true, pornographic and so on, we can see the emergence of another kind of bad information in which the World Wide Web as curiosity cabinet becomes the site of the articulation of technocratic power.

7

From Android to Synthespian
The Performance of Artificial Life

Dan North

As pianist Jim Peterson picks out the final bars of his solo, Yuki Terai bites her lip coyly and steps up to the microphone at the centre of the nightclub stage to sing the last chorus of her hit single *Fly Away Alone*. She has been stepping and swaying gently during the break from her vocal duties, occasionally glancing across at Peterson for a cue, but mostly she appears to have been dancing for herself, perhaps recalling the lost love at whom the song is directed. She pinpoints every high note of the soaring refrain precisely, emoting her paean to a beloved deceased with such clarity and truth that we want to forget that she's miming. Maybe the English subtitles that translate the Japanese lyrics don't preserve their poetic subtleties ('Fly away alone, away into an unknown sky/Your human form, it has flown away'), or maybe such subtlety was never there, but the sincerity of her delivery is affecting. As the song concludes, Yuki turns to the camera, to us, and bites her lower lip again, a shy gesture that belies her status as a top-selling pop star. As she acknowledges the external spectator (the nightclub is empty), she seems almost embarrassed to have been watched in such a display of emotional vulnerability. All of a sudden, she fades from the scene, and we realize that this is not Yuki's fantasy of remembrance, but Peterson's; it is she who is the spectre of his ecmnesia. She is an ethereal performer, forever excluded from the material world. It is a fitting revelation, since Yuki Terai is entirely computer-generated.

Yuki is a virtual idol created by Japanese animator Ken-Ichi Kutsugi in

Fig. 12. Virtual idol Yuki Terai sings her hit single 'Fly Away Alone',
from *Yuki Terai: Secrets* (Escapi Entertainment, 2000).

1998; she first appeared on Kutsugi's own homepage as part of his
experimentation with 3-D computer graphics, but her appearance on the
centre pages (a space usually reserved for young, flesh-and-blood bikini
models) of *Weekly Young Jump/Shukan Yangu Jarpu*, to which Kutsugi
usually contributed comic strips, brought her to a larger audience.[1] Yuki
is perhaps best described as a complex piece of cartoon animation,
delivering a performance built partly on keyframe digital animation (i.e.,
the movements are plotted in advance by animators) and partly on
motion capture data, for which live performers are videotaped from
multiple angles and their movements plotted as digital coordinates from
key anatomical reference points, producing a skeleton of data onto which
Yuki's digital form is then mapped. The transferability of this data
means that she can be composited into any situation, playing various
short film roles in a number of geographical and temporal settings, while
also releasing pop albums and appearing in advertisements. In addition,
she has featured in a Playstation console game, '*Primal Image*'. This
qualifies her for the title of *virtual star*—she is a versatile performer
rather than a fictional character of fixed identity, exhibiting enough
distinctive characteristics that she can be seen as a cohesive star text in
her own right.

86

Rémy Brun, director of motion capture director at Attitude Studio, the makers of Eve Solal, a French virtual star and Europe's nearest equivalent to Yuki Terai, refers to his art as 'very high-tech puppetry'.[2] Since such figures are not sentient or artificially intelligent (though emotionally nuanced performances are designed to imply that they may be), all of their movements are plotted by human operators. Roman Paska points out that puppets are almost always discussed in terms of their 'symbolic relationship with human models, the puppet being primarily cast in the role of a surrogate human'. The puppet is thus a 'diminished, artificial human proxy'.[3] The kind of computer-assisted puppetry exhibited by cyberstars such as Yuki Terai alters the link between the puppeteer's body and its avatar in a manner which is analogous with the shifting relationship between images and their referents with the advent of digital (rather than indexical/photochemical) processes. The human puppeteer who creates a physically present (though concealed) manipulation of the puppet endows it with inflections which are vestigial traces of his or her own physical idiosyncrasies. The digitally animated character is different in that, while still connected to the animator's hands and body (techniques such as motion capture, Direct Input Devices and key frame animation ensure this), the real-time causal link has been severed. The digital character/synthespian is thus a puppet without a direct indexical link to its performative source.

In cyberspace, the avatar is always connected, like a puppet, to its user. The virtual star has at least the illusory appearance of being separated from a 'user', just as a star persona is somewhat distinct from the human being which is its physical vessel. Richard Dyer states that stars exist, sociologically speaking, within certain texts, but that star iconography is always inflected by the private person (however our knowledge of that person is mediated) behind the icon.[4] With no private autonomy, the cyberstar such as Yuki Terai is a piece of *pure stardom*; its intertexts are technological, not personal. It is ostensibly separate from its puppeteer, just as the automaton is capable of acting independently of its creator, who has programmed those actions meticulously in advance. The mechanical automata I will presently discuss are similar to marionettes in that they fulfil this role of surrogacy for the operator, but distinct in that they are seen to operate independently of a human agent.

Yuki Terai represents the advance guard of what we might term the synthespian, the cyberstar, the virtual actor or, to indulge the less persuasive neologism, the *vactor*. The synthespian is a quasi-mythological concept, imagining the usurpation of the human actor by a pliant, mutable and tireless digital stand-in. This mythos has a basis in actual technological forays in cinema: virtual performers have expanded crowd scenes in *Titanic* (James Cameron, 1997) and *Gladiator* (Ridley Scott, 2000) and enacted impossible, i.e. superhuman, stuntwork in recent films such as *Spiderman* (Sam Raimi, 2002), *Star Wars Episode II* (George Lucas, 2002) and *The Matrix: Reloaded* (The Wachowski Brothers, 2003),[5] mostly based on computer scans of actual human actors and motion capture data.

The most ambitious use of these maturing technologies has also been their biggest setback—Hironobu Sakaguchi's *Final Fantasy: The Spirits Within*, released in the summer of 2001, was entirely computer-generated, featuring a cast of the closest approximations of photorealistic humans yet seen on screen. Despite the unprecedented detail of its animation, technical milestones were not enough for it to recoup much more than half of its estimated US$137 million budget. This enormous, crippling financial failure stalled similar projects and made the virtual actor, as an attraction in its own right, a risky proposition rather than a utopian ideal. Despite this setback, there is still a prevailing belief that this mimetic digital animation will develop an artificially intelligent performer indistinguishable from an organic human actor. The completely simulacrous virtual actor is a wishful futurological trope whose realization is far less imminent than we might be led to believe by commentators within the graphics, special-effects or artificial intelligence (AI) industries.

In May 2003, Will Anielewicz, a digital animation supervisor at George Lucas's special-effects facility, Industrial Light and Magic, opined, 'Within five years, the best actor is going to be a digital actor.'[6] Experts in the field have a more succinct mantra for the future. Kelly Tyler, a producer of the popular science broadcast and website NOVA Online, has identified the photorealistic human simulacrum as 'a new digital grail'.[7] Damion Neff, an artificial-intelligence designer of Microsoft video games has called it 'the Holy Grail of character animation'.[8] In his keynote address to the 1997 Autonomous Agents Conference, Danny Ellis listed the emotionally intelligent virtual actor as one of four 'holy grail' in the field.[9] In May 2003 John Gaeta, discussing his visual-effects work on *The Matrix Reloaded* in the *Los Angeles Times*, referred to a believable digital human as 'the holy grail' for the profession.[10] It seems that the grail analogy has found some currency, at least amongst those working in the relevant creative industries. This frequently uttered analogy sums up the suggestion that technologies of visual representation have been working inexorably towards a final goal, but they might also inadvertently hint that such a goal is essentially elusive.

The development of special effects over time thus often relies on a teleological narrative of technological progress towards an already established conclusion, whereby the development is advanced by a series of refinements and improvements to existing mechanisms. Certainly, computer-generated imagery, with its increasing photographic verisimilitude permitted by faster processing speeds and more efficient rendering software, appears to be advancing at a quantifiable rate, implying a final destination of absolute simulation, a point where a digital human being can be depicted with a level of detail that makes it indistinguishable from images of actual flesh and bone, and can possess enough (artificial) intelligence to be a star offscreen instead of just a hyperreal cartoon upon it.

So, how can this teleology by questioned? How do we construct a more continuist approach to historicizing these spectacles in the face of such persuasive technological progress? We could begin by drawing the focus away from the dazzling verisimilitude of illusory technologies and focusing on the conceptual questions which underpin their fascinating surfaces. We can also observe antecedents of the virtual actor and note that the same spectacular strategies, prompting the same ontological questions, were in play. To this end, I have chosen to examine the mechanical automata which provided similar kinds of fascination in the eighteenth and nineteenth centuries. Both phenomena provoked speculation that the human body might one day be superseded by its artificial counterpart.

When making such comparisons, there is always a danger of indulging in what some historians of science refer to as 'Whiggism', that is, judging the past exclusively in terms of how it informs the present. Rather, I hope to point towards some continuities within the contemporary discourses around mechanical automata and virtual actors in order to show these developments as culturally and phenomenally repetitive, as opposed to distant points on a linear course. What comparable reactions do the mechanical android and the synthespian provoke in the spectator and what issues do they raise?

Lister et al suggest that cyborgic developments 'call into question the settled edge between the biological and the technological',[11] and we can see that synthespians prompt similar lines of enquiry, inviting the spectator to assess the virtual body at all times in relation to its organic referent—that is to say, the synthespian's success lies in its ability to mimic human motion. By examining how the automaton and the synthespian perform, we can see that, despite the differing means by which they are produced, each performs the same function of *suggesting* or *enacting* the achievement, or at least the imminent achievement of simulation's Holy Grail, without actually *being* it. The nurturing of the myth is part of the process of consuming the illusion and believing in the astonishing capabilities of the virtual performer.

In this sense we can describe the virtual actor as a 'pnambic' phenomenon.[12] In a consideration of Alicebot, a 'conversation engine' (originally named 'Pnambic') which was created with the intention of simulating verbal exchanges that could be mistaken for human (and by implication *intelligent*) verbal communication, Richard S. Wallace defines 'pnambic' as follows

1. A stage of development of a process or function that, owing to incomplete implementation or to the complexity of the system, requires human intervention to simulate or replace some or all of the actions, inputs, or outputs of the process or function.
2. Of or pertaining to a process or function whose apparent operations are wholly or partially falsified.[13]

Virtual actors impersonate the surfaces of the human form and in doing so suggest that those surfaces relate to a correspondingly human identity, but their 'bodies' are only a mask for underlying technical processes; we are enticed into viewing Yuki Terai as an emotive performer rather than as a mesh of algorithms. Since these digital bodies are representing humanness instead of emulating its basic properties (Yuki blinks because an algorithm makes her do so periodically, not because she needs to spread moisture across her eyes; her chest rises and falls because it is programmed to appear that way, not because she needs to take in oxygen), we can best understand them not as the actualization of a technological imperative to incarnate human doubles, but as a mere speculative pretence in the direction of such achievement.

The automata in which I am particularly interested are those which we term androids, recognizably human in shape, movement and usually in scale. In the eighteenth century, the construction of automata attained its highest status as an art form, and, as Jessica Riskin has noted, this is also the period when they become less machine-like in appearance, as their manufacturers begin using organic materials such as leather and wood.[14] The most prestigious attractions were the large androids (recognizably

Fig. 13. The Jacquet-Droz android harmonium player,
from *The Jacquet-Droz Androids* (Neuchâtel: Talia Films/
Musèe d'Art de d'Histoire, 2001).

human in shape, movement and usually in scale), such as those constructed by the father-and-son team Pierre and Henri-Louis Jaquet-
Droz between 1772 and 1775. One surviving trio of Droz figures,
consisting of a harmonium player, a writer and a draughtsman, comprise
some of the very few remaining examples of eighteenth-century androids
which are still in working order.[15] The profuse apocrypha that are the
only records of famous devices often exaggerate the automaton's abilities,
leading to a mixture of historical fact and hyperbolic, indirect reportage
of contemporary rumour.[16] The Jaquet-Droz androids still perform
for eager crowds once a month at the Musée d'Art et d'Histoire,
Neuchâtel.[17]

Perhaps most striking of the Droz trio is the harmonium player.[18] The
production of music is not the main attraction of this machine—it is far
more than a humanoid music box. The real achievement is a mimetic
reproduction of *performance*, a female mannequin whose dress conceals
the barrels, fusee wheels, bellows, cranks and cams moving her body,
which in itself offsets the mechanical nature of the musical reproduction.[19] Her chest rises and falls in imitation of respiration, even between
melodies; her eyes follow the movement of her hands, and at the
conclusion of her piece, she nods demurely as if to acknowledge an

appreciative audience. The Jaquet-Droz harmonium player is an out-standing accomplishment of intricate mechanical motion, but what the machine itself achieves (producing music) is not the same as what the player seems to be doing (playing an instrument). Innovations in anthropomorphic design are camouflage for the machinery within.

A letter to the editor of the *Scientific Gazette* in 1826, describing the operations of an automaton capable of writing on paper, remarks that the outer casing of the instrument is 'a mere piece of framing', a means of anthropomorphizing it and, correlatively, masking its machine-ness.[20] In his *Letters on Natural Magic* of 1832, David Brewster describes automata as the testing ground for more significant and practical utilities, claiming that their intricate workings 'reappeared in the stupendous mechanism of our spinning-machines and our steam-engines'.[21] It is this dual identity as an illusory performer and a technological servant which characterizes the android automaton.

It is customary to separate the fake automaton from the genuine android, to see the latter as proffering a posthuman machine capable of performing the tasks or characteristics of human beings, and to see the former as fogging the state of progress in such develops by exaggerating it or diverting its course. For every painstakingly automated figure there is a trick automaton, a shell mechanism whose apparently spontaneous movements are actually directed by a hidden operator, or remotely, via wires or compressed air. It would seem to me to be reductive to dichotomize these two kinds of automaton; their performative aspects are as important a part of their history as is their actual composition. They are all illusory forms, and their common aim is the concealment of their true motive force. What they also share is an illusion of interaction with their environments, and, by extension, an illusion of consciousness born out of the appearance of *wilful* self-propulsion. It could be argued that all of these androids are tricks, since the acts they perform are misdirectional feats designed to imply spontaneous responses and thus to distract from the machine-ness of the mechanisms at work beneath clothing and casing.

Jacques de Vaucanson's famous defecating duck, for instance, not strictly an android, but certainly an early example of a re-enactment of a natural body by mechanical means, was first displayed in 1739. To the spectator, it seemed that the duck could take food pellets in its mouth and, shortly afterwards, excrete the end product, processed by a mechanical approximation of a digestive system. The implication was that the creature could feed and sustain itself, like a pseudo-organic perpetual-motion device. What it was actually doing was storing the pellets and pumping out a pre-prepared paste, another case of theatrical metamorphosis, claiming that a second item is the first in a new form.

Vaucanson was not just intent on producing mechanical tricks, however. Voltaire commended the social value of his plan to create a mechanical man with mimetic circulatory, digestive and respiratory systems:

> He claims that by using this automaton we shall be able to carry out experiments on animal functions, and to draw conclusions from them which will allow us to recognize the different states of human health, in order to remedy his ills. This ingenious machine, by representing a human body, will be able to be used eventually for demonstration purposes in anatomy courses.[22]

It would appear from this evidence that the improbability of such a feat of engineering had not occurred to Voltaire. No matter, because the very suggestion of its possibility was sufficient to add to the speculative wonder excited by the contemporary state of automaton engineering. Technological spectacle, as well as providing an instant fascination, not only demands that the viewer compare earlier attempts at the same technical feat but also invites imaginings of how the technology might be reapplied in future contexts. Vaucanson's project of producing mechanical men was never realized. The Industrial Revolution depended upon the acceptance that machines needn't be built like humans in order to outperform them. Automata, deprived of their scientific potential, nevertheless retained their status as performative wonders on the stages of the nineteenth-century magic theatre.

Jean Eugène Robert-Houdin (1805–71), the French illusionist often credited with exerting a profound influence on the magic entertainment scene by his gentlemanly dress code and elegant presentation, was most renowned for his mechanical effects and exhibitions of automata. These virtual performers, including an acrobatic trapeze artist (Antonio Diavolo), were not mechanically animated, but operated by hidden agency, whether by wires and pneumatic mechanisms or, as in the case of a clockwork pastry cook who delivered wine and cakes to the audience, by the magician's young son Eugene encased in a hollow suit.

The androids exhibited from 1873 to 1904 at London's Egyptian Hall by John Nevil Maskelyne (1839–1917), proprietor and resident magician, with his partner, George Alfred Cooke, included several musicians but, most famously, an android in Oriental garb named Psycho, who could play hands of whist against audience members. As well as playing cards, Psycho could spell out words given to him by the audience; in addition, 'he was an arithmetician and gave answers to calculations by sliding numerals in front of an aperture near his hand. He could pick out marked playing cards and by striking a bell denoted values. He shook hands with his partner in whist before leaving the stage.'[23] This highly dextrous mechanism exhibited some true technical skill in its movements, but the actual choice of which card to play was made remotely by an operator supplying variable levels of air pressure to the device. Maskelyne even offered a reward of £2,000 for 'a genuine Automaton capable of producing Psycho's movements'.[24] He clearly wanted to provoke speculation about the machine's composition, but surely the automaton's movements were a secondary source of wonder for the audience—by seeming to interact spontaneously with a human opponent, Psycho was appearing to perform acts which required consciousness and intelligence.

Perhaps the most famous trick automaton of all time is Baron von Kempelen's 'Turk', a mechanical chess-player and a match for almost any opponent, first appearing in Vienna in 1770. Like Psycho, von Kempelen's chess player is distinct from the Vaucanson or Jaquet-Droz androids in that the attraction lies not in his simulation of movement so much as in his imitation of powers of reasoning and tactical manoeuvres. This machine provided a long-standing puzzle to spectators. When the machine was under new ownership, Edgar Allan Poe's essay 'Maelzel's Chess Player', published in the *Southern Literary Journal*, April 1836, situated his proposed solution (that it was operated from inside by a confederate) within a broader consideration of the history of automata, but even before this Kempelen had urged audiences to work out how the illusion was achieved; when public suspicion was gravitating towards the possibility that the Turk was moved by concealed magnets, he began placing a lodestone next to the Turk in order to frustrate the possibility of such a solution. What set it apart was its ability to *respond* rather than to simply carry out pre-ordained procedures. Of course, Poe's solution was ultimately correct, but the performance of machine intelligence was sufficient to enrapture audiences.[25] As a spectacular fiction, the show urged them to muse upon the possibility of intelligent, autonomous machines.

All of these famous androids and synthespians are tied to comparative performances alongside human counterparts. Psycho and von

Kempelen's Turk compete with human opponents, allowing a fascinating spectatorial conceit whereby the android's imitation of human movements is juxtaposed with a real human, providing a constant point of comparison which can only serve to emphasize the residually mechanistic qualities of the automaton. The confusion also encapsulates general attitudes to the relationship between science and magic in this period—it is difficult to separate popular science from its use in narrativized, spectacularized demonstrations in magicians' acts.

The drive to facsimilate the human form can be seen partly as the experimental continuation of physiological and philosophical debates of the seventeenth century and beyond. As Thomas Huxley stated in an 1874 address to the British Association for the Advancement of Science, the work of William Harvey in explaining the circulatory systems of the human body confirmed 'the idea that the physical processes of life are capable of being explained in the same way as other physical phenomena, and, therefore, that the living body is a mechanism'.[26] This was furthered by Descartes' anatomical study, *De Homine* (written in 1633 but not published until 1664), and Julien Offroy de la Mettrie's *L'Homme Machine*, published in 1747. Patricia S. Warrick has suggested that Descartes' view of animals as merely machines (as opposed to humans, who had minds and souls) may have come from his observations of the many animal automata that appeared in his lifetime, including those of Jacques de Vaucanson.[27] Mettrie posited that the human body is a self-regulating machine which can act automatically—that is, independently of the 'self' of which it is the receptacle. He allegorized the human being as a machine, with thought being one of the properties of matter, rather than a separate space in a Cartesian duality.

In the twentieth century, the possibility of machines thinking like humans, rather than being similarly embodied, was energized by investigations of artificial intelligence. Again, though, the starting points were part of a confrontational dynamic that pitted human and machine against one other in order to define the properties and potential of each. This reached a crucial point with Alan Turing's test for computer intelligence, first proposed in his paper 'Computing Machinery and Intelligence' (1950).[28] In the Turing test, a set of questions is put to both a machine and a human. An examiner should not be able to distinguish between the two sets of answers. Turing predicted that computers would have the capacity for a 30 per cent success rate by the year 2000, but so far no computer has passed. Peter Millican states that the Turing test was considered a good criterion for defining intelligence because '[i]f the computer were able to give sufficiently humanlike responses to resist identification in such circumstances, then it would be quite gratuitous to deny that it was behaving intelligently, irrespective of its alleged lack of a soul, an inner perspective, consciousness, or whatever'.[29] The test is perhaps most useful as a philosophical inroad to the issue of machine intelligence, but it represents an attempt to assess a machine's capabilities against a human, organic measuring pole, rather than to define an essential machine-ness. Machine intelligence is thus defined by its deficiencies in relation to the human model, and the test establishes a template for machine intelligence which is principally performative. As Robert M. French puts it, the basis of the test's effectiveness is the belief that '[w]hatever *acts* sufficiently intelligent *is* sufficiently intelligent'.[30]

It would seem like the search for a perfect synthespian has become, as Henry Jenkins puts it, 'a new kind of Turing Test by which computer modellers and AI specialists hone and measure their skills.'[31] The synthespian is, like the prototypical automaton as described by Jean-Claude Beaune, 'a *techno-mythological idea* or, more precisely, the mythic distillation of technical processes and machines and, by extension, of tools or instruments'.[32]

What connects the areas which I've outlined here is their performative nature, the sense that what the android and the synthespian seem to be able to do is far more important than what they are actually doing. Yuki Terai, the virtual idol who began this discussion, seems to be able to wave to her fans from a television or monitor, to carry out all the signature acts of stardom. The coyness that Yuki Terai exudes at the end of her song, and which the Jaquet-Droz harmonium player displays when bowing to the crowd after finishing her recital, are distinctly human characteristics performed by the machines to help downplay their *machine-ness*, but also to spectacularize their technical achievements in the light of such mechanical self-effacement. In *Human Robots in Myth and Science*, John Cohen lists blushing as one of those human tics that robots can neither *do* biologically nor *require* practically, and the incorporation of these most human articulations into the synthespian's performance is calculated to distract from the true (mechanical) constitution of the performance.[33]

Many of Yuki's animated adventures are short episodes which cause her to question the reality of her own being. The short film *Mirror* (Ken-Ichi Kutsugi and Hiromi Hayashi, 2000) finds her fleeing from innumerable expressionless clones of herself, while *A Life* (Hiromi Hayashi, 2000), the final melancholic episode, concludes with her selecting the best outfit in which to commit suicide. These existential musings serve to embed the possibilities of synthespianism into her life story. Rather than being urged to suspend disbelief in her substance and to fetishize the tactility of digital surfaces, Yuki's fans are encouraged to think about her virtuality. In this sense, we can see that the anthropomorphic exteriors of Yuki or the Jaquet-Droz androids are a spectacular coating for the real state of the mechanisms beneath, inviting the spectator to consider the presence of autonomous action while masking its absence.

Brooks Landon has argued that the recent prominence of virtual human characters in cinema represents 'a fast-approaching degree of synthetic agency for synthespians or virtual humans that should itself be thought of as a science fictional phenomenon'.[34] There is certainly something new, or at least something inherently 'electronic', about the way in which the virtual star can be transported across a range of texts and manipulated to suit each new diegetic space. Nevertheless, if we are to account fully for the novelty of the phenomenon, then we must look back to its antecedents and the similarly illusionistic strategies they deployed, namely the performative tics consciously added to the virtual character in order to meet the expectations upon which science is as yet unable to deliver. The science-fictional narrative trajectory Landon attributes to synthespians owes as much to popular imaginings of a technological future as it does to the finalized achievements of the laboratory.

The digital performers that are incorporated into mainstream cinema preserve the mythological aspects of virtual performance by suggesting the full achievement of the technological targets in play. That is to say, the synthespian turns in a fully synthesized performance that appears to represent autonomous interaction with human performers as if both are taking cues from the same director, spatially consistent and fully vocalized, but which is, in fact, only a partially technologized piece of puppeteered and overdubbed mimicry. Each serves as a diagram of new technology in its most identifiable, anthropomorphic form, inviting comparisons of the technology's value and quality with known qualities of the human body. Each one 'scientizes' traditional modes of performance while turning science into a performative showcase. That is to say, since each 'virtual human' addresses its audience through a musical or physical rendition of a familiar nature, the human body becomes a measuring pole against which the technology can be assessed by the spectator.

8

As Seen On TV
Kinaesthetic Crossover and the Animation of Social Dance Pedagogy

Jonathan Bollen

In April 1978 Australia's music television show, 'Countdown,' hosted a disco-dancing contest. On a perspex dance floor lit with coloured lights from beneath, contestants danced to songs from the *Saturday Night Fever* soundtrack and a large cut-out figure of John Travolta, striking that archetypal disco pose, presided over the event.[1] Predictably enough, the winning contestants were the couple (from Sydney) who performed the most recognizably accomplished and rigorously choreographed imitation of disco dancing, *Saturday Night Fever* style. Their prize was a return trip to the United States to meet the Bee Gees, the featured artists on the movie soundtrack. But before they left they were invited to draw the winning entry in an audience competition. The lucky viewer's prize? A videocassette machine—not only the latest in home-entertainment technology but a handy piece of equipment for a budding disco dancer eager to learn the latest dance moves *as seen on TV*.

This essay is concerned with the cultural politics of social dancing, with techniques of social dance pedagogy and their relationship to innovations in media technology, and with the phenomenon of kinaesthetic crossover, a process whereby Anglo-European dancing was infused with the movement qualities of African-American dance. It argues that the crossover of an African-American kinaesthetic coincided with the emergence of an 'animatic' conception of movement, mediated by the dissemination of photographic, cinematic and television technologies. This argument arises from a survey of twentieth-century social dance manuals, sourced in second hand bookshops and local libraries in Australia and in a digitized collection of dance manuals at the Library of Congress. It also draws on archival film footage from Ron Mann's documentary film *Twist*, from the British Broadcasting Corporation's television series 'Dancing In The Street' and from the Australian Broadcasting Corporation's music television show 'Countdown'.

Writings on dance negotiate a difficult relation between dancing and writing. Writing is unidirectional and set out on a two-dimensional surface. Once written, it is timeless and inert. Dancing, on the other hand, is multidirectional and unfolds in three-dimensional space during discrete periods of time. It is of the moment, fleeting and animate. Dance manuals seek to resolve these tensions by drawing on various pedagogical techniques for representing movement on paper. But what seems inevitable in these paper-bound representations is a halting of flow, a fixing of motion, a taxonomy of moves. Dance written down makes visible what the cinematic reliance on 'persistence of vision' covers over. Dance action is solidified, snap-frozen and shattered into myriad postures and positions, gestures and steps. Something of the dance is lost: its momentum always escapes. This halting of flow in dance manuals and the way dancing resists such an arrest suggests a narrative trope, one that pitches the fixative force of writing against the fluid resistance of dancing.

In the writing of dance manuals, dances are given names, their movements are broken down into sequences and each action is described in detail. Labelled at each step in the sequence, these bits of choreography become the building blocks with which entire dance routines are taught, learnt and performed. The acquisition of dance proficiency thus entails progress from the simple to the complex, from individual steps, postures and gestures to combinations, patterns and sequences. This taxonomic approach to writing down dance formed a basis for the institutionalization of social dance pedagogy. Social dancing academies and societies of dance instructors wrote manuals prescribing their steps, trained dance instructors according to their prescriptions, established hierarchies of accreditation in expertise, and through these means sought to exercise regulatory control over the teaching and performance of social dancing.

When dance instructors wrote dance manuals, they rarely invented new dances. Rather, they sought to intervene in the performance of social dancing, to codify, define and refine existing dances, to promote and ensure their correct and proper performance. For instance, Victor Silvester relates his history of modern ballroom dancing to civilizing narratives of colonial adaptation:

> In the past, the steps associated with a new dance in the early days of its ballroom career rarely proved a permanent part of the dance. Quite often they were complicated and sometimes positively eccentric. Even when taken from the original folk dance, they needed a good deal of adaptation to become acceptable in the smart ballrooms of their day.[2]

Silvester was a founding member of the committee of the Ballroom Branch of the Imperial Society of the Teachers of Dancing, which was formed in 1924. The first task of the committee was to publish by the end of their first year an examination syllabus which would control admission to membership of the Ballroom Branch. The syllabus comprised three components defining distinct areas of competency:

1. A rudimentary knowledge of music as required for modern ballroom dancing.
2. Carriage of the arms, head and body.
3. A knowledge of the basic steps of the Foxtrot, Waltz, One-Step and Tango.[3]

What this syllabus documents is a kinaesthetic for social dancing, a style of bodily movement valued at that time. The key feature of this kinaesthetic is a distinction between the 'carriage of the arms, head and body' and 'a knowledge of the basic steps'. This distinction specifies a relatively stable upper body held in place (the hold) while the loco-motional apparatus of the lower body executes the progressive movement of the dance (the path). Cultivated in dance teaching and embodied in dance practice, the 'hold/path' kinaesthetic underscored a standard system for representing dance on paper. It enabled a postural comportment—the hold—to be established prior to the step-by-step instructions for a progressive sequence of steps—the path—typically depicted with the aid of footstep diagrams. Furthermore, the 'hold/path' kinaesthetic was complicit in the maintenance of gender roles. The relational configuration that disposes dancers into gender-differentiated couples is sustained throughout the progression of the dance. Indeed, it is the path that realizes the gender differentiation of the hold. For as long as the hold is held, the man always leads, stepping out forwards, directing the movement with decision, whilst the woman is led, stepping off backwards, following her partner's direction (see Figure 14).[4]

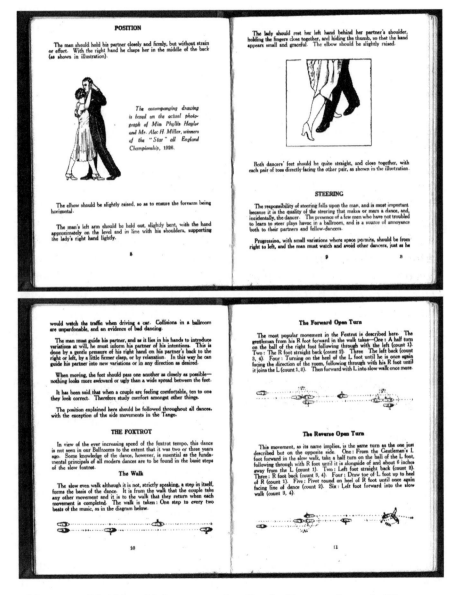

Fig. 14. 'Hold/-path' documentation for the Foxtrot, from An Expert, *The Modern Ballroom Dance Instructor* (London: Geographica, *c*.1926).

Founded on the 'hold/path' distinction, social dance manuals cultivated a traditional Anglo-European kinaesthetic to which a number of dances would prove resistant. The Foxtrot and the Charleston, the Lindy, the Jitterbug and the Jive, the Twist and the dancing that came to be called 'disco' were all subject to pedagogical regulation that sought to adapt them to the 'hold/path' kinaesthetic. Sourced in African-American tradition and channelled through the style economies of Anglo-European youth, these dances presented an energetic, improvisatory performance that occasioned a prescriptive, civilizing response from established institutions of social dance pedagogy. In particular, these dances introduced a stationary, non-progressive style of dancing that emphasized gestural action over locomotional progression and, in this regard, proved resistant to 'hold/path' analysis and confounded the differentiation of gender roles.

That the Charleston, for instance, proved resistant to the civilizing regulation of social dance pedagogy is evident in the enduring cultural memory of the dance. Importantly, this memory is sustained not through social dance manuals, but in the visual record, in historical photos and film footage that document young women, the 'flappers' of the 1920s, performing the Charleston without partners and with evident enjoyment. Nevertheless, a trace of this resistance is evident in *The Modern Ballroom Dance Instructor*, a British dance manual from the 1920s. In the section that teaches the steps for the Charleston, the standard footstep notation system is abandoned. Evidently, the stationary and gestural action of the Charleston demanded a different documentation strategy. Indeed, such action was barely conceivable within the 'hold/path' kinaesthetic of social dancing and could hardly be represented using the standard approach. Instead the movement of the 'original Charleston' and its characteristic 'Foot-Twist' are depicted as an animatic sequence of illustrations (See Figure 15).

The footstep system for recording the path of a sequence of steps may be traced to the Beauchamp-Feuillet notation system, which was invented around 1700 and used throughout eighteenth-century Europe for the pedagogical documentation of social dancing.[5] In contrast, the animatic approach used in documenting the Charleston of the 1920s is part of a much younger movement-notation tradition that conceptualizes movement as a sequence of static images. Such a conception may be dated to the nineteenth-century interest in 'persistence of vision', the perceptual phenomenon whereby a sequence of images, passed at sufficient speed before the eyes, generates the illusion of movement. But

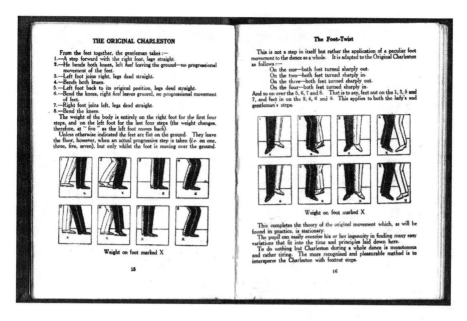

Fig. 15. 'Animatic' documentation for the Charleston, from An Expert, *The Modern Ballroom Dance Instructor* (London: Geographica, *c*.1926).

it was the pioneering work in motion photography undertaken by Eadweard Muybridge in the late nineteenth century and the subsequent development of cinematography, animated films and cartoon strips in the early twentieth century that would have popularized the animatic conception of movement. Irene and Vernon Castle's experimental use of film strips in 1914 was a novelty which, in failing to document the 'hold/path' kinaesthetic of their dancing, was not adopted in subsequent ballroom-dancing manuals (Figure 16).[6] On the other hand, the application of an animatic conception of movement in the 1920s to document the non-progressive gestural action of dances like the Charleston, which were sourced in the African-American tradition, prefigured a major shift in the twentieth-century dissemination of social dancing.

Like the Charleston, the Twist of the 1960s is a stationary, non-progressive dance that emphasizes gestural action over locomotional progression and may be performed without a partner. And, as with the Charleston, the popularization of the Twist articulated relations between an African-American culture of origin and the derivative fashionability of white Anglo-European youth. What was new about the Twist is that it was in all probability the first dance to be disseminated via television.

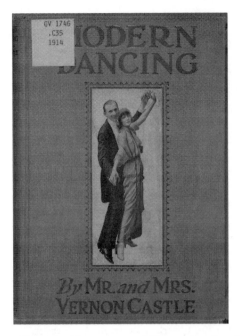

THE CASTLE WALK

Fig. 16. Experimental film-strips for the Castle Walk, from Irene Castle and Vernon Castle, *Modern Dancing* (New York: World Syndicate Co., *c.*1914), Library of Congress, Music Division.

Featured on television shows like 'American Bandstand' and countless others, the Twist was performed by American teenagers at 'record hops' in television studios and broadcast to an audience of American teenagers, many of whom, we may imagine, were dancing along at home. This televisual dissemination of the Twist was reproduced across the world in those countries like the United Kingdom and Australia which, in the postwar period, took their pop-cultural cues from the United States.[7] Consider the introductory paragraph to an instructional chapter on the Twist taken from *Everybody Dance: It's Nice 'N' Easy*, a British social dance manual published in 1962 (emphasis added):

> As previously mentioned this dance is extremely popular at the time of writing. The music appeals to young and old, the steps are simplicity itself, and the dance has received tremendous publicity in the press, magazines, and television. *There can be few readers without some mental picture of the Twist being performed.* An added advantage to the Twist is that the dancers do not move about but remain almost in one place, therefore you can practise the Twist movement

at odd times in the home when radio or television is playing the music.[8]

Note how the expertise of the dance instructor is held in deference to the kinaesthetic experience of the reader and note how this deference and appeal to the reader's experience is premised upon an assumption that the reader has participated in the mass-mediated moving-image dissemination of the Twist. In my view, this passage signifies an unprecedented moment in the history of social dancing, a moment when social dance pedagogy moved off the pages of instructional dance manuals and onto the television screen and when the dissemination of social dancing moved beyond the regulation of institutional dance instructors and into the market economy of a burgeoning pop-culture industry.

This moment, of course, is far from clear-cut, and the authors of *Everybody Dance* go on to teach the Twist using the standard step-by-step approach. But their instructions for the Twist are offered without the footstep diagrams used elsewhere in the manual. Indeed, the inadequacy of footstep diagrams as a pedagogical device for teaching a dance like the Twist is evident in Ron Mann's documentary film *Twist*. In an unidentified television segment from the early 1960s a woman attempts to teach a man to dance the Twist. Both the man and woman are white and in their 30s. As an aid in teaching the dance, the teacher turns to a footstep diagram, explaining the movement as follows:

> I have a little pattern here for the Twist. The starting position, our feet are slightly apart and one of our feet, the right one or the left one, is a little bit ahead of the other one. On number two you turn to the right. On number three you turn to the left. And from then it's just a continuous repetition.[9]

The emphasis on the feet and on turning and the absence of attention to the action of the torso is a legacy of the 'hold/path' kinaesthetic. Indeed, the kinaesthetic is reproduced in the learner's first attempts at performing the dance. As he swivels on his feet, his torso is held rigid and his pelvis, upper torso and arms move as a unit without isolation and in directional alignment with the feet. The man does eventually learn to isolate his pelvis from his upper torso and to counterbalance the pelvic movement with his shoulders and arms. But he learns this from the teacher's demonstration. Neither the footstep diagram nor her explanation represents the torso-pelvic action that is the key to performing the dance.

In marked contrast is the explanation offered by Chubby Checker, the singer who first popularized the dance in 1960 when he performed Hank Ballard's song 'The Twist' on 'American Bandstand':

> I taught people my concept of what the Twist was to me. You remove your hands from your partner, putting out a cigarette with both feet, wiping off your bottom with a towel, to the beat of the music. People understood that.[10]

Checker emphasizes the bodily involvement of the torso, in particular, the isolation between pelvic action and upper-body counterbalance that is the key to performing the dance. Checker's explanation finds a visual representation in Mann's film with a set of animatic illustrations that appear to be taken from a booklet accompanying Joey Dee's record 'Dance The Authentic Peppermint Twist'. Instead of a bird's-eye view of footsteps, these snapshot illustrations depict the whole body, viewed from the front and caught in mid-action. A large curved arrow passes through the pelvis, making the site of movement initiation—the pelvis, not the feet—the focus of pedagogical instruction.

Almost everybody interviewed in Mann's film has something to say in retrospect about 'the dance where you moved your hips'. But it is Chubby Checker who, with excited and emphatic repetition, works hardest at recapturing the significance of dancing the Twist:

> It was this [moving arms]. No it was this [moving torso and hips]. It was people moving their hips. It was hips. It was hips. If I'm—and it was doing hips. And that was nasty in 1959, 1960. They don't do things like that. I mean we just got over the Jitterbug. We just got over Elvis doing gyrating. We just got over kids going crazy dancing to Little Richard, 'Tutti frutti, ah rooty'. I means, now we got this. This very suggestive movement. (Interviewer: The Twist wasn't nasty when you did it?) Nothing's nasty when I do it. I make everything nice. I have the talent. I do.[11]

Checker's talent at making 'everything nice' lay in his ability as a clean-cut, baby-faced black teenager to perform covers of rhythm-and-blues songs in such a manner that the producers of 'American Bandstand' could broadcast him into the family rooms of white America without fear of losing advertising revenue. In contrast, Hank Ballard, the black rhythm-and-blues singer who wrote the song Checker sang, was never invited to appear on 'American Bandstand'. With his band, the Midnighters, Ballard had built a career performing in black clubs on the east coast and recording songs for black radio that featured what he calls 'dirty lyrics'. And whilst the lyrics of 'The Twist' weren't quite as 'dirty' as those of other songs, the movement referred to in the lyrics certainly was:

> I was watching my group going through a routine and they were twisting about and the lyric came to me—'Twist'. When they were doing the Twist, their leg would come up, real low-down and dirty, yeah baby, and they'd go back [demonstrates]. (Interviewer: They picked that up from the kids on the street?) No, I don't know where they got it from. I really don't. I think they just made it up as they were going along. Because their gimmicks were just spontaneous on stage. Anything that would grab attention, you know, had some shock value.[12]

Whilst Ballard's career remained confined to the black segment of a racially segregated music industry, Chubby Checker's performance of the Twist on 'American Bandstand' is an example of 'crossover'. In the American music industry of the 1950s and 1960s, 'crossover' was a marketing phenomenon whereby music producers took the 'dirty' out of black music by hiring white musicians with rock-and-roll talent and black musicians with crossover talent to perform toned-down covers of black rhythm and blues for an expanding white teenage market. Whilst the 'dirty lyrics' of rhythm-and-blues songs often survived the crossover to rock and roll, vocal and kinaesthetic styles were subject to some modification in accordance with Anglo-American standards of decency and decorum. This was especially the case for performance on television, where, unlike on radio, an African-American kinaesthetic could not be so easily disassociated from the music.

White performers performed rock and roll with a distinctly Anglo kinaesthetic. In the first episode of 'Dancing in the Street', Pat Boone's finger-snapping yet otherwise straight-laced performance of 'Tutti Frutti' for television contrasts markedly with film footage of Little Richard's hyperactive nightclub performance of the song, in which he breaks into a version of 'snake hips', a classic African-American dance move. Whilst the famous furore over Elvis Presley's pelvic-centred dancing led television producers to instruct their camera operators to film him from the waist up,[13] from the other side of the market, black performers committed to crossing-over were trained in finishing schools and took dancing lessons to lighten their African-American kinaesthetic and give 'class' to their presentation in performance. Motown, the Detroit record company that spearheaded the crossover of black musicians through the 1960s, hired Maxine Powell to set up a finishing school and train the performers in kinaesthetic style. Interviewed for 'Dancing in the Street', Mrs Powell, as she was known, still displayed traces of the 'classy' kinaesthetic that became the trademark of Motown performers:

> Everything had to be done in a classy way. So if they were doing the Shake or whatever, well we didn't do it in a vulgar way. With Diana Ross and the Supremes, we worked on singing, expressing yourself, looking pleasant. And with a smile and maybe a gesture. And how to handle the mike so the mike don't handle you. I don't want you to ever lean forward. You do not protrude the buttocks.[14]

Motown also hired Cholly Atkins, a black tap-dancer and choreographer to devise dance routines for Motown performers. Combining steps from his tap-dancing past with moves from current rhythm-and-blues performers, Atkins lightened the kinaesthetic in order to achieve crossover appeal:

> Sometimes we would find a move, might be quite primitive, something that you would just see on the R & B circuit . . . So what we would do for the presentation and the crossover, we would try to bring it up and give it a little bit more sophistication.[15]

But it was on shows like 'American Bandstand', where social dance pedagogy was explicitly harnessed to the marketing of music, that a crossover kinaesthetic was most keenly developed and most widely disseminated. Dancing alongside crossover performers like Chubby Checker, white teenagers on 'American Bandstand' introduced dances they had learnt from black friends, claiming on occasion to have invented the dance themselves. Drawn from the choreographic repertoire of African-American dance but danced by white teenagers for a mass television audience, these 'new' dances harnessed a racialized kinaesthetic to the construction of teenage style. From an African-American perspective, however, the effects of kinaesthetic crossover were somewhat absurd:

> White kids were trying to dance like black kids. But they had a way of dancing where they wouldn't move their hips, especially on 'Bandstand' and those type of shows. And if you dance without moving your hips, it just ain't happening.[16]

Certainly, Checker's twisting on 'American Bandstand' is a toned-down version of the move that inspired the song. Checker keeps both feet on the ground and his torso is held upright and kept relatively uninvolved. But, as the camera zooms out in time for the chorus, it is evident that, under his long-cut jacket, Checker is indeed moving his hips.

Popular-dance historians are fond of quoting the response of America's foremost dance instructors, Mr and Mrs Arthur Murray, to the Twist phenomenon. Whereas 'Mrs Murray considered the dance "a nice exotic thing, good for reducing weight, and not at all vulgar", Mr Murray thought it "not a dance at all—no steps, pure swivel"'. Nevertheless, the Murrays were soon advertising 'six easy lessons for $25'.[17] It is hard to imagine how teaching the Twist could take up six lessons. Presumably the kinaesthetic of the Twist was so completely alien to the 'hold/path' kinaesthetic of the social-dancing tradition represented by Murray that he expected students would require detailed step-by-step instruction over a number of sessions. But the reason the Murrays' commercial proposition seems so amusing is that the mass-media dissemination of the dance had rendered dance lessons obsolete.

Taking advantage of the new medium, the Murrays had already moved their pedagogical enterprise in social dancing onto the television screen. In Mann's film *Twist*, there is a segment from their television show in which Arthur Murray teaches the Mambo with exemplary 'hold/path' separation but it's evident that his traditional approach to social dance pedagogy sits somewhat uncomfortably on television. During the Mambo lesson, the standard aspect ratio of the television screen necessitates cutting between close-up shots of stepping feet, depicting the path but not the hold, and full-body shots tracking the dancers across the floor, depicting the hold but losing the detail of the stepping as the feet are often cut off by the bottom of the screen. In contrast, the Twist seems ideally suited to televisual presentation. Danced solo and without progression, it could be shot front-on, with no cutting between takes and no need to track dancers across the floor.

Most important, it could be shot with the pelvic action of the dance centre-screen.

Providing a 'mental picture' which writers of dance manuals would later recall,[18] such televisual representations of the Twist disseminated a new kinaesthetic for social dancing, a crossover kinaesthetic of African-American derivation, which came to characterize a raft of 'new' dances: the Millie, the Fly, the Watusi, the Hully Gully, the Mashed Potato, the Monkey, the Swim, the Jerk, the Frug and so on.[19] Emphasizing gestural action over locomotional progression, bodily involvement over 'hold/ path' separation, and solo gender-indifferent pleasures over the relational dependency of the ballroom hold, these were the dances that established the kinaesthetic style and choreographic repertoire of disco—or what Victor Silvester would call 'the ultimate free-for-all of the twentieth century'.[20]

It would be wrong, however, to regard this rhetoric of freedom as evidence of liberation from pedagogical regulation, for when the appropriation of African-American dance is figured as a 'liberation' from the regulation of an Anglo-European kinaesthetic, such rhetoric belies the regulatory function of a pop-cultural industry that disavowed the African-American derivation of its 'innovations' in order to present them as the latest 'in' thing to do. Rather, disco dancing was easy and free because there was no need for it to be explained by dance instructors in social-dance academies. One didn't learn it by reading books, deciphering diagrams and following instructions. One could simply watch it on television and learn by imitation, without the discursive intervention of traditional social-dance pedagogy. This apparent state of 'free-for-all' ushered in by disco dancing was of concern to the guardians of social-dance pedagogy. In a final, page-long chapter on 'Disco Dancing', Victor Silvester chastises the 'dancing profession' for not intervening with appropriate pedagogical regulation and 'laying down a few simple figures to act as a guide for those who wish to learn this form of rhythmic movement'.[21] But he should not have been so concerned, for by the end of the 1970s a bevy of disco-dance manuals had been published.

In some respects, these manuals continue the traditions of social-dance pedagogy established in earlier manuals. They are written by self-proclaimed experts for a beginner readership and impart their expertise in step-by-step instructions. Furthermore, following the lead of the immensely successful *Saturday Night Fever* (1977), disco-dance manuals thoroughly recuperate the gender differentiation of the 'ballroom hold'. But the representational techniques used in disco-dance manuals differ markedly from those of their predecessors. None of the disco-dance manuals I have collected makes use of footstep diagrams. Rather, they adopt an animatic strategy, representing movement with freeze-frame illustrations and photographs of bodies caught in mid-action. Indeed, *Dancing Madness*, an early manual from 1976, which documents disco pre-*Saturday Night Fever*, even includes in the margins of its pages flip-book animations for the New York Hustle and the Bump. Here is how two disco-dance manuals from 1979 explain their representational technique:

> In this book we've attempted to give disco students the next best thing to a live teacher: step-by-step photos of every essential move-ment in each dance. These photos allow you to stop the action on each dance so that you can see exactly what the dancers are doing. All you really need to do is look at each photo and imitate the movements you see. Once you can do each step, the music's irresistible beat will help you tie them all together for a smooth and rhythmic dance.[22]

> This easy-to-follow guide will help you develop an individualized style and the self-confidence that will put you in the spotlight. Notice that even in the more complex dances, there is very little need for confusing footstep diagrams to follow. This is because our main philosophy is to develop first a basic vocabulary of steps and movement patterns. Once you've mastered these, you will be well on your way to any disco dance . . . Step-by-step, the text, illustrations and photos tell you *exactly* how to achieve the disco look.[23]

In both manuals, the pictures show 'exactly' how it is done and all the learner need do is 'imitate' the movements as shown. That this repre-sentational technique should be regarded as innovative and 'easy-to-follow' in contrast with the directional instructions of 'confusing footstep diagrams' could suggest that it emerged in response to the kinaesthetic demands of disco dancing. Yet, like the Charleston and the Twist, with which it shares a crossover kinaesthetic of African-American derivation and for which innovations in animatic representation had already been developed, disco dancing would receive its most effective documentation within a pedagogical approach that mobilized an ani-matic conception of movement to invoke a mimetic response from the learner (see Figure 17).

THE SMACK

In the Smack, a line dance with 16 counts, the hips take the lead. Unlike most of the dances in the previous lessons, weight transfer is accomplished mainly through a shift of the hips, rather than by stepping from one foot to the other. Throughout most of the dance, both feet remain on the floor, as the dancer thrusts one hip to the side and then the other. To do this dance effectively, concentrate on your hip area, your center of gravity, rather than on your feet and legs.

COUNT 1.
Stand with your feet spread apart comfortably and your hands on your hips. Place most of your weight on your right foot and thrust your hip to the right side.

COUNT 2.
Now transfer your weight without moving your feet. Merely thrust your hip to the left side, so that most of your weight is on the left foot. Your hands are still on your hips.

COUNT 3.
Transfer your weight again. Thrust your hip to the right side so that your weight is mostly on your right foot. Leaving your left hand on your hip, extend your right arm straight out to the right side from the shoulder. Note that your fingers on the right hand are spread with the palm facing downward.

COUNT 4.
Now thrust your hip to the left side so that your weight is on the left foot. Leaving your right arm out to the side, lift the left arm and extend it out to the left side, remembering to spread the fingers.

COUNT 5.
Transfer your weight again, thrusting your right hip to the right side and putting your weight on your right foot. Also, bend your elbows at ear level and place your hands just behind your ears against your head.

COUNT 6.
Now transfer your weight to the left foot, thrusting your hip to the left side, as you throw both arms overhead, straight and in a "V" position, with fingers pointed upward.

Fig. 17. 'Animatic' representation of The Smack, a disco line-dance, from Jennifer Meloney, *You Can Disco* (New York: Exeter Books, 1979).

In superseding the instructional footstep diagrams of earlier dance manuals with innovations in animatic-mimetic representation, disco-dance manuals might have established a new pedagogical standard. In fact, they mark the demise of printed social dance pedagogy in the twentieth century. Published in the wake of 1970s disco cinema (for which *Saturday Night Fever* was only the vanguard) and on the verge of a burgeoning market in televised music videos, disco-dance manuals derived their animatic-mimetic pedagogical approach from an increasingly cinematic and televisual dissemination of social dancing that would eventually eclipse the publication of printed dance pedagogy.

Section Three

Media Consumption and Interactivity

9

Depth, Colour, Movement
Embodied Vision and the Stereoscope

John Plunkett

The stereoscope was one of the most popular and enduring of all nineteenth-century optical recreations. It first achieved commercial success in the early-to-mid 1850s following the interest it aroused after being displayed at the Great Exhibition of 1851. The London Stereoscopic Company was set up in 1854 and, by 1856, claimed over 10,000 pictures in its trade catalogue. Its co-founder, George Nottage, went on to become Lord Mayor of London in 1885. This essay explores the fascination exerted by the stereoscope in the first decade of its popularity. Much of its appeal undoubtedly stemmed from its immersive and embodied, yet virtual, viewing experience. However, whereas previous critics have emphasized the novelty of this experience, I argue that the device's success stems from the way it extended a mode of viewing employed by preceding optical recreations, whose effect similarly depended on the illusion of virtual space. The panorama, diorama, and the numerous varieties of peep show, were equally concerned with creating the impression of bodily immersion, of imbuing flat painted scenes with three-dimensions. What did mark the stereoscope out though was the way the large number of stereographs available gave users a new form of interaction with its mode of viewing.

That the stereoscope was closely linked to existing optical formats is evident in its crossover with other imaging technologies. Thus, while the stereoscope was initially a device that created a 3-D effect for an individual viewer, during the 1850s numerous efforts were made to create both projected and animated 3-D images by combining it with the magic lantern and the phenakistoscope, respectively. The resultant devices typify the intermediality of nineteenth-century screen practice. Attempts to create these hybrid devices were made by both notable scientific figures and photographers, with papers presented before bodies such as the Royal Society and British Association for the Advancement of Science. This essay focuses on the period up to the early 1860s in order to demonstrate the depth of fascination exerted by a fully immersive device that would potentially combine the reproduction of three-dimensional space and movement.

The stereoscope emerged out of a large body of experiments on the physiology of vision in the 1820s and 1830s. It thus has the same origin as the thaumotrope and phenakistoscope, which were products of physiological research undertaken by, amongst others, Paul Roget, Michael Faraday and Joseph Plateau. The stereoscope was first described by Charles Wheatstone, Professor of Experimental Physics at King's College, London, in a paper given to the Royal Society in June 1838. (His initial research on binocular perception, however, dates from late 1832[1]). The originality of Wheatstone's reflecting stereoscope stemmed from its demonstration that the perception of objects in three-dimensional space depended on the uniting of dissimilar pictures seen by left and right eyes.

Several critics, particularly Jonathan Crary, have argued that the growth of interest in physiological optics, and concomitant devices such as the stereoscope, challenged the positivism of Enlightenment conceptions of a stable, transparent, external world.[2] The stereoscope called attention to the phenomenology of vision, demonstrating the active role of the self in producing sensation and its own experience of being-in-the-world. As David Brewster declared, 'The laws of binocular vision, when studied in all their generality, throw much light upon many physical and metaphysical questions of high importance.'[3] Debates provoked by the stereoscope, especially between Wheatstone and Brewster, concerned the relationship between the perceiving self and the external world, and the intermeshed but equally indistinct relationship between mind and body. Brewster, for example, used the stereoscope to reject George Berkeley's theory of vision, according to which depth-perception was learnt from experience, in favour of his belief that the eye perceived distance directly. In contrast, Wheatstone gave the mind a greater role in spatial perception. While the finer details of learned discussion did not translate into popular descriptions of the stereoscope, the device did question assumptions concerning the relationship between the material and ideal, the internal and external, imagination and reality.

The very first paragraph of Wheatstone's paper demonstrates that the stereoscope's success was part of an already established embodied mode of viewing. Despite the scientific origin of the device, Wheatstone saw it as exploiting similar principles used by the panorama and diorama. He asserted that, when scenes were viewed at a great distance, there was no difference between their appearance to two eyes and to one eye only. The implication of this was that in such cases there was

> no difference between the visual perception of an object in relief and its perspective projection on a plane surface; and hence pictorial representation of distant objects, when those circumstances that would prevent or disturb the illusion are carefully excluded may be rendered such perfect resemblances of the objects they are intended to represent as to be mistaken for them: the Diorama is an example of this.[4]

For Wheatstone, the diorama manipulated the physiological perception of depth so as to make a painted transparency seem like a three-dimensional scene. Whereas the stereoscope relied on imitating the fact that we see two dissimilar images of nearby objects, the panorama, peep show and diorama worked in a similar but converse fashion in that they tried to prevent binocular perception. The single lens of a peep show, for example, very obviously denies the use of binocular perception, which would reduce the effect of the viewed scene. Panoramas and dioramas, with their darkened interiors and far-off scenes of illuminated cityscapes or landscapes, similarly tried to confuse the perception of depth-cues in order to mitigate the flatness of the scene.

The design of Wheatstone's reflecting stereoscope, which initially used drawn geometrical pictures, underwent significant revision before the stereoscope became a popular artefact. Brewster devised a lenticular stereoscope in the late 1840s that was a significant improvement upon Wheatstone's version, which was expensive and bulky to construct. It was Brewster's stereoscope that was made by Jules Duboscq, a famous Parisian optician, for the Great Exhibition of 1851. It was the advent of photography, though, which was vital in facilitating the initial craze for stereoscopic pictures. The indexical realism of photography combined potently with the phenomenal realism of the stereoscope.

In Wheatstone's initial paper he claimed grandiosely that objects 'might thus be represented so as not to be distinguished by sight from the real objects themselves'.[5] Although this claim for a fully simulated 3-D image was overstated, popular descriptions often lauded the stereoscope's ability to physically take the viewer to the three-dimensional scene. One oft-repeated advertising cry of the London Stereoscopic Company was 'Seems, Madam, NAY IT IS!', while the *Leisure Hour* declared that the stereoscope 'transports you to the spot. You are not sensible of a picture—do not think of it as a picture; the illusion is complete, and the mind as well as the eye, dwells on the actual scene.'[6] The opening issue of the *Stereoscopic Magazine*, launched in July 1858, similarly declared that stereoscopic pictures were able to transport the viewer to domestic and foreign scenes: 'The temples in which our fathers prayed, and the fields upon which our fathers fought, for the liberty which we enjoy, may be impressed upon our minds without moving from our homes; and the child may be schooled in that love of country, which produced our Arthurs and our Alfreds.'[7] The stereoscope removed the physical and psychological distance between the viewing subject and the scene portrayed. The mode of viewing fostered the popularity of stereographs of national and international sites, which in turn promoted the creation of a mobile self which extended itself beyond the local, corporeal limits of the body. The tele-visual nature of the device was thus deeply implicated in the way nineteenth-century modernity embedded the private interiority of the self into the national and global.

The appeal of the immersive realism of the stereoscope is evident in the different attempts to augment this effect. The three-dimensional quality of stereographs was often artificially enhanced through taking the two pictures at a larger angle of separation than that of the human eyes. Much heated debate took place in photographic circles concerning whether the left and right stereoscopic pictures should be taken at a differential angle that replicated the interocular distance. Underlying this debate was the traditional discourse of natural theology, which promoted the divine perfection of the human senses and concomitantly regarded the eye as the ideal optical instrument.[8] Brewster recommended that most stereoscopic pictures should be taken using the interocular distance. He declared that to add 'artificial relief is but a trick which may startle the vulgar, but cannot gratify the lover of what is true in nature and in art'.[9] Not all photographers agreed, however: for stereoscopic pictures of distant objects in particular, where the effect of binocular vision was negligible, a 3-D effect could be accentuated by taking the pictures at a greater angle of separation. Antoine Claudet's stereo-daguerreotypes of the interior of the Great Exhibition, which accompanied Brewster's stereoscope at the same event, were taken using this larger angle. The *Illustrated London News* declared that 'instead of seeing the object itself, you see a miniature model of it brought close to the eyes; so that, in this instance, the stereoscopic Daguerreotypes actually surpass the reality'.[10] In 1858 the *Leisure Hour* similarly complained that there was a general tendency to use too wide an angle in order to sell startling and exaggerated effects: 'truth is sacrificed and we have a false representation of nature.'[11] Distant landscapes were particularly impressive when experienced through accentuated perspective; plunging valleys, ravines, and waterfalls, large statues, mountains and monuments, all took on more spectacular qualities. Enhanced relief created a viewing experience that went beyond mimesis in the cause of greater sensation. The stereoscope was thus like other optical devices in that, while demonstrating an aspect of the physiology of vision, it also exploited the contingency of visual perception.

The addition of colour is another way that the impact of stereoscopic pictures was accentuated. The stereoscope is most commonly associated with black and white photographs (although the London Stereoscopic Company would supply hand-coloured pictures for sixpence extra in the 1850s). To overcome the monochrome effect of photography, numerous stereoscopes were either produced or patented which imparted colour to stereoscopic pictures using different-coloured reflectors.[12] In 1856, for example, the London Stereoscopic Company advertised a colour-reflecting stereoscope that used different-coloured glass at the shuttered back to reflect tints on the transparent pictures. Picturesque effects of moonlight, sunset and sunrise could therefore be created.

The fascination with spatial perception also involved numerous experiments on the way that the phenemenology of colour helped to create a sense of depth. In 1841, Wilhelm Heinrich Dove, a German scientist, demonstrated that the stereoscopic combination of complementary colours produced white light. Dove's work demonstrated that if one of a pair of stereoscopic pictures was outlined in blue on a white background, and the other outlined in red, a spectator furnished with red and blue glasses would see the picture as a combined 3-D image. Dove conducted all manner of experiments to demonstrate the way colour affected the perception of distance and depth. In October 1852, Dove's use of red and green lenses to create stereoscopic effect was described by John Tyndall in a paper published in the *London, Edinburgh and Dublin Philosophical Journal*.[13]

Brewster was aware of Dove's research and began work on his own chromatic stereoscope in 1848. It was briefly mentioned by Brewster in a paper given at the British Association for the Advancement of Science meeting that year, 'On the Vision of Distance as Given by Colour', and fully reported at the subsequent meeting in 1849, and in a paper given to the Royal Scottish Society of Arts in December of that year.[14] Brewster noted in a letter to William Henry Fox Talbot that it was a stereoscope 'in which distance, and consequen[tly] solidity, is given by colour alone without form'.[15] Like Dove, Brewster argued that greater relief could be given to plane figures by the application of different colours to signify the distance of different objects from the eye, thereby heightening the perspective. Red and green were usually used because they were the colours with the greatest degree of difference in their refrangibility. Brewster noted that 'in coloured decorations of all kinds, the *red* or less refrangible colours should be given to the prominent parts of the object to be represented, and the *blue* or more refrangible colours to the background and the parts of the object that are to retire from the eye'.[16] Tinted stereoscopic pictures often had different areas coloured in red and green on their reverse in order to accentuate their perception of depth.

While the success of the stereoscope owed much to its viewing experience, it would be a mistake to overstate its role. The device's popularity was sustained by the large number of stereoscope designs that were able to make available its mode of viewing to different social classes of consumer. Tellingly, the second advertising motto of the London Stereoscopic Company was 'No Home Without a Stereoscope'. (In 1858, the *Liverpool and Manchester Photographic Journal* commented, 'Wherever there was an available place for the operations of the bill sticker we were sure to be assaulted with the words "NO HOME WITHOUT A STEREOSCOPE".')[17] The mutability of the viewing experience was vital in achieving the widespread dissemination of the device. The price of different packages of viewers and slide sets available in the mid-1850s ranged from twenty guineas, for a set designed for a gentleman's dressing table, to two shillings for the London Stereoscopic Company's open japanned-tin stereoscope.[18] The numerous varieties of hand-held stereoscopes were complemented by large column stereoscopes that were ideal adornments for the genteel drawing room. More home-entertainment systems than cheap portable toys, the appeal of many large stereoscopes derived from their decorative value as much as their optical fascination.

The primacy of the stereoscope's mode of viewing also has to be

Fig. 18. Selection of stereoscopes c.1860–1880.
Courtesy of the Bill Douglas Centre, University of Exeter.

qualified by the fact that, as the device's initial novelty inevitably faded, emphasis moved from its immersive effect to the quality and usefulness of the pictures. In 1859, the *Liverpool and Manchester Photographic Journal* noted that at first any card that displayed the principle of the instrument was enough to gain a viewer's interest. Stereographs were a secondary consideration to the stereoscope itself. As time progressed, though, commercial success could be maintained only by the production of better stereographs:

> The demand, of course, was complied with, and eventually it occurred that the stereoscope and stereographs changed places. Purchasers ceased to buy the latter to show off the former, and began instead to procure stereoscopes, because they were *necessary*, in order to enjoy fully the beautiful illustrations that were everywhere offered to the public.[19]

The stereoscope thus prefigures subsequent popular media, such as cinema and personal computers, whose appeal underwent a similar shift. The enduring success of the stereoscope, as a piece of 'hardware', stemmed not from its novelty but from the range and attraction of visual material, or software, it was able to deliver.

Unlike preceding optical toys, the large number of stereographs available offered users an unprecedented degree of choice. Small moving panoramas, peepshows, thaumotropes, which were all similarly consumed within the domestic sphere, were usually limited to the single scene or narrative that originally accompanied them. In contrast, the range of stereographs gave users the freedom to satisfy their own tastes. Users were also able to create their own visual narrative through controlling the order in which they viewed their pictures. This was particularly true for large-column stereoscopes that were able to hold between fifty and 200 stereoscopes. The range of stereographs available prevented the device being simply a novel philosophical toy and meant that high hopes were held for its educational and utilitarian potential. Brewster, for example, claimed that it would provide an improved mode of teaching natural history and geography, while, as an aid to three-dimensional design, it offered numerous possibilities for engineers, architects and sculptors. The success of the stereoscope thus stemmed not simply from its embodied mode of viewing, but the interaction that the user had with the device.

Many different genres of stereoscopic pictures were produced: still lives, topography, architecture, narrative scenes from novels or plays, comic tableaux, pornography. Numerous stereoscope sets were produced to function as tours round the Lake District, the Highlands and other picturesque locations. Pictures available from the London Stereoscopic Company in 1856 included Kenilworth Castle, Anne Hathaway's cottage, Windsor Castle, and Mrs Caudle's Curtain Lecture. Most areas of Britain soon had their own topographical set, which were often proclaimed as an inexpensive substitute for the pleasures of travel. There were also high hopes for the stereoscope as an educational tool with sets

Fig. 19. *The Ghost in the Stereoscope c.*1860.
Courtesy of the Bill Douglas Centre, University of Exeter.

of pictures produced as guides to, for example, classical antiquity and wonders of the ancient world.

Topographical pictures, whether of British or foreign scenes, obviously played upon both the immersion and extension of the self that characterized the stereoscope's mode of viewing. This haptic discourse of realistic transportation was complemented by pictures that similarly exploited the simulated yet corporeal viewing experience, and the stereoscope's larger questioning of the relationship between the material and ideal. Of these, the most popular was a picture called 'The Ghost in the Stereoscope'. The effect was achieved by introducing a figure into the picture after the exposure had been partially taken. Various ghost pictures were available, including 'The Mother's Grave', showing a group of children around their mother's grave with her spirit departing.[20] Other stereographs that similarly played with the boundaries of perception by materializing mental or spiritual phenomena included 'The Orphan's Dream' and 'The Fairy'.

The mutability of the stereoscope's mode of viewing, its adaptation for different markets and the different means of achieving or enhancing its effect, constitutes only one half of its story. It was a short step from an internal mutability to its crossover with other forms of screen practice. From the early 1850s the success of the stereoscope led to attempts to create moving 3-D images by combining the stereoscope with the phenakistoscope. These devices are significant because, as Mark Gosser has argued, they are among the first to use photography to create moving images.[21] In 1852, Charles Wheatstone, Antoine Claudet and Jules Duboscq all attempted to build stereo moving-picture devices. Claudet published a brief account of their work in the French photographic journal *La Lumière*, where he noted that, although Wheatstone was seemingly unaware of the work of the other two, 'Mr. Wheatstone and the inventor of the Phenakistoscope have been both struck for some years with the possibility of applying the principle of the stereoscope to the effects of the Phenakistoscope, but hitherto without success'.[22] Wheatstone's experimentation with a stereo phenakistoscope began as early as 1849: in a paper of that year, Joseph Plateau, inventor of the phenakistoscope, noted that Wheatstone had communicated with him over a plan to arrange sixteen daguerreotype images around two discs that were to be used in a reflecting stereoscope.[23]

Wheatstone did not patent any of his designs. He did, however, pick up his stereo work much later. In November 1878, the *Photographic News* noted that Wheatstone had recently demonstrated a stereo peepshow device to the Prince and Princess of Wales.[24] In Wheatstone's apparatus, pictures were placed upon a continuous band which was fastened to the outside of a spoked wheel. The viewer saw the stereo pictures through eyepieces at the top of a wooden peepshow cabinet. Wheatstone's stereo device, though, did not have a shutter or any other registration mechanism so the motion effect must have been very imperfect.

Antoine Claudet and Jules Duboscq were similarly notable figures who tried to combine 3-D space with movement. Duboscq was the first to actually patent a stereo moving picture, a stereo phantascope or bioscope, on 12 November 1852. Duboscq experimented with two designs; in the first, two series of binocular photographs were fixed around a revolving phenakistoscope disc, one above the other. Two small mirrors placed at the correct angles reflected the two sets of images onto the same horizontal line, and the images were viewed through two prismatic lenses. Each eye, during the revolution of the disc, had consecutively the perception of one of the series of photographs. Duboscq's second device placed two series of images onto the inside zones of a cylinder. Duboscq's designs were only partially successful, though, as the two sets of picture were either curved when placed inside the cylinder or moved at a different velocity when placed around the disc at different diameters.[25]

Antoine Claudet, the third major figure working on stereoscopic movement, studied under Daguerre and, under license from him, set up one of the first dageurreotype studios in London at the Adeleide Gallery in 1841. He was an active figure in photographic and scientific circles, and in 1853 was both made a fellow of the Royal Society and given the title of Photographer to the Queen. Claudet took out a British patent on 23 March 1853 (no. 711) for several stereoscopic devices. His most basic idea for a moving stereoscopic picture was for the left and right pictures to show two phases of motion; thus, to show 'a man taking off and putting on his hat, one picture must be made with the hat on, and the other with the hat off and in the hand'.[26] In conjunction with the pictures, Claudet used a sliding bar with viewing holes that could be moved left and right so that one picture and then the other was successively revealed. Persistence of vision created a crude movement effect. This contrivance was relatively successful, as in 1865 the *British Journal of Photography* noted that, for several years previously, there had been a fashion for pictures showing two phases of motion.[27]

A more elaborate design by Claudet used a modified Brewster

stereoscope, again with the moving eye-bar. A series of eight stereo-scopic pictures were pasted onto a cross-hair device rotating around a central shaft. A mechanism connected with the sliding bar brought each image consecutively into view. The device was arranged 'so that the observer may, in succession, see eight different pictures, all in different attitudes'.[28] Claudet's device was not commercially marketed but achieved some public exposure, as it was reported in an 1852 article on photography in Dickens' *Household Words*. The authors reported using Claudet's ingenious device to view a boxing match and a needlewoman sewing.[29]

Another high-profile attempt to solve the difficulties of moving stereoscopic images was made by William Thomas Shaw, a researcher from Middlesex. On 22 May 1860, Shaw patented a stereo apparatus on the principle of the reflecting stereoscope, using synchronously revolving picture discs (no. 1260). A paper describing a second device, which Shaw called the stereotrope, was read at the Royal Society in December 1860; it was also demonstrated at a photographic society soiree at King's College in 1861, which over 500 people attended.[30] On an octagonal drum, Shaw mounted eight stereographs of successive phases of motion of, for example, a steam engine. The drum turned on a horizontal axis. Between the outside of the drum and the lenses was a cylinder pierced with eyeholes. The holes were cone-shaped and arranged geometrically so that the stereo picture was revealed and then passed out of sight almost instantly. Shaw's device, like others, was a relative failure. The *British Journal of Photography* noted that, although the device created a stereoscopic effect, 'the dark screen, with slits, which revolves between the eye and the picture, has a disagreeable effect, which will be under-stood by supposing yourself to wink as fast as you possibly can when looking at an object in motion'.[31]

Patent records and photographic journals from the 1850s and early 1860s indicate numerous attempts to combine the reproduction of time and space. In 1856, for example, patents were taken out by Phillipe Benoist, a well-known French lithographer and painter, and A.D. Jundzill (for a device called the kinimoscope).[32] There were at least four other British patents in the 1850s and early 1860s.[33] In the photo-graphic press, Thomas Sutton, the editor of *Photographic Notes*, noted in December 1860 that he had been working on two designs for moving stereoscopic images, one of which he subsequently described fully in order to establish priority of claim over Shaw's stereotrope.[34] Sutton's design is notable in that he proposed showing stereoscopic views taken

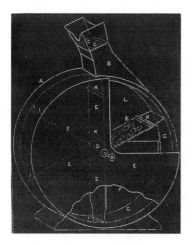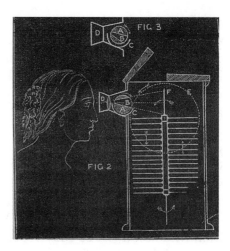

Fig. 20. Coleman Sellers, two designs for the Phantasmascope, in *British Journal of Photography*, 1 October 1862, p. 366 (left), p. 367 (right). Courtesy of the British Library, p.p.1912.h.

instantaneously at intervals of a second or less, and of momentarily illuminating each picture (printed on thin waxed paper to make it transparent) via a slit in the back of the cylinder.[35]

The international interest in animating stereoscopic pictures is reflected in an American design patented by Coleman Sellers on 5 February 1861 (no. 31,357). Sellers was a renowned engineer who would go on to become president of the Franklin Institute between 1870 and 1875. His Phantasmascope, which was widely reported in the British photographic press, arranged a series of stereoscopic pictures around the inside of drum. Like other inventors, Sellers realized that the central problem of animating stereoscopic images was that 'it is absolutely necessary, that the pictures should be entirely at rest during the moment of vision'.[36] Thus, in his Phantasmascope, each pair of images had a flap at the end so that only one image could ever be seen at a time, thereby preventing the blurring of one image into the next. Sellers also produced another design for when the motion sequence required a large number of stereoscopic photographs, as his drum design was only suitable for simple repetitive motion sequences.

The attempt to create moving stereoscopic images was matched by a desire to project them. Projecting 3-D images to a large audience would overcome the primary commercial limitation of the stereoscope, the fact that only one person at a time could view its pictures. Many attempts were made. One early suggestion was made in January 1856 in *Photographic Notes*. Its editor, Thomas Sutton, suggested using two magic lanterns to project the left and right stereoscopic images; prism-spectacles cut at the correct angle would combine the images.[37] Nineteen months later Sutton returned to the subject, claiming that, of all the applications of photography, 'there is probably none in which the public would be more deeply interested, could it be accomplished, than that of exhibiting stereoscopic pictures upon a screen in such a way as that *a considerable number of spectators* might each *at the same time* perceive a single solid figure.'[38] The collective viewing experience of stereoscopic projection was so attractive because it was the converse of the solipsism of the hand-held device.

Two methods of projecting stereoscopic images, which formed the basis for many subsequent devices, were described by Joseph D'Almeida in 1858 in a paper to the French Academy of Arts and Sciences.[39] D'Almeida's first method used two magic lanterns, one with a red filter

Fig. 21. ViewMaster stereoscope *c.*1955 and three reels. From left to right: *Queen Elizabeth's Coronation, Queen Elizabeth Visits Nigeria, Wonders of the Deep.* Courtesy of the Bill Douglas Centre, University of Exeter.

and one a green filter, projecting superimposed images. Seen unaided, the mingled picture looked grey and indistinct. Yet if looked at through red and green glasses, which allowed only the corresponding colour to penetrate, the resulting impression was a black and white picture seen in relief. D'Almeida's second method, while similarly using two magic lanterns, relied on two complex shutter mechanisms. One revolving shutter was in front of the magic lanterns and one was in front of a set of stereoscopic viewing lenses. If both shutters worked in perfect unison, the left picture would be seen only by the left eye and the right picture would be seen by the right eye in a continuous sequence. The after-image of the blocked-out picture would combine with the projected one so that persistence of vision would create a stereoscopic effect. D'Almeida ended his paper by noting that he was attempting to add motion to his projected pictures through using the principle of the phenakistoscope, thereby creating fully-immersive stereoscopic moving images.

D'Almeida's work was widely reported in British and American photographic journals. Intriguingly, J.H. Pepper, renowned Professor and director of the Royal Polytechnic Institute, seems to have attempted to exploit the commercial potential of D'Almeida's work. Pepper took out a patent on 21 April 1859 (no. 1011) for projected stereoscopic images; significantly it focused more on the exhibition requirements than on the projection technology. In addition to using two magic lanterns to project side-by-side images, each seat in the theatre was to be accompanied by a pair of glasses with focal lenses appropriate to its position in relation to the screen. Each audience member thereby saw 'the two projected pictures as one largely magnified picture'.[40] Nothing indicates that Pepper was able to execute his patent, but the fact that it was envisaged for the Royal Polytechnic, a principal London exhibition venue, exemplifies the fascination with large-scale 3-D projection.

Most early experiments concerning projected and moving 3-D images were relative failures, or at least were never able to realize any commercial success. During the first flush of enthusiasm produced by the stereoscope, these efforts were nevertheless at the forefront of work on moving pictures and the phenomenology of vision, sometimes pre-figuring the later work on chronophotography. In 1860, for example, Thomas Rose, projectionist at the Polytechnic Institute, suggested using 100 stereoscopic pictures in a row, giving exposures of one-sixth of a second at intervals of the same duration, and subsequently mounting the stereo-positive pairs on a large phenakistoscope disc for projection.[41]

With the advent of cinema, there were obviously many attempts to create stereoscopic moving pictures in the nineteenth and twentieth centuries, by figures such as Louis Lumière, Theodore Brown and William Friese-Greene, with occasional spates of success, such as the fashion for 3-D cinema in the 1950s.

In contrast to 3-D moving pictures' lack of widespread appeal, the stereoscope itself prospered as a popular toy throughout the twentieth century, metamorphosing through various brand names such as the Vistascreen Viewer, the Coronet Picturescope and the most successful of all, the Viewmaster. Like their predecessors, these devices continued to offer the prospect of a transparent and immediate experience, whereby, as Jay David Bolter and Richard Grusin have pointed out, the aim is to erase the medium and 'leave us in the presence of the thing represented'.[42] Contemporary virtual and augmented reality devices belong to a long genealogy of attempts to recreate an embodied immediacy. These attempts, at their most idealized, continue to reach for the prospect of a fully immersive device that combines the illusion of movement with an experience of three-dimensional space.

10

Penny Gaffs and Picture Theatres
Popular Perceptions of Britain's First Cinemas

Andrew Shail

> *Out of the magic lantern, out of the shadow play,*
> *Out of the dreary sideshows of the fairs of yesterday,*
> *Out of the panorama, and the primal penny gaff*
> *Man made himself a plaything—called the Cinematograph*
>
> W.A. Williamson,
> 'The Cinematograph: A Fantasy and a Forecast', 1912.[1]

In the above quotation, the practices that Williamson believed to be the closest relatives of the current mode of cinematograph display in the 'picture theatres' of 1912 (the venues first established by the 1908–1914 boom) are very revealing. The first, the projected—often scene-changing—lantern image, and the second, the shadow drama, seem clear predecessors. Of the remaining three, the novelty attractions of the fairground and the panorama have less clear correspondences but both were installed and synthesized touring views. What of the penny gaff, however, either defined as unlicensed penny theatre, with its music, pantomimic sketches and sensational re-enactments, or the 'penny shop show', with its fat lady, 'savages', 'automatic machines' and waxwork 'chamber of horrors'? This essay will argue that the parentage of 'the primal penny gaff', particularly its association with criminality and a resolutely working-class audience, was a strong influence on the mode of audience participation seen as appropriate to kinematograph display even after 1908.

Debates on early cinema currently stress that the kinematograph practice for at least the first ten years after 1895 is more accurately described as the late period of several earlier 'cultural series', from magic to illustrated press reporting.[2] Not only were participants in the production, display and viewing of the first film shows understanding film images using borrowed models, they largely did not understand the 'kinematograph' to be distinct from a range of older amusement practices. In addition, the 'second birth' of cinema—when it reputedly emerged as a 'distinct' form—may have been equally determined. Cinema's distinct formal properties as they 'emerged' after its industrialization from 1908 were the result not of formal evolution but of its discursive reinvention. This occurred as much through widespread consumption of the publicity formats of the new institutions of cinema after 1908 as in the alteration of film form. The emergence of national forms of film culture in this second period—most notably in the form of the industry-determined national popular film magazine—enabled as much as evidenced the new phase of cinema. The popular film magazine, with its motion-picture short stories and its nationally disseminated iteration of equivalence between cinema and literary fiction, is just one example of a continuing intermediality, whereby cinema's 'independence' was produced through newly established contact with more bourgeois forms.

The Importance of Crime

A desire to disassociate itself from the penny gaff was fundamental to the dignifying practices of the industry-led film discourse of the early picture-theatre period in the UK. The voices championing the new venues as dignified and respectable put much more effort into describing the cinematograph as anathema to and distanced from representations of violent crime than they put into asserting, for example, its upwardly mobile class status. 'To-day in moving picture fields,' *The Pictures* magazine asserted in May 1912, 'you see no bank robberies, train robberies, murders and so on, as in the early days . . . The stories are told for the uplift as well as the entertainment of those who see them.'[3] Faced with a widely circulating story about children's being admitted to a film in which a man cuts his own throat,[4] this magazine stated that '[t]here is an old film, a version of Othello, where the Moor of Venice did cut his throat, and the thing is still lingering somewhere in railway arches before being consigned to the junk waggon.'[5] The venue under a railway arch being shorthand for the pre-'picture theatre' penny film show of the 1906–10 period, this was an effort to describe the contemporary product and venue as entirely foreign to a preceding popular production and exhibition practice oriented around representations of violence.

Shelley Stamp argues with reference to the early development of cinemas in the United States that the film fare was not as important as the idea that cinema was what went on behind dingy urban storefronts.[6] Popular perceptions of what kind of urban amusements the picture theatre succeeded were similarly influential in the UK; notably, though, the films themselves were often perceived as continuing a representational tradition focused on violent crime. One May 1913 article in *The Pictures*, an initially distributor-owned popular film magazine launched in October 1911, demonstrates its view that the content of contemporary films did not adequately distinguish film from criminal fare: 'Surely, there are enough pleasant and clean dramatic stories in the world to render it unnecessary to drag on to the screen replicas of the "penny dreadful".'[7] Even as late as September 1916 the drive to uplift by declaring the absence of representations of crime was still active; one journalist in *Pictures and Picturegoer* wrote that *Ultus and the Grey Lady* 'does not attract by methods of criminality, thus proving the contention that films can be sensational without holding up a mirror to crime.'[8]

The industry's drive to voluntarily self-censor in late 1912 was also impelled by, amongst other factors, by the perceived need to distance the picture theatre from representations of crime. Harry Furniss, another champion of the new 'institution-cinema'[9] of the post-1908 period, was in sync with the efforts of the new British Board of Film Censors, founded in January 1913, when he remarked in 1914 that '[t]he pictures themselves have in character and artistic merit improved by prodigious leaps and bounds'.[10] 'The old doubtful character of the cinema has vanished,'[11] claimed a January 1914 article in *Illustrated Films Monthly*. Such assertions, common at the time, enabled the industry to produce a narrative about a minority of bad films which pains were supposedly being made to eradicate. In advertising *The Stolen Symphony* to picture-theatre managers in December 1912 the distributor's publicity organ, *The Top-Line Indicator*, implied that dangers of similarity were present: 'Not only the originality, but the keen human and love interests are conspicuous in this film. It will put moving pictures another long stride away from the "penny gaff", and make a deep appeal to every good-class spectator.'[12] Clearly, the picture theatre's overwhelmingly working-class audience was a problem as much for its associations with the penny gaff as for its lack of cultural respectability. Valentia Steer claimed in 1913 that kinematograph display was only newly divorced from being seen as 'an adjunct to the "Fat Lady" and the "Two-headed Calf"!'[13] While I have argued elsewhere[14] that this indicates a recent popular divorce between kinematograph display and its preceding performance contexts —in this case the penny shop show—it also indicates that the persistent fear of association led to an ongoing desire to assert difference and deny continuity.

'Blood-stained pictures': The Picture Theatre Prefigured

G.A. Williamson's use of 'primal' denotes perceived origins in the common aspect of the multiple types of nineteenth- and early twentieth-century 'penny gaff'—violent crime and a disreputable, if not delinquent, working-class audience. James Ewing Ritchie wrote of the penny theatres in 1859 that 'never did the scum and refuse of the streets so liberally patronise the entertainment as when deeds of violence and blood were the order of the night',[15] while the 'running patterer', or penny shop show exhibitor, interviewed by social reformer Henry Mayhew for his *London Labour and the London Poor* (1861), told of a waxwork exhibition career subsisting on violent crimes, listing, as a sample, eleven murder cases to date: "'Since Dan'el Good there had been little or nothing doing in the murder line—no one could cap him" he commented, "— till Rush turned up a regular trump for us.'"[16] This article will concentrate on the second type of penny gaff, the shop show, and specifically on the prefiguring of cinema by the waxworks. Later in the nineteenth century the tradition of 'Chamber of 'Orrors'[17] exhibition was still a cornerstone of shop show amusements.[18] Around 1890 Montagu Williams, entering a building in Whitechapel Road he knew had previously been an undertaker's but which was now advertised outside by a canvas depicting 'a Fat Lady' and 'a Black Dwarf', saw that, as he later wrote, 'the solemn realities of death had been succeeded by a coarse burlesque of murder':[19]

> In the body of the room was a waxwork exhibition, and some of its features were revolting in the extreme. The first of the Whitechapel murders were fresh in the memory of the public, and the proprietor of the exhibition was turning the circumstances to some commercial account. There lay a horrible presentment in wax of Matilda Turner, the first victim, as well as one of Mary Ann Nicholas . . . The heads

were represented as being nearly severed from the bodies, and in each case there were shown, in red paint, three terrible gashes reaching from the abdomen to the ribs.[20]

Charging a penny per head and holding an audience of 'some hundred persons',[21] the venue, with its waxwork chamber of horrors, fat lady, contortionists and female weight-lifter, was the standard province of what Williams called the 'East End showman'.[22]

Williams detailed the wider trend in penny gaffs of waxwork and peep-show scenes of crime (in the latter the painted canvas would be viewed through holes in an intervening screen). At one,

> Jack Sheppard, Charles Peace, and a host of other similar celebrities lived again on the canvas screen, and there repeated, before an audience of awe-stricken and admiring East End youths, some of the more daring acts of their graceless lives. Outside one show stood a coloured man scowling over a representation of the murder of Maria Martin in the Red Barn.[23]

These scenes recycled long-standing crime narratives that, in the case of Jack Sheppard, went back to W.H. Ainsworth's eponymous 1838 novel. In 1901 Arthur St John Adcock similarly remarked on the widespread production of waxwork crime scenes in both the 'peripatetic waxworks that wander about London restlessly'[24] and permanent waxwork shows (both still charging only a penny):

> The shop and the floors above are rich in waxen allegories symbolising the might of the British Empire; also in wax models of statesmen, warriors, thinkers, with here and there distributed among them renowned ruffians who have been crowded out of the Chamber of Horrors, which galaxy of great criminals is on the third floor here.[25]

Upwardly mobile and with a ticket girl controlling a turnstile, these venues were similar to the 'respectable' picture theatres of just a few years later. The term 'peep show' was certainly easily applied to the picture theatre. *Kinematograph and Lantern Weekly* quoted from *The Nation* in January 1911: 'The old peep-show boasted a certain individuality and variety. The modern peep-show [the cinema] has discovered the fundamental fact of the identity of human tastes . . . To the habitues of these peep-shows no land can be foreign.'[26] The newness asserted here and associated with film's supposed autonomy runs side by side with the continuing trope of peeping at views.

The Pictures magazine typifies early efforts to dignify picture-theatre kinematograph display by linking the institution with established bourgeois cultural forms, asserting in March 1913 that 'living pictures', the best pictures, 'reproduce chiefly works of great authors successfully'.[27] But while the term 'living pictures' as used in the 1908–1914 period may have tried to root kinematograph practice in *tableaux vivants*—variety acts imitating fine art compositions and statuary and one definite predecessor of early film form—the term established just as many roots in the waxwork chamber of horrors. Assertions of cinema's unrivalled imitation of real life established a direct resemblance to the realism of the waxwork. A handbill for two turn-of-the-century waxwork shows in Hartlepool and Durham advertised

> The Dying Afghan Chief
> This beautiful life-like Figure fitted in
> Glass Case, 9ft x 6, has death
> depicted on the Features, the Flowing
> of the Blood from the Bullet Wound,
> and the heavy Breathing is like life
> itself.—*Vide Press*[28]

Similarly, cinema was *still* discussed in the 1908–14 period as 'lifelike' rather than 'a recording of life', continuing to situate cinema amongst the uncannily realistic representational traditions that had produced the waxwork. Its realism was still often referred to not as a faithful transcription of life but 'as if' it might come to life. The dominant account impressed by industry-led film culture of the picture-theatre period referred to cinema as 'as nearly a perfect presentation of real movements as I believe we shall ever attain';[29] the effect of this upon the extant belief in a naive 'lifelike' cinematic realism is suggested by one February 1913 joke:

> At a certain theatre Biograph's Battle picture was being shown, when an elderly gentleman was seized with a violent fit of coughing. The manager sympathised with him, and was surprised when the sufferer informed him that so realistic was the film that the smell of the gunpowder had brought on the attack.[30]

Such common narratives of audience naivety attempted to inject a class dimension to what was more likely a willing suspension of disbelief in the full knowledge of the syntheticness of the image. This bourgeois account of the 'bumpkin', the elderly or the uneducated regarding the image as more real than real indicates the felt necessity, by those discursively reinventing the institution cinema, to disavow perceiving the image as disturbingly 'lifelike', which in turn suggests that this regard for the cinematic image—drawn from an earlier mode of audience inter-action—was still widely extant.

The inclusion of penny-gaff fare in music-hall entertainment, one other popularly perceived genealogical predecessor of the picture theatre, demonstrates its pervasive influence on more genteel entertainment. In 1901, Whitechapel's 'Wonderland' music hall contained, around the auditorium and available to view in the intervals between the acts, 'certain side shows consisting of all sorts of armless, legless, skeletons, or spotted "freaks"'.[31] That the correspondence between the new picture theatres and the penny gaff was greater even than that between picture theatres and the music hall is suggested by a statement in the *Daily Mail* in December 1912, which noted that 'the London County Council's new license restricts them to instrumental music and incidental to the pictures only' because 'an attempt was being made to turn some of the picture shows into *little* music-halls'.[32] The small size of many of the picture theatres of the boom period clearly distinguished them from the typical music hall but not from the small penny gaffs, which employed a variety aesthetic like that of the music hall and which were capable of holding, as Williams remarked, 'some hundred persons'. Similarity between the pricing structures of some picture theatres and penny gaffs was also embarrassing for a *Rinking World and Picture Theatre News* trying to uplift the popular image of the institution as early as 1910. At Hurndell's Kings Hall, it stated, '[c]onsidering the high-class character of the films, the prices are altogether ridiculous. One penny admits to a chair in the body of the hall, twopence to the balcony, and threepence to a plush tip-up stall.'[33] This parity was linked to the fact that, as the paper stated in as positive a matter as it could, picture theatres were 'largely patronised by the mass rather than the classes'.[34] It also stated that one-penny and two-penny cinemas or 'exhibitions' were usually below their notice, suggesting both that these continued and that the history of threepenny shows it preserves was part of a conscious effort to commemorate only certain cinemas.[35]

Motion Pictures in the Penny Gaff

While the picture-theatre version of kinematograph display was made 'out of . . . the primal penny gaff', the similarity of motion-picture amusements to the mode of display and consumption used in these shows was also iterated by the fact that the technology, for many, seemed to have originated *in* the penny gaff. As Fig. 22 shows, in 'sideshow London' the public would experience moving pictures—in the form of mutoscopes and kinetoscopes—in the same context as the 'freak' installation. Adcock told how in the penny shop show he had visited,

> [t]he public enter gratis and, sooner or later, succumb to the fascinations of one or other of the machines, and drop in a penny or a half-penny as the case may be, to set little leaden figures under glass playing cricket or football, or peer down a glazed opening and turn a handle to witness, in a series of biograph views, a scene from a familiar melodrama, the changing of the guard at Buckingham Palace, or some ludicrous episode of domestic life.[36]

Notably, as with the waxwork crime tableau, the motion picture could also be understood not in terms of motion but as 'a series of biograph views'. Joe Kember and Simon Popple's research into the memoirs of penny shop show exhibitor Tom Norman also highlights that the presence of projected kinematograph displays in penny gaffs, which were exhibited alongside 'freaks' in the ensuing years to around 1906, closely conditioned public perceptions of the technology.[37] Charles Urban was certainly frustrated with this when he insisted in 1907 that cinema was intrinsically a scientific tool, writing, 'The Cinematograph has become, not—as some people imagine it to be—a showman's plaything, but a vital necessity for every barracks, ship, college, school, institute, hospital, laboratory, academy and museum.'[38]

Jon Burrows has recently detailed the existence of a 'transition' phase of kinematograph exhibition venues in the form of penny film-only shows from 1906 in London.[39] His work has also provided evidence that the popular image of the mode of public participation appropriate to the picture theatre was conditioned by this predecessor, a direct link between the penny shop show and film-only shows that was accentuated by their shared high concentration in working-class areas.[40] This can only have been confirmed by the persistence of these 'nickelodeons' into the new 'picture theatre' phase of exhibition. One journalist for a popular film

A FAT LADY.

Fig. 22. The Interior of a London penny gaff c.1901, from
Arthur St John Adcock, 'Sideshow London', in George Sims (ed.),
Living London, vol. 2 (London: Cassell, 1902), p. 285.
By permission of the British Library, 10349.k.13.

magazine wrote in March 1914 that 'inside any of our best picture
palaces . . . one seldom, if ever, sees the old-fashioned cowboy drama, or
the lurid, sensational film, both of which have gone right out of favour,
except in the "penny gaffs".'[41] As Burrows has shown, the term 'penny
gaff' was very rarely used of the penny film shows while they were in
their ascendancy, mainly being used in the period *after* 1910 when
'picture theatres' had become largely identified with kinematograph
practice. The use of 'penny gaff' here suggests an attempt to displace
onto the penny film shows the expectations held of the picture theatre,
expectations derived from the various forms of penny gaff. It denoted
everything that the kinematograph was not, or, more accurately, a
continuing preoccupation with crime that industry commentators wanted
the public to regard as an error of infancy rather than as a characteristic
of the medium. It was one of the key ways that the 'picture palace' was
marked out as distinct. One 1918 account of a pre-picture theatre
kinematograph exhibition venue made sure to associate the fraudulent

use of still magic-lantern slides and scratched motion pictures with the penny admission price and its location in a shop.[42] 'Three short years [sic] picture theatres were few and far between,' one commentator wrote in August 1912. 'They partook in many instances of the "penny gaff" system, well dressed and refined people hardly liked to patronise them.'[43] Referring to film exhibition *after* the first picture theatres, this commentator indicates that this 'system' based on representations of crime, at a penny admission, was a part of kinematograph exhibition even in its 'new' era.

'It is the horrible that draws': The Status of the Picture Theatre

One industry magazine article, of September 1912, praised film's capacity for 'stimulating the imagination . . . and enlarging the outlook on life'.[44] By this time, popular perception of kinematograph display was probably somewhere between this praise and critics' belief that it was not only saturated with, but promoted, criminality, claims exemplified by H.D. Rawnsley's article 'The Child and the Cinematograph Show and the Picture Post-Card Evil' (1913). Perhaps drawing on an understanding of moving pictures formed by their association with penny shop shows, Rawnsley explained that what he perceived as a public taste for horror was a result of the picture theatre boom:

> It is not improbable that the cinematograph film has a good deal to answer for in this matter of the public demand for horror and sensation. On many of the hoardings near the cinematograph halls and pavilions, beneath the sensational programmes are written such words as 'nerve thrillers,' 'eye-openers to night,' and when we turn to these programmes we cannot help noticing that it is the horrible that draws.[45]

Rawnsley's account was typical of reports cited by the trade as evidence that the picture theatre's detractors had never entered one. Nevertheless, even if Rawnsley's experience of motion pictures was slight, he typified, albeit to an extreme, popular conceptions of the equivalence of kinematograph display with displays of violent crime. He referred to films as 'the items of horror or fierce excitement or degrading sensationalism which . . . are still being exhibited up and down the country'.[46]

Harry Furniss, in spite of his alignment with industry concerns in his capacity as a scenarist for Edison, reveals much in his description of the

Driving the public away.

Fig. 23. Drawing of cinema poster by Harry Furniss,
in *Our Lady Cinema* (Bristol: J.W. Arrowsmith; London: Simpkin,
Marshall, Hamilton, Kent & Co., 1914), p. 146.
Courtesy of the Bill Douglas Centre, University of Exeter.

newly conceived 'Photo-Play World' in *Our Lady Cinema* (1914). 'There
is no gainsaying the fact that the cinematograph moving pictures have
attracted the masses in every civilised country under the sun. The
question, however, cannot fail to present itself to one, Why is it they
have not yet to any extent touched the classes?'[47] For him the answer lay
in 'the common, vulgar, garish posters placed outside the cinematograph
theatres in order to advertise the show within. They are absolute
atrocities.'[48] The posters, for Furniss, were 'fifty per cent. worse even
than the most atrocious poster advertising the most plebeian play in the
vilest and most poverty-stricken purlieus frequented by the veriest riff-
raff of the amusement-going public'.[49] Typically, it was the penny gaff,
specifically in this case the penny theatre, which provided Furniss with
his closest comparison. Furniss's industry-friendly concerns can be seen

Fig. 24. Drawing of cinema poster by Harry Furniss,
in *Our Lady Cinema* (Bristol: J.W. Arrowsmith; London: Simpkin,
Marshall, Hamilton, Kent & Co., 1914), p. 148.
Courtesy of the Bill Douglas Centre, University of Exeter.

in the fact that he blamed this popular conception of violence solely on bad poster art, but he also provides evidence that expectations of crime tableaux pre-existed the posters, writing that those who do not go to the cinema habitually will 'hesitate to enter on the score of the possible vulgarity of the entertainment to be witnessed', and so will look to the posters for explanation of particular narratives and have their worries confirmed.[50] This suggests that the popular image of cinema, because of its perceived genealogies, evoked expectations that it would deliver the

Fig. 25. Drawing of cinema poster by Harry Furniss,
in *Our Lady Cinema* (Bristol: J.W. Arrowsmith; London, Simpkin,
Marshall, Hamilton, Kent & Co., 1914), p. 150.
Courtesy of the Bill Douglas Centre, University of Exeter.

specific sort of 'vulgarity'—depictions of violent crime—characteristic of the penny gaff. Furniss's drawings of posters certainly seem to confirm popular expectations of violence and crime (see Figs 24–5). '[T]he masses,' Furniss wrote, 'crowd the picture shows nightly,'[51] and for an institution that would not begin to attract any meaningful proportion of middle-class patrons until circa 1916, continuing to cater to a working-class public meant crime. The first piece of editorial matter in the new *Illustrated Films Monthly* of November 1913 demonstrates this association, referring to the viewers of matter that tends to 'degrade' cinema as 'that class which has supported the cinematograph so solidly in the past',[52] a class that continued to do so.

In addition to its concentration on violent crime, the interested voice of *The Pictures* magazine propagated a narrative of social and aesthetic uplift that centred on class, typified by one November 1911 article:

> A newspaper says that certain persons interested in the Motion Picture business have made the suggestion that the ocean liners be equipped with Motion Picture appliances so that the steerage passengers might have entertainment during the six or seven days of tedious travel. Whoever these certain personages were, it seems strange that they should suggest such high-class entertainment only for the steerage passengers.[53]

Even these narratives of upward class mobility tended to lament the stigma of criminality endemic to the various forms of penny gaff. A December 1911 piece of 'news' commented, 'Public taste is being more and more cultivated in regard to pictures, with the result that the lower ranks of the workers, who used to pack some of the picture halls in the city, and who in a large measure delighted in the sensational, are gradually fading away.' Given that this public had resolutely *not* given way to 'better-class audiences',[54] attempts to assert that they had indicate an effort to disassociate cinema from the sensational in general and representations of violent crime in particular. It was even asserted explicitly in February 1912 that 'the modern cinematograph theatre has become entirely dissociated with, and is a thing apart from, the "gaff" or penny peep-show'.[55] This statement was motivated specifically by the impulse to distance the picture theatre from such associations rather than an effort to create a distinct space for cinema (for example, associations with the legitimate stage were being actively cultivated at this time).

'Out of the lurid peepshows, with their once immoral sway'[56]

For Burrows, the almost total absence of London's 'nickelodeons' from historical memory is the result of deliberate suppression occurring as early as the 'zenith of their success and influence'.[57] Furniss, for example, provided an account of the rise of the picture theatre that erased the penny film show, explaining, that 'Only a few years ago it [the cinematograph] was of the nature of a scientific experiment appealing to a few.'[58] This erasure can be partly explained by the effort in the 1908–14 period to disassociate film from shop-show exhibition, an effort which in turn illuminates the widespread validity of a repressed genealogy for film in penny-theatre or waxwork portrayals of violent crime.

The transformation of cinema away from its immediate relatives was effected not by the rise of the picture theatre but by the emergence of new forms of film discourse. Where the term 'cinema' or 'kinema' previously related closely to the apparatus, cinema's formalization as a realm of national popular discourse from 1910 allowed for a widening of the subjects covered by the term. Cinema as the result of, and displaying the marks of, the director/producer's influence, as discrete event narratives with duration in time rather than length in feet, as an evening's entertainment, as a realm of achievement for the 'picture personalities': these all entered the interpretive schema of motion pictures as a consequence of the re-description of cinema by the Edwardian/Georgian era's newspaper and magazine personnel, who replaced the turn-of-the-century magicians, showmen and music-hall artistes as the engines of film discourse. The knowledges that the term 'cinema' came to refer to in popular discourse were now of a realm variously called 'Picture-Land'[59] 'film-land'[60] or 'the "movie-world"'.[61] Accounts of high-expenditure filmmaking endorsed a transformation in the public perception of the cinema industry away from cheap penny amusements. An article on the production of *The Golden God* (1914) explained that it would be the most expensive film ever made in America at $45,000–50,000, with the majority spent on large battle scenes.[62] Such headlines as 'Warren Kerrigan in "Samson": The Costliest Set Ever Erected for a Moving Picture Spectacle is Wrecked in One Minute'[63] performed the same 'distancing' function. The production values ascribed to film could even exploit association with a stage adaptation; *Vanity Fair* reported in September 1913 that the building of the castle of Elsinore for Johnstone Forbes-Robertson's film version of *Hamlet* 'called for an expenditure of £2,000', meaning that just one two-minute scene 'cost over £15 a second'.[64] This nonetheless took time—only in 1917 did the Mather and Crowther advertising agency's annual list of British publications see kinematograph exhibition as distinct enough from amusements to move the entries for film magazines from 'amusements' to a new 'cinematograph' section.

The production of cinema as a national institution was rooted in how practices of reception around the early 1910s relinquished previous associations and advanced new ones.[65] In trying to make new connections, through providing what James Donald and Stephanie Hemelryk Donald describe as 'structures of visibility, modes of conduct, and practices of judgement, which together constitute a culture of public participation',[66] the film discourse of this period was clearly trying to combat an existing visual exhibition culture founded on working-class participation. If the 1906–10 heyday of penny film shows established kinematograph display as a common part of the urban texture of at least London earlier than has been previously thought, it is crucial to note the continuing lack of distinction from cinema's predecessors, which even the 1908–14 picture-theatre boom did not remedy. As André Bazin pointed out in his late writings and Christian Metz commented in 1964, cinema had to *invent* itself as a distinct singular medium, not because of a drive to independence, but to dissociate itself from the multiple forms it derived from and drew on, including the penny gaff.[67] *The Pictures* noted in 1912 that the buildings being converted into 'picture theatres' included tram depots, warehouses, garages and pubs.[68] In spite of the shift in exhibition practice from the continuous performance mode shared with the penny gaff to twice-nightly showings involved in the rise of the feature film from 1912, there was little to distinguish these converted buildings from existing venues for the exhibiting of amusements, as also evidenced by the persistence of the term 'exhibition' to refer to film into the 1908–14 period. If the implicit and explicit descriptions of films, picture theatres and picture-going produced by the institutional film culture of the picture-theatre period were all directed in part towards re-purposing the institution away from its immediate predecessor, these compensatory acts suggest that in common perceptions the 'gaff', particularly the shop of horrors, was the most explicit of these.

11

From Museum to Interactive Television
Organizing the Navigable Space of Natural-History Display

James Bennett

Introduction

In late 2001, the BBC rebranded its interactive services, BBC Online, BBC Text and BBC Interactive, as BBCi, bringing all these new, digital media sites together under a single identity. The flagship television programme for this rebrand was 'Walking with Beasts', which the BBC heralded as bringing interactive television into digital-TV households in the UK.[1] Although interactive television had accompanied the launch of digital television in the UK in 1998, 'Walking with Beasts' was the first programme that would be interactive to viewers on all three digital platforms: satellite, cable and terrestrial. The series was the second in the 'Walking with . . .' trilogy, following 'Walking with Dinosaurs' (1999), both in the BBC's format of what Karen Scott and Anne White call 'un-natural' history programming, using computer-generated imagery (CGI) to recreate extinct life.[2] The introduction of interactive features, which were altered for the following 'Walking with Cavemen' instalment (2003), allowed digital-television viewers to access a range of extra video, text and aural content. This included 'Making of', 'Evidence' and 'Alternate Commentary' audiovisual streams, which were promoted in the title sequence as spaces and content that the viewer could 'explore' and 'delve deeper' into for more information on each episode's 'beasts'. The series achieved the fifth-highest ratings for 2001 and, with an audience of over eight million for the first episode, contributed to BBC1's much publicized trumping of ITV1 as Britain's most popular channel under Greg Dyke's directorship. In a significant endorsement of its interactive featues (by the public), 'Walking with Beasts' achieved a high user rating, with over two million viewers (of an available eight million digital-television homes at the time the series was aired) 'pressing the red button' during the course of the series; the interactive application also received a British Acadamy of Film and Television Arts award for 'enhancement of a linear media'. However, the programme was also lambasted by critics, most notably by David Attenborough, who dismissed it as both 'tacky' and full of the 'bells and whistles' of CGI spectacle. Attenborough and others saw 'Walking with Beasts' as being about 'entertainment' rather than education, positioning the series within the discourses of 'dumbing down' that were rife at the time and, as Helen Wheatley implicitly shows, outside the discourses of quality, public-service broadcasting[3].

I start with this short overview of the production, text and reception of 'Walking with Beasts' to suggest that, as Alison Griffiths' work has demonstrated, the display of natural history and anthropology has always been a 'site [of] complex negotiations . . . between anthropology, popular culture and commerce in attempting to strike the right balance between education, spectacle and profit'.[4] In this essay I aim to trace the history of this precarious balancing by public institutions from the late nineteenth century to the present day, from the exhibition of natural history in the museum to its display in interactive television. In particular, my concern is with the relationship between the activity of the spectator, that is, the perceived virtual and actual mobility of the spectator, and this balancing act. As Griffiths' and Tony Bennett's work have demonstrated, the development of the museum as a public institution led to an attempt to display natural history that focused on the didactic aims of the museum, differentiating itself from the 'vulgar' display of anthropology and natural history in amusement parks, cabinets of curiosity and fairs.[5] The simultaneous development of an increasingly mobile citizenry and gaze (due to nascent developments in transport technology and types of public spaces available), which Anne Friedberg describes as *flâneur*-ism, meant this concern was often focused on an attempt by the museum to counteract and differentiate itself from the distracted spectatorial glance and behaviour of the *flâneur*. It is important to note that as Friedberg's work demonstrates, this mobile spectator was connected to a virtual gaze, which although apparent across all forms of visual representation was 'produced most dramatically by photography' and the cinema, which 'combined the "mobile" with the "virtual"'.[6] As a result, similar concerns regarding spectators' physical mobility accompanied the introduction of moving-image technology into the museum space and the didactic aims of natural-history display. The museum was therefore part of a larger cultural milieu in which mobility intersected with various modes of spectatorship. Henry Fairfield Osborne, President of the American Museum of Natural History (AMNH) between 1908 and 1933, stated that the museum itself might be thought of as 'journey for those who can not [sic] travel'.[7] Bennett positions this concern to regulate the spectator's movement as a form of 'organised walking', whereby the museum, the fair and the permanent amusement park all share 'a concern to regulate the performative aspects of their visitors' conduct . . . each, in its different way, is a place for "organised walking"'.[8]

The prominence of discourses of mobility is reprised by the current development of interactive, nonlinear spaces, which often—as interactive television and 'Walking with Beasts' do—attempt to constitute the spectator as mobile, active and immersed within the navigable space of digital environments. In turn, the interactive spectator's perceived 'activity' is conceived as an attempt to capture and engage the television viewer—traditionally perceived as distracted and passive. Such interactive spaces and discourses have perhaps been best theorized by John Caldwell, who posits that rather than having created dispersed, amorphous worlds within which we can freely roam the vast halls of digital information and display, digital networking 'has made the need for content programming . . . even more compelling'.[9] Caldwell terms these forms of rationality 'second shift aesthetics', which represent a much looser notion of the 'text'—from a production, reception and analytical perspective. Second-shift aesthetics therefore recognizes that

> instead of linear textual compositing models, TV/dot-com synergies now must learn to master *textual dispersals* and user navigations that can and will inevitably *migrate* across brand boundaries. In essence, programming strategies have shifted from notions of network *program* 'flows' to tactics of *audience/user* 'flows'.[10] [Emphasis in original.]

Although the television text has always been considered malleable and messy (terms such as viewing strip, supertext and flow attempting to deal with the lack of a central organizing voice in the television-viewing experience), digital, interactive programming allows a marked shift in the ability of viewers to personalize their experience. However, like the discourses that surrounded the citizenry's newfound mobility around the turn of the nineteenth century, Caldwell's work is suggestive of a concern to regulate the movement of the 'active' spectator, albeit from a commercial perspective. My interest here is therefore twofold: first, to demonstrate the links between spectator mobility in the display of natural history from museum space to interactive television and, second, in so doing, to provide a 'second-shift aesthetics' model of the interactive television text that enables a tracing of the concern to balance issues of education and spectacle across public institutions. Thus, I argue that by considering the navigable space of interactive television's display of natural history as an extension of the museum-goer's 'organised walking', we are able not only to understand the current moment of digitalization as importantly connected to earlier technologies of visual display, but also to have a basis for considering interactive programmes, such as 'Walking with Beasts', in relation to discourses of quality and public-service broadcasting that are (ostensibly) motivated by digitalization.

Spectacle and Education in the Display of Natural History: From Display Hall to Screen

> The primacy of the visual as a conduit of scientific knowledge, the emphasis on spectator mobility, both real and virtual, and the values of didactic consumerism linked the nineteenth-century experiences of the department store shopper, the natural history museum-goer, Midway gawker and early film spectator.[11]

The tropes of spectacle within natural-history display might be broadly broken into three categories, which have remained remarkably consistent across the history and sites of its exhibition. First, there is the sense of wonderment and awe that nature in the aesthetic of the sublime can evoke, often aided by the framing, staging or production of those involved in its display. These 'generic' moments of natural history spectacle are, or attempt to be, framed invisibly (in a Classical Holly-wood sense)—whether in cinema, television or the museum—and the spectacle is of a 'natural' moment, object or specimen itself; for example, a taxidermic display of a life group such as a grizzly bear, reared on hind legs. Within the cinematic and televisual display of natural history this is most often the moment of predation, where the narrative (or, in this case, the educational lesson) is suspended in order for a dramatic moment to be played out, usually to the accompaniment of a musical score that reinforces its visually arresting and visceral nature.[12] Second, there is the spectacle of verisimilitude: recognizing that what is on display is man-made nature. For Scott and White, this spectacle of immediacy is achieved through the claims to lifelikeness of digital technologies' CGI rendering of prehistoric beasts and dinosaurs.[13] However as Griffiths' work attests, attempts to imitate nature have always been aligned with the spectacular in natural-history display, leading some museum curators to advocate the use of anti-realist representational strategies in order to retain 'the pedagogic impression [rather] than a totalising verisimilitude.'[14] Third, there is the spectacle of the display apparatus itself, which we might most easily align to Tom Gunning's work on the early 'cinema of attractions', whereby the narrative or content becomes secondary or, in his words, a 'frame upon which to string a demonstration of the magical possibilities of cinema'.[15] This final trope is most evident in the use of interactivity in television's display of natural history, which I will discuss below, but might also be apparent in the use of 'interactive displays' in museums and in those moments of frozen narrative discussed above. These forms often coalesce but, importantly, are intimately connected, across the various technologies of display, to the mobility of the spectator in the balancing of spectacle and entertainment. As the above quote from Griffiths attests, it is the primacy of the visual and its relationship to spectator mobility that links these different experiences of natural history and is most evident in this negotiation of spectacle.

Bennett's discussion of 'organised walking' suggests that the arrangement of exhibits across the architectural space of the museum is designed to use sequential locomotion to present the visitor with an itinerary that reveals an evolutionary order of things. However, as Griffiths implicitly argues, spectacle often forms as much of a guiding principle under which Bennett's notion of 'organised walking' is played out. She argues:

> the spaces between the museum life groups experienced by the museum-goer can . . . be read as anticipatory, since they largely consisted of supplementary materials that failed to attract the spectator's attention in the compelling manner of the life group tableaux.[16]

That these life groups, through their visually arresting presence in size and verisimilitude, act as a form of spectacle is borne out by Donna Haraway's work and the visceral experience of the AMNH. Haraway describes the layout of the AMNH's Akeley Hall of African Mammals as dominated by the display of African elephants, standing in the centre of the room 'like a high altar in the nave of the great cathedral'.[17] She implicitly realizes their awe-inspiring size and verisimilitude as a form of spectacle, positing that they stand so large and lifelike that a moment's fantasy would see them awaken from their dream-like stasis. Similar to the life-sized replica of the blue whale in the British Museum of Natural History (BMNH), the display of African elephants dominates not only the entire second-floor gallery, but the third floor as well, which is terraced around the exhibit to allow a bird's-eye and/or close-up view of the spectacles. The positioning of this display as a 'must see' spectacle is confirmed by the museum's floor plans, which specifically pick out displays of spectacle by providing a shadowed illustration of the exhibit, rather than simply naming the gallery (as is generally the case). Such layouts seek to visually guide the visitors' overall trip to the museum, while the domination of space by such life groups privileges the moment of spectacle and encourages the visitor to stop in awe of the exhibit. Visitors pass through the gallery with a focus on one exhibit, which is accompanied by very little explanatory text, bypassing many other exhibits, dioramas and explanations of natural history. The presence of other spectacular exhibits, marked on the floor plans, then continues this pattern of organized walking and distraction as visitors organize their time around the 'must see' exhibits; thus perennial favourites such as dinosaurs similarly appear in iconic form on the floor plans of both the AMNH and BMNH.

Griffiths' work demonstrates that the scale and verisimilitude of the 'life group' often serves to stupefy and entertain, rather than educate the museum-goer. For pioneering anthropologist Franz Boas, himself a onetime assistant curator of the AMNH, the danger of life groups is that its realism would distract the spectator's attention from the intended scientific aims, displacing the anthropological object-lesson 'in favour of a fascination with the technical means of the human facsimile'.[18] In a similar vein, the mimetic properties of film and the predominance of the 'big hunt' films at the turn of the century caused a similar anxiety about the use of film in the museum's display of natural history.[19] Haraway demonstrates that these debates coincided with the development of film technology and its use to counter 'hoax' activity regarding 'wildest' Africa in anthropology and natural history. On the one hand, filmmakers such as Osa Johnson proclaimed that the 'camera cannot be deceived' yet, on the other, aligned this truth-telling function with discourses of spectacle and profit, proclaiming, that 'This Big Feature is going to be the biggest money maker ever placed on the market . . . It will be *so spectacular* that there will be no danger of another film of like nature competing with it.'[20] Thus, as Griffiths argues, cinema was perceived as a threat to the newly established didactic regime of the rest of the museum environment. The eventual introduction of film to the AMNH (one of the first museums to experiment with film) was on condition that it be accompanied by a lecture, whereby its meaning could be mediated via the scientific authority vested in the lecturer.[21] To this end, the introduction of moving-image technology added greater tension to the balancing act of education and spectacle: cinema's capacity for visual splendour was thought to inherently invoke irrational, emotional responses that the museum sought to contain. As Friedberg's work on the *flâneur* and cinema suggests, the immobility of the cinema spectator is compensated, or rewarded, by the imaginary mobilities that such fixity provided.[22]

To complete this trajectory of mobility, spectacle and moving-image technology it is worth briefly situating television's relationship to these debates and the place and style of natural-history programming. Television's inception, like that of cinema, was linked to discourses of mobility surrounding other nascent telecommunication and wider technologies.[23] Thus Jason Jacobs, in linking television's origins with the mobilization of civil life through technologies as diverse as the telephone and public-transport systems, argues that 'early television itself was also promoted in terms of mobility—from the "transport" of images to the home, to the invitation to journey *from* the living room with the broadcasters to distant events and locations'.[24] This 'window on the world' logic, as we have come to recognize it, has continued to affect our thinking about television and its capabilities, functions and definitions. Digital television and its current pre-eminent, interactive, form can similarly be thought of as influenced by the aesthetic and technological capacities surrounding its birth; for example, the Internet, World Wide Web and the possibilities of convergence with other media all affect screen aesthetics and medium use. As a result, we now see a greater use of 'windowed' aesthetics, in programmes as diverse as '24' to 'This Morning' whereby the screen is fragmented into a series of smaller windows, mimicking or remediating, the aesthetics of desktop computers. Further, the term 'channel surfing' becomes more appropriate in multichannel television-homes; the terms 'flicking' or 'zapping' no longer suit the sheer size of the television environment that the viewer now has to navigate, traverse and explore.

Finally, Helen Wheatley's work on 'The Blue Planet' and natural history demonstrates the continuing relevance of debates about the balancing of spectacle and entertainment in its display on television, with the BBC standing in for the museum as public institution. Often marketed as 'event' television, natural-history programming has tended to be held up in public-service broadcasting debates as an example of quality programming because it ostensibly fulfils the traditional edict of educating and informing whilst doing so in a visually spectacular way that not only entertains, but does so in large numbers. Drawing on Charlotte Brunsdon's work on quality television drama, Wheatley repurposes Brunsdon's categories of quality for natural-history television as 'proven scientific fact', 'best of British presenting', 'export value' and expensive production according to 'upper-middle-class taste codes'.[25] Wheatley's detailed textual analysis of 'The Blue Planet' convincingly positions it as an example of 'quality' television, in contrast with 'Walking with Beasts' identity as the flag-bearer for digital services.

Here the status of 'The Blue Planet' as quality, public-service television is owed to its careful balancing of spectacle and education that leads to a display of 'visual pleasure' in accordance with the codes of upper-middle class taste. That is, whilst the educative aims of the programme were somewhat subverted by the emphasis on visual display, the series' use of a specially commissioned orchestral score, cinematic lighting, film stock and languid editing pace all served to place a primacy on visual pleasure, rather than the raw, visceral moments of spectacle that are usually based on moments of predation. Thus, as I suggested above, the primacy of the visual and its relationship to perceived and actual spectator mobility echoes throughout the halls of natural history display's trans-media history, continued by the emergence of digital, interactive media forms.

Spectacle and Public Institutions: From the Museum to the BBC

Janet Murray's work on digital, interactive texts argues that, with digitalization, 'environments can present space *that we can move through*'.[26] Within digital television, this often takes the form of interactive applications, which present the viewer with a range of content to choose from that is spatially laid out. In the UK, interactive television applications, such as those for BBC's and Sky's news and sports coverage (both building from the application designed for 'Walking with Beasts'), have utilized a screen aesthetic that allows the viewer to navigate across streams of audiovisual content, placed in 'video windows', laid out horizontally and vertically across the screen. The movement here is, therefore, essentially planimetric: the viewer scrolls across a two-dimensional X–Y axis. However, this movement, particularly in 'Walking with Beasts', is supplemented by the limited introduction of what Jeremy Butler usefully terms a third axis, the z-axis, which 'pokes out at the viewer or recedes into the background'.[27] This z-axis is essentially contained to the moment where the viewer chooses to 'press red' and access the interactive television application. By pressing the red button on the remote control at any time during an interactive television programme, the viewer is taken to either a specific interactive application or a range of interactive services offered by the channel, such as home shopping, games, competitions or sites for flagship programmes. These applications exist almost 'behind' the programming being broadcast on the channel proper. The sense that one is journeying to a space behind the screen is heightened by what the industry terms 'the blue screen of death',[28] which is experienced by viewers as load time and the wipe-over replacement of normal programming by a blue or channel ident screen while they wait to reach the chosen interactive application.[29]

This sense of movement makes the text nonlinear and, in the liberatory thinking of some cyber-theorists (and, more importantly, its promotion by the industry), allows viewers to create their own version of the programme. However, whilst Murray may indeed be correct about the ability of digital technologies to create immersive, navigable environments, it is important to bear in mind Caldwell's assertion that such spaces are, nevertheless, rational and constrained by those who author them. As a result, although a nonlinear text, ostensibly malleable and personalized to the viewer's choices, may complicate the notion of the programme as a stable entity in terms of its production and reception, by thinking about forms of rationality that have always existed in the display of natural history, it is possible to pin down a 'Walking with Beasts' text for analysis. Thus I argue that the interactive structure of 'Walking with Beasts' can be considered a remediation of 'organised walking', here termed 'organised viewing', to borrow Dan Harries' term for the modality of watching and using interactive texts.[30] Such a 'second-shift aesthetic' model allows for an analysis of the programme that enables it to be placed within the discourses of public institutions, relating the programme to the BBC's public-service broadcasting remit.

The broadcast version of the programme—which was available to watch as a straightforward linear programme throughout the interactive transmission via the main feature video stream—was narrated by Kenneth Branagh, although digital viewers had the choice to access an alternative, more scientific, commentary voiced by Dilly Barlow (who was a prominent reporter on the BBC's flagship current affairs programme, *Horizon*). This mainstream mimicked the natural-history genre by narrating the life stories of various CGI beasts in their un-natural habitat, following an invented narrative that saw them experience the traditional trials of life: birth, mating and, of course, moments of predation. Consequently, the interactive application—as a form of spectacle in its own right—had to negotiate, and be sure not to undermine, the twin forms of spectacle already apparent: CGI verisimilitude

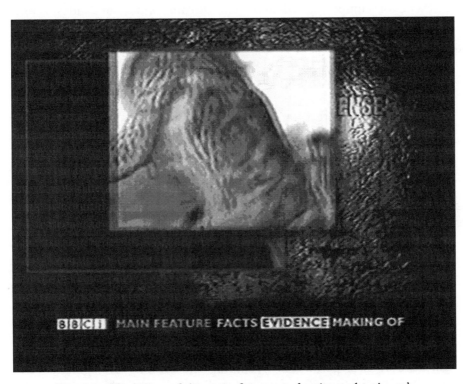

Fig. 26. The tiling of the main feature to dominate the viewer's screen is timed so as to allow the viewer on subsidiary streams, such as the 'Evidence' one here, to enjoy the moment of spectacle. Still from *Walking With Beasts* (BBC, 2001).

and the generic moments of predation written into the programme's narratives. As a result, 'Walking with Beasts' had to perform a double balancing act, weighing spectacle against educative aims whilst simultaneously pitting different forms of spectacle against one another.

The interactive application provided the digital viewer with a sense of being able to 'move around' and explore the programme (and by implication the 'fascinating world of beasts') by containing a further two, supplementary, streams of audiovisual content: 'Evidence' and 'Making of' (a 'Facts' stream being simply a series of pop-up text boxes that gave information on climate, biology, etc). The interactive application is displayed in Figure 26, showing the BBC's onscreen i-bar indicating the planimetric movement between streams that was available to viewers via the use of their remote control; in all, five streams were set out for the viewer to explore. The sense of movement, as the viewer chose to switch streams, was reinforced by the series' attempt to mimic the 'replacement' aesthetic of computing whereby one stream 'wipes' or 'slides across' another, moving to dominate the screen, whilst the main stream is 'tiled' into the top corner. When viewers changed streams, there was a brief pause in transmission as they jump between transponders to access new content, further underlining the sense of movement in the application's navigable text.

These streams were formatted into short segments, such as an interview with a series producer or a scientific expert, which occurred at fairly regular intervals. Importantly, at the end of each segment, the viewer was provided with an aural prompt relating to the narrative events in the main stream's story, which acted as cues to return to the main feature stream. These cues effectively provided a means for organizing the viewer's movement between streams, ensuring they were presented with a text that was more coherent—as to watch one stream of content was to miss what was going on in another, including, most problematically, the main feature's narrative and moments of spectacle. For example, in the episode entitled 'Sabretooth', the narrative follows the life story of the CGI smillodon character Half-tooth, which includes various moments of predation and conflict with fellow smillodons. For the viewer watching the 'Evidence' stream, the balancing of spectacle and educative aims is performed by timing the running of segments with interviews and scientific data to end when particularly spectacular moments are due to played out on the main feature. As in Figure 26, at these moments the small video window of the main stream is tiled back to dominate the viewer's screen, accompanied by an aural rejoinder to

DESERT STORM
Creating floods and then making the animated beasts splash through them were some of the biggest challenges the crew faced.

BBC1 MAIN FEATURE FACTS EVIDENCE MAKING OF

Fig. 27. The moment of spectacle is reinforced by its
presence in both 'Main' and 'Making of' streams.
Still from *Walking with Beasts* (BBC, 2001).

return to the narrative to 'watch Half-tooth do battle'. Such timings and reminders acted as a form of regulation on the viewer's exploration of the text's navigable space so as to ensure that the viewer on any stream is able to enjoy this dual moment of spectacle, involving both predation and a high degree of verisimilitude as the smillodons fight. The use of spectacle as an organizing principle is most apparent in the episode 'Land of Giants', in which a chase between two beasts is slowed into bullet-time (super-slow motion), the camera rotating around the adversaries as they slip in the wet conditions. Not only is this moment presented as spectacle in the main feature—by completely suspending narrative and educative aims (both commentaries pause during the chase)—but the timing of the evidence stream's segmented content coincides to allow the viewer to return to this visceral encounter and the 'Making of' stream is devoted to an account of how this moment was achieved, allowing the spectacle to be present in both windows on this stream's screen as well (Figure 27). Thus the organized viewsing experience of 'Walking with

Beasts' ensured that those viewers who responded to the accompanying map or guide were not lost in the technical wizardry of interactivity or the (comparatively) vast spaces of digital content, but as with the shaded icons on the museum's floor plan, were guided through their journey via the prominence of spectacular moments and images.[31]

The timing and interrelationship of this series' many streams demonstrates that the application was not simply an amorphous world of digital content to explore, but rather a highly rationalized space, organized to showcase its high production values and moments of spectacle. The programme's concern to regulate user flows remains remarkably similar to the principles of display and organization of exhibition space in the museum. However, representing as it does a public institution, the organization of the text's navigable spaces around principles of spectacle remains problematic for the question of balancing education and spectacle. David Attenborough's denouncement of the programme's showcasing of 'whistles and bells' technology indicates that the programme's need to balance forms of spectacle against one another undermined the negotiation of spectacle and educative aims. Further-more, the promotion of interactivity as a form of spectacle in its own right, combined with the use of CGI to recreate beasts whose verisimilitude was to be judged against the blockbuster graphics of *Jurassic Park*, meant the programme failed to conform to the codes of middle-class taste that Brunsdon and Wheatley show to be so crucial in the category of quality television. Whilst the programme's interactive structure sought to organize the space of natural history's display, the desire to promote the programme as a spectacular advertisement for the BBC's new digital service resulted in the programme's denunciation. This criticism was fed by broader anxieties over the introduction of new moving-image technologies into the didactic regime of the BBC as public institution.

The subsequent development of interactive television's display of natural history has continued to rehearse debates that go back to museum exhibition practices. The organized viewsing of 'Walking with Beasts' arranged around the principle of spectacle was followed by 'Walking with Cavemen', which although signifying a retreat from the level of interactivity and its hyping of spectacle in its own right, never-theless was largely predicated on the display of spectacle, outweighing the programme's educational value. Here, interactivity came in the form of pop-up text boxes that sought to provide the viewer with a greater degree of scientific veracity than that offered by Robert Winston's rather whimsical presentation and commentary. However, these pop-up text boxes, akin to the timed segments of the 'Walking with Beasts" subsidiary streams, never obscured or undermined the moments of spectacle within the broadcast version of the programme, allowing moments of predation and verisimilitude to stand as spectacle in their own right. As a result, the series was similarly lambasted as a critical failure, destabilizing the BBC's hard-won status as provider of quality natural-history programming.

Ultimately the attempt to balance spectacle and education in the use of interactive television has led to a return to the anxieties that accompanied the introduction of moving-image technology into the museum. 'The Life of Mammals' series (2002–03) thus employed the reassuring presence of David Attenborough to guide the viewer through the interactive application, both visually and aurally. 'The Life of Mammals' replicated the introduction of film into museums, whereby the technology's potential to stupefy was mediated via scientific authority vested in the lecturer. 'The Life of Mammals', unlike the 'Walking with' series, was produced by the BBC's Natural History Unit and contained all the trappings of quality that Wheatley details in her discussion of 'The Blue Planet' with a specially commissioned score, David Attenborough's presentation and the restrained sense of money spent as dictated by upper-middle-class taste (best encapsulated by the series' title sequence, which depicted various mammals in slow motion, often shot against the golden tinge of a setting sun and accompanied by a grandiloquent orchestral score). Similarly, the interactive application was not available throughout the duration of the programme, but rather (arguably as a mark of respect for the quality of the main feature) appeared only during the programme's final minutes, at which point Attenborough, seated in a cinema theatre, introduced the interactive supplement and invited viewers to 'press the red button' and test their skills on the topic of the 'fascinating world of mammals'. The multiple-choice quiz that viewers then accessed was similarly structured as a form of organized viewsing that rationalized the interactive space by allowing choices that determined what the viewer saw and heard next. However, by structuring these choices around an educational quiz and rewarding correct answers with more spectacular footage than that accessed if the viewer answered incorrectly, the programme effectively organized the display of natural history around a careful balance of both education and spectacle.

In using David Attenborough to moderate the interactive elements in

'Life of Mammals', the BBC ensured it had a figure who both represents the 'best of British presenting' and is vested with 'proven scientific' knowledge, thereby producing interactive programming that fits within the discourses of both public-service broadcasting and quality television. In particular, the use of interactivity at the programme's conclusion ensured that the spectacle of technology did not upset the upper-middle-class taste codes of visual pleasure that the main feature strove to present. This, combined with the restricted mobility the programme offered the viewer, is suggestive of both how digital spaces are rationalized and how debates about quality television and digitalization, in the display of natural history at least, are intimately related to longer histories of visual culture.

12

Imaginary Spaces
User Participation in Networked Narrative Environments[1]

Andrea Zapp

> The idea of networks and links as spaces or environments is some-
> what of an enigma, still to be forged and integrated into thought,
> rather than an accepted notion.[2]

A decade after Margaret Morse wrote those words, we experience digital
networking and the Internet not only as leading platforms for artistic
ideas, but as extending far beyond their political and social arenas,
influencing many aspects of our everyday lives. In this constant merging
of real and virtual spaces and existences, the 'networked narrative
environment' is defined as a *modus operandi*, reflecting not only creative
but also social processes, and facilitating the experimental combination
of artistic devices, disciplines and languages.

This essay examines the research models in which a public installation
and theatrical space linked to the Internet is designed and employed to
create a participatory field of dramatic action. The *network* provides the
technical backdrop that enables a remote and open-ended dialogue
between these spaces. The resulting *narrative* demonstrates interactivity
as a user-controlled construct. The *environment* is the physical architecture of the installation creating a stage for real and virtual role-play,
with site specifics underpinning metaphors and supplying 'plots'.
Human presence is addressed as increasingly subject to a flow of online

contributions, material and data. How does this realign our collective understanding of the physical and the virtual, the real and the imaginary? How can the logistics of a networked participatory platform challenge the idealistic potential of an allegedly 'virtual existence'? This type of open system or artwork can be understood as an 'interval', as it tests media art and its reception on a transitory stage between natural and digital space and between their communities, acting as a symbolic passage or point of transfer between provinces of 'pure potentiality'.[3]

Work in Progress

> . . . by connecting our similar yet distributed activities in physical space on a global scale, our methods of connection between ourselves and information become as important as the information contained within the transmission. Digital information has a meaning and networks are not only for data . . .[4]

Networks are not only for data—and they create a relationship between its users. The subtext of the above quotation raise one of the Internet's most current issues, namely that it should be understood not only as an instrument for the transfer and distribution of information, but also as an open resource for participation. The Internet is a unique cosmos of invented identities, partakers, and accomplices in joint pursuits, hidden in the endless labyrinth of home(sic!) pages, chat rooms and communities, comprising the largest theatre in the world, offering everyone fifteen megabytes of fame.

These cinematic and performative elements of the Internet serve as an intriguing aesthetic motif with which to explore it as a dramatic setup for user participation and as a testing ground for innovative 'actor' or character constellations. Moving on from solely Web- or browser-based works, I am interested in approaching these issues by combining physical installations with online dimensions to create a more compelling multichannel arena of communication.[5] As these creations often provide only the frame for unforeseen content, they must be regarded as works in progress, in which individual user contributions appear first as arbitrary anecdotal fragments but eventually become footage for evaluation and documentation of an open-ended dynamic chronicle (formerly known as 'a story'). As opposed to information channelled through a post-production filter and editing procedure, we are now looking at the synchronized effects of immediate real-time exchange. This produces a short-lived episodic and transient content, originated by the textual and visual dialogue between participants of the online and remote physical environment.

Imagination and Illusion

imaginary, *adj.*: fantasy, make-believe, made-up, unreal, invented, pretend

One of my recent projects, *The Imaginary Hotel* (2002/03), consists of an installation in a public art gallery linked to a website.[6] Gallery and website visitors alike are invited to play with the idea of occupying their ideal room. The installation is set up as an open platform, with two adjoining walls simulating a stage for (inter)activity and reflecting the concept of the room's spanning inner and outer areas, the actual room and the network. The installation architecture replicates a typical hotel

Fig. 28.   Andrea Zapp, *The Imaginary Hotel* (2002), installation view, http://www.azapp.de/tih_02.html

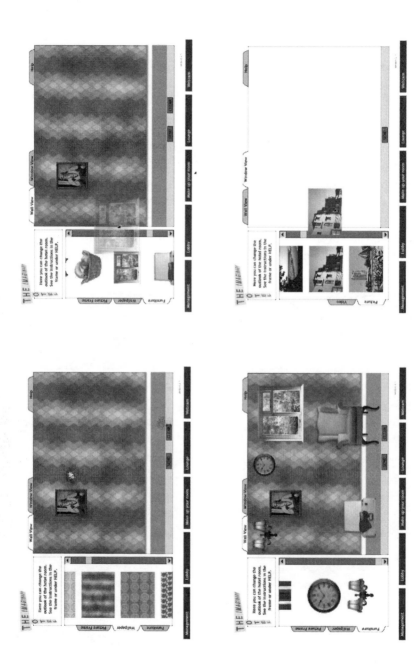

Fig. 29.   Andrea Zapp, *The Imaginary Hotel* (2002), part of the TV and Web interface, http://www.azapp.de/tih_02.html

room, with its characteristic furniture, carpet and appliances. The usual text display on the room's TV is replaced by a computer application which is accessed via a remote-control mouse provided on a coffee tray on the bed. The software offers a wide range of images for modifying the look of the room. Using a simple drag-and-drop interface, visitors can alter the interior face of one of the walls and refurbish their room with different furniture, wallpaper or pictures; they can also 'transfer' the hotel to another location by choosing for the other wall an alternative window view created from photographic images. Their final room design is transferred via the Internet to projectors and displayed life-size on the walls.

At the same time, Internet users can interfere and occupy the room virtually from a remote location. The TV interface also appears on the website, enabling remote visitors to alter the projection and add their own material. A search interface collects their personal images from their hard drive to be displayed on the window wall and in the (real) picture frame on the other wall. These are then inserted into the database choice on the TV and website. A webcam is constantly streaming real-time video from the 'hotel', documenting the visual changes and communication.

The website further reinforces this virtual architecture by providing a 'hotel lobby' with a chat lounge. From the 'lobby', users are able to ring the telephone in the 'real' hotel. A special Internet–telephone interface makes it possible to send text messages from the website to the installation telephone, where they are translated into voice messages.

Given that today a wide range of collaborative projects are presented on the Web, *The Imaginary Hotel* was remarkably popular during its premiere in October 2002. Data and log file statistics gathered over ten days show over 2,000 different wall designs in which 10,790 objects were placed, whilst 378 images were uploaded to the database and 507 users registered themselves into the chat lounge (not to mention the ones who checked in anonymously), and many users returned to the hotel site several times. The hotel 'guests' came from places as diverse as Barcelona, Geneva, Marienbad, Dortmund, Tokyo, Rotterdam, San Francisco, Melbourne and Montreal, to mention but a few.

The Narrative Environment

The hotel metaphor was based on the idea of a hotel as an empty shell in which neutral rooms become personal hideaways for a certain period of time. A hotel as such stands for an anonymous social melting pot in a constant state of flux, similar to the digital network. Like a blank canvas, the vacant room is successively shaped by its short-term inhabitants of various identities. Real and virtual guests arrive from out of nowhere, meet, and disappear, leaving their personal traces, reflecting the seamless border between physical and figurative places of being. Accordingly, the walls function as projection screens in a more direct sense: the contributed material makes the walls a piece of scenery, a backdrop for the personal narrative, referring through the photo-realistic image to the personal background. However, the theatrical space now adds a fictional dimension to the found footage from the individual desktop. Most of my works have experimented with this particular type of individual, or user-originated, imagery streaming into an installation or context frame to fill it with episodic or sporadic prototypes of story. Peter Weibel describes the general allegorical value of found footage in a media artwork as follows:

> . . . what we have are media-oriented observations of a second order, in which visual culture as a whole is exposed as a ready-made object for analysis. Consequently, observation of the world gives way to the observation of communication. The unconscious character of the visual code becomes evident in a kind of symptomatic reading . . .[7]

The viewer's persona in front of and reflection on the computer screen seems to fuse with the virtual counterpart beyond it, the picture frame on the installation wall becoming a figurative object comparable to a mirror (the majority of the images sent are portraits or similar personal items). In an equally emblematic way, the projection wall becomes a window on the outer—but here digital—world. The public-installation setting of the *Hotel* project, with its invisible surrounding wiring and obscure, circulating information, highlights the theatrical backdrop as a crucial principle. It becomes a gateway to the Internet as the main source material, and the boundaries between the individual and dramatic domains become less blurred. The networked platform then hints at the cinematic scenario, in which the actor or performer is replaced by the participant's own visual vocabulary filling the screens. To support this analogy, *The Imaginary Hotel* is explicitly designed as a wide-open stage, delineated by the carpet and accentuated by the two fragile walls, curtains and props reminiscent of a shoddy TV set. Thus it plays with the idea of a material facade for the imaginary and illusionary.

I Spy with My Little Eye

The work as an immanent model of the circular 'cause and effect' between the physical and digital arenas, of the interference and distortion of the installation setting, is realized in the webcam image.

If the Internet and the 'mirror world' of cyberspace are spatially abstract, webcameras can be interpreted as mediating devices—points of contact between the virtual and the real, or the spatial 'anchors' in a placeless sea. Webcameras open digital windows onto real scenes within the far-flung geography of the Internet. The networked computer enables the exchange of text-based information with distant persons or machines; webcameras add to this a degree of real-time visual knowledge. As Garnet Hertz puts it, webcameras constitute an attempt 'to re-introduce a physical sense of actual sight into the disembodied digital self'.[8]

Webcams and related surveillance technologies have become widespread tools in internet-based artistic practices and have further led to numerous related voyeuristic media formats in television and cinema. In a recent project, titled *05 March/10:43 pm*, I have illustrated—in a literal way—the above-mentioned paradigm of the webcam as an open window onto a distant world. However, in comparison to the creative interactive nature of the *Hotel*, this work touches upon more ambiguous and darker characteristics of networked identity. Though it runs offline and without significant user input, the link to the Internet and the problematic issue of represented space couldn't be stronger, as it employs a physically distanced, yet emotionally immersive, mode of participation.

05 March/10:43 pm consists of a small-scale model of a suburban house mounted on a plinth and linked to a computer underneath. Peeping through the window into one of the rooms, the viewer discovers the live video image of a male person, collapsed on a chair, with a computer and webcamera running on a table next to him.

The image is thrown from a small LCD monitor, located on the ceiling of the room, onto a small sheet of perspex placed diagonally inside the room. This trick of projection creates an optical illusion in which the scenery seems to be floating and filling the space. To achieve this, the video footage ('actor' and objects) was screened in front of a black background, and the walls of the projection room in the model house were also painted black.

This 'live image', with the computer constantly flickering, reminiscent of a characteristic webcam scene, seems to be abruptly frozen in frame,

Fig. 30.   Andrea Zapp, *05 March/10:43 pm* (2004),
installation view.

coming to resemble a decorative mobile. It recalls a recent incident in which a young man—his monikers being 'the Ripper'—killed himself with an overdose of prescription drugs, at home in front of an internet audience and apparently encouraged by fellow participants in a chat room.

The model house of the installation represents the personal or 'genuine' terrain, while its miniature dimensions and 'icon' shape remind the viewer of how the internet can be a virtual home in which to model a second self. But the ambiguous visuals inside contradict the neat and tidy scenery. They reveal an online presence that has come to a shocking and tragic end. The actual facts and consequences can only be insinuated within an imaginary surrounding that turns increasingly into a disconcerting construct of reality in which, for the remote viewer, the obvious truth can't be told from the fiction.

By looking through the windows, the audience 'arrives' at the scene of the crime too late to do anything but wonder about the circumstances of the suicide. The spatial and temporal remoteness of the event gives a sense of uncanniness: critical questions—about how our online activities, our virtual alter egos, psychologically influence our moral responsibility and physical existence—fill the house and the exhibition room. What happens when the 'small' private world links up with the global network?[9]

A Hole in Reality

As the 'networked narrative environment' serves as a processor for unpredicted action and interpretations through exchanges between physical and digital spheres, the space and time continuum as defined in media history is called into question, becoming a surreal and timeless experience. The possible narrative in this has moved on from being a mode of message-communication or documentation, a linear story axis, to being a circular context, a matrix-like structure of accessibility and open variables. Genre-specific media art theory has been coining quite a few new terms throughout these debates.

In the well-known concept of the 'spatial montage', Lev Manovich sets the 'sequential narrative' as a tradition of film language against the spatial arrangement of story segments. In the installation settings described above, dispersed spatial and geographic parameters generate (new?) meanings and associations? Manovich relates such models of synchronized action and perception to the network in referring to an early vision by Michel Foucault:

> We are now in the epoch of simultaneity: we are in the epoch of juxtaposition, the epoch of near and far, of the side by side, of the dispersed . . . our experience of the world is less of a long life developing through time than that of a network that connects points and intersects with its own skein . . .[10]

In a telepresent setting, the montage is a sequence of networked geographical locations and different parallel fields of activity that produces a variety of allegories. Stated more directly, it

> allows the subject to control not just the situation but reality itself. Telepresence provides the ability to remotely manipulate physical reality in real time through its image. The body of a teleoperator is linked in real time to another location where it can act on the operator's behalf: repairing a space station, doing

underwater excavation, or bombing a military base in Baghdad or Yugoslavia.[11]

Slavoj Žižek identifies the virtual space as a topological structure, and so as a 'hole (or fracture) in reality', becoming the opening to the 'phantasmatic room' and supernatural universe in a kind of topological inverse or 'turning in on itself' of reality: 'No longer at home in the material world, in search of the other scene, however, it will stay forever virtual, a promise in itself, a floating anamorphotic shimmer, accessible only through a glance out of the corner of one's eye.'[12]

In addition to this, Söke Dinkla, in her discussion of the viewer representation in an imaginary construct, elucidates the 'floating' work of art:

> Part of the authorship transfers from the artist to the user in the floating work of art through the imaginative act . . . the user feels the effects of his own behaviour, which is determined by social norms and rules, and which he is reluctant to put aside . . . In the cybernetic circle his own gaze, which is determined by social conventions, is thrown back at him and makes him realise that it is he who generates reality with his gaze. In the floating work of art the user becomes conscious that he is an accomplice in a fundamental sense. However, he only seemingly occupies an omnipotent position that allows him to control events, since he is always victim and perpetrator at the same time. In a web of relations he is only one of many controllers. This becomes particularly clear when the floating work of art is extended directly into the Internet. In this case it is possible to try out 'shifting personalities', which are capable of continually changing their appearances and adapting them to new conditions.[13]

Everything Flows

Söke Dinkla curated the media art exhibition 'Connected Cities—Processes of Art in the Urban Network' (1999), which focused on the former German coal-mining region known as the *Ruhrgebiet*. The commissions were spread throughout a metropolis of urban sprawl and former industrial landscapes, the artistic statements and experiments addressing the radical social, cultural and architectural changes forced by the move from the industrial to the digital age.

Consequently my own project for this venue—*A Body of Water, Waschkaue Ewald/Schlägel und Eisen II*—created a very site-specific net-worked narrative. The work was produced in collaboration with the artist Paul Sermon, using the telematic interface technique he had developed for most of his previous installations. This allowed the projection of a whole body of remote viewers through a network and video conferencing system into one interactive space of fictive-documentary imagery.

The installation was located simultaneously in the Wilhelm Lehmbruck Museum in Duisburg and the 'Waschkaue' (a local term for the miners' changing rooms) at the disused Ewald colliery in Herten, a small neighbouring town. A video camera captured images of the audience in Duisburg, standing in front of a chroma-key blue backdrop, and these were sent to Herten and mixed with a camera image of the audience there. The joint image was then projected onto a fine wall of water, sprayed from high-pressure showerheads, in the *Waschkaue* shower

Fig. 31.   Andrea Zapp, *A Body of Water* (1999), the *Waschkaue*.
Photo: Frank Schuberth.

Fig. 32.   Andrea Zapp, *A Body of Water* (1999),
shower room and water projection.
Photo: Frank Schuberth.

room. A camera captured an image of this water curtain and fed it to monitors in the other participating venues, so that all of the networked participants were interacting with each other in the virtual water wall.

The water screen was located in the centre of the shower room and had two different image sequences projected onto it simultaneously from either side. Floating independently on the water, the two images did not overlap and appeared as completely different scenarios. The audience were able to walk around the water screen and experience the images changing from the colourful telematic link with Duisburg to the black and white documentary footage of former miners showering after work in the original *Waschkaue*.

The flowing medium forms the heart of the installation and is its key metaphor; it transports the public interaction and at the same time reflects the area, the *Ruhrgebiet*, as a pulsating web of rivers and waterways. All the visual and conceptual layers meet here. On the one hand, the viewers are confronted by the new era, the interactive platform of networked communication, as a possible future. Yet on the other, they discover the ghostlike shadows of the past miners showering in the water—a flashback to the abandoned space and its former working culture.

The *Ruhrgebiet* and its inhabitants have always been characterized by a strong local profile, individualism, and pride in local traditions resulting from the working culture. The coal mine Ewald/Schlägel und Eisen II with its impressive shower and changing rooms closed down in 1997, once having one of the largest mines in Europe, employing over 7,000 miners. Each day, over a thousand miners per shift used the *Waschkaue*.

The local context plays an integral part in the 'networked narrative environment' in general. It raises the essential question about our representation in between the two societies, the digital and the (corpo)real. Linking the past or present to the future, the site-specific network not only connects mutual (historical) backgrounds in a shared environment, but speculates about the effects on the local community of the growing networked space. The disappearance of the individual and its 're-emergence' in the network, as experienced in *A Body of Water*, puts the ordering parameters and established patterns of societal identity into question.

Likewise, *The Imaginary Hotel* and, to a certain extent, the model house in *05 March/10:43 pm* examine the global village itself and review the prototype of an already digitized or dislocated and iconized identity. Their conceptual network emphasizes the insignificance of location within a supposedly borderless existence, in which the individual room is inhabited whilst a personal history is produced.

The documented artworks focus on distinctive conceptual metaphors, yet they represent a widespread approach within the new media circuit: a mixed-media or mixed-location technique that concentrates on a physical stage and as a result interrelates the disciplines, namely architecture and design, with internet and installation art. If architecture can be defined as 'structural design', then media art might be termed 'designed structures', leading to a simple formula in which a networked installation equals a physical room in a hybrid space producing a generic content. The 'networked narrative environment' recaptures a creative approach that uses networked technology as crucial artistic equipment to achieve new, open-ended configurations of a multi-channel 'story' space that are open to different readings. Finally, it explores its surrounding terrain with the intent to fuse the two types of existence, the digital and the real, into an ephemeral silhouette within a momentary illusion.

Conclusion

The crucial point of this artwork is not only that the human being is a 'zoon technikon' that puts artificial technical environments, its second nature, between itself and its raw natural environments, but that the status of this 'second nature' is virtual in an irreducible way. To return to the example of the interface: the room that we can see on the screen of the interface is virtual, this universe made out of signs and shiny images, through which we are free to surf. It's the universe that is projected onto that screen and that evokes a false impression of depth. In the moment when we cross its threshold and encounter what really lies beyond the screen, we see nothing apart from useless digital devices. This phantasmic scenery and the symbolic order are strictly correlative: there is no symbolic order without the phantasmatic room, no ideal order of the logos with the pseudo-material, 'virtual' other scenery, in which the phantasmagoric phenomena can appear. Or, as F.W.J. Schelling, a key figure of German Idealism, expressed it: 'There is no spirit without ghosts, no truly spiritual universe of ideas without the obscene, ethereal, phantasmatic physicality of "spirits" (the undead, ghosts, vampires . . .).'[14]

Section Four

Visions of Convergence:
Bringing Media Together

13

'The Lady of Shalott'
Optical Elegy[1]

Isobel Armstrong

The editor of one of the earliest film fan magazines made an analogy between the 'shadows' in Tennyson's poem and screen images.[2] He intuited the visual technologies immanent in 'The Lady of Shalott', one of the great lyrics of nineteenth-century modernity. We do not need to read the poem in terms of a teleology culminating in film, however. Rather, the poem explores the nature of the mediated world of the mid nineteenth century, disclosing a pre-history to screen culture that has its own optical consciousness.

1) Catoptrics

Dark Chambers

'The Lady of Shalott' begins twice over—in Part I with a landscape inhabited by an unseen woman, who is conjured verbally, though not visually, like an optical illusion or after-image of language—'Who hath seen her wave her hand?/Or at the casement seen her stand?' (ll. 24–25)—and, in Part II, with a woman in a dark room. She is weaving here, not waving, incorporating the reflected images of the landscape passing through a mirror into her web.

The poem is a thesaurus of optical images, its multiple references deriving from many lens- and mirror-based sources, old and new. In addition to the mirror, the lens and the screen, components of the nineteenth century's visual technology, are inferentially present. And yet these are so enigmatically indeterminate in their reference, so open in their visual readings, often superimposing nineteenth-century modernity over an archaic visual experience, that the same figure can signify more than one optical situation, with multiple and sometimes contradictory meanings.[3] (Just as the poem gestures to more than one woman weaver in classical myth.) The shadowy interiority of the second 'beginning' in the poem's second section, though, its enclosedness only relieved by the hyperaesthesic intensity of the mirror's coloured images, warrants the hypothesis that Tennyson is gesturing to the visual conditions inherent in the ancient camera obscura and the modernized magic lantern. The human eye itself, habitually described in writings on optics as a series of chambers (the retina is said to be 'painted' with images) is also part of the visual lexicon of this poem. The reference is suggestive and not literal, but the components of the camera obscura and magic lantern appear—the Lady seems to be working by means of their elements, responsive to mediated images transmitted through a lens and screened by the mirror.

To begin with this beginning. The Lady lives in a drama of shadow and colour. She alternates delight—'But in her web she still delights/To weave the mirror's magic sights' (ll. 64–65)—with desire—' "I am half sick of shadows," said/The Lady of Shalott.' Desire suspends the almost automated paratactic anaphora of the poem as the pace of the stanza slows with the suspended line. A curse whose origin is unknown forbids her 'To look down to Camelot'(l. 40)—to turn to the casement, to circumvent the mediated image. She, or the poem, is in mourning. The text is a threnody drenched in grief, an elegiac ballad. Something terrible happens to the lyrical world of the poem. The taboo is broken. Lancelot's appearance makes a traumatic assault upon the mirror, and the mirror shatters as she turns from it. The curse takes effect. The causal relations between taboo and trauma are as mysterious as the taboo itself.

But one might see the enigma of the taboo as itself a curse. 'And so she weaveth steadily'(l. 44). She lives with representations transmitted through the virtual images of a mirror, to which her own act of mimesis is subordinated. It is displaced by a form of image making in which representation is accomplished by light acting on light itself, through reflection. Traditional mimesis, in which one object is interpreted *by an agent* through something other to it—the human body by paint, for instance—is repudiated, and the mirror substitutes the screened image formed 'in the air', as analysts of optical images termed it, convergent with matter but not *of* it. (If we relate the mirror to Tennyson's lens-based culture there is also the fear, less of *distortion*, than that the image is a function of the lens itself—the '*mirror's* magic sights'—a technologized image bearing a questionable relation to the body it mediates, and establishing a lesion between image and it.) Has the *mirror* cast a spell transmitted to the 'magic' web? Is there something trance-like, even mechanical, about this perpetual motion? Does the curse create estranged labour even of the aesthetic?

Furthermore, the Lady is trapped in repetition. It seems that the suspended moment of desire is repeated, 'often' (l. 66), over and over. She is caught in a repeated moment of grief. Just as the duplicated images are sealed in the mirror, so she is sealed in claustrophobic anaphora, the act of repetition constantly affirmed formally in the structure of the poem. Repetition occurs at the level of the smallest particle and lexical item. From the morpheme to the line, from rhyme scheme to the double refrain, patterns of formal pairing, parallelism and coupling occur. The poem works through duples, insistent doublings and correspondences. This compulsive anaphora brings to mind Martin Meisel's brilliant attribution of such serial repetition to optical devices and particularly optical toys.[4] The repeatability of lens-produced experience is not only a function of the image itself but of the body— the constant shaking of the kaleidoscope, the repeated peering into the stereoscope's uncanny lustrous solidities.

To return to the psychic and somatic experience of the darkened camera obscura/magic lantern experience, both archaic and modern, as I have said. The camera obscura models a concealed psychic interiority here. I will look at two sources for this figuring of interiority. The physics of light and the erotics of light, registered by Arthur Hallam's iconophilia, also authorize the-subject-in-the-darkened-room.

The camera obscura and its extension in the magic lantern is a corollary of the foundational narrative or primal scene that popular nineteenth-century physics and optics invariably repeat, Newton's discovery of the spectrum by splitting light. Light is now known through darkness. The familiar story of the beam of light entering through a slit in a shutter, taken through a prism, and projected onto a screen split up into intense component colours, or the beam of light passed through shutter and lens projected as an inverted image of the outside world on wall or screen—Tennyson has understood the new conditions of seeing entailed in this recurrent myth of discovery. The sensoria are routed through the eye. We have to remember that even the most detached and consciously objective explications *trope* this experiment. The domestic shutter, and the darkened domestic room—the core space of the nineteenth-century subject—are retained as the context of experiment even when laboratory conditions make this wholly unnecessary in practical terms.[5] An emergent laboratory of the subject in a scopic world, internally transformed by changed sensoria, is being signalled in these accounts.

It was the educated eye, the 'eruditus oculus' of Tennyson's new poetry of sensation and the specular that Arthur Hallam celebrated. His iconoclastic, insouciant confidence in a modern poetry of sensation, in which the sensoria 'tremble' into emotion from colours, sounds, and movements, was the basis of his aesthetic and his ethics.[6] The world is made permeable through the primacy of the eye, an idea that could come into being through a Lucretian account of light's materiality, whose atoms dissolve the boundaries of self and world. The Epicurean materialist ethics explored in Hallam's essay on Cicero explicitly found the moral self on sensuous experience.[7] Sensory associative networks bring thought alive. We do not think in images by an act of translation: *images think* by conferring *cognitive power* on corporeal experience. (Hallam had warrant for this in Kant's essay on orientation in thinking (1786), in which Kant models orientation in thinking through a dark chamber and *bodily* orientation.)[8] The knowledges of an optical consciousness or unconscious were reparation for the deep wounds of the division of labour in modernity. Its fragmentation of both world and mind at least produced a compensatory splitting off of acute sensation and a healing eroticization of sight—'energetic love for the beautiful'.

Mirrorings

The replications of the mirror, the 'colours gay' mediated to the web, have a peculiar patina, a brilliance and scintillating intensity created entirely through a comparatively sparse language of red and blue. The 'red cloaks of the market-girls' (l. 53) or 'long-hair'd page in crimson clad', pass through the 'mirror blue' appropriating to themselves an uncanny brightness. 'The sensation of red could only be called forth . . . by a more saturated red than has ever been seen in the world,' Helmholtz said.[9] Language here makes that saturated red known only in the mind's eye a possibility. It's how Tennyson confers cognitive power on corporeal existence, as Hallam saw. (Red is also the primary colour that shows at long distance, as Lindsay Smith has pointed out.)[10] But these images, are, the poet insists, 'shadows of the world'. Chiaroscuro supersedes colour, or co-exists with it. These are virtual images. In his essay on the characteristics of modern poetry Hallam ignores mediation, the fact of *remote seeing* put in place by the mirror. It is interesting that the insistence on simulacra means we have to ward off other simulacra and their associations here—Plato's shadows and the images of the photographer also haunt this part of the poem. But, to continue with the mirror, Tennyson's language—'the mirror clear' (l. 46)—calls forth, first, the hard-edged, polished brightness of plane mirror images, images, John Herschel said, more clear and perfect in their replication than any other form of light-transmitted image including the radiant projected image, more polished and perfect, perhaps, than the world they figure.[11] But the language also manages, second, to call forth the virtuality and distance of the image sealed in a mirror, the phantom nature of the shadows it reflects.

The world of this glistening mirror replicates the doubling and pairing associated with the idea of mirror reflection. Churls, girls, damsels, shepherd-lad, page, Abbot and knights, 'riding two by two', suggest the symmetry and hierarchy of a feudal society, marked by both gender and social stratification (girls, damsels), by ecclesiastical and peasant work patterns, and an economy of use-value (barter in the market). But this binary world does not correlate or 'match' with the world outside it, with the mercantile wharfs and burghers that appear in the last section of the poem. There is a slippage within the patina of the image itself, as the 'whirls' of the river eddy momentarily assimilate the 'churls' syntactically into its disorder. How far is the mirror a screen rather than a reflector? This doubling without correspondence—a consequence of the collaboration of mirror and lens—seems to take us further and further from the real rather than nearer to it. It is not surprising that the mirror sequence ends by displacing collective life with the night-time chiaroscuro scenes of funeral and lovers, death and desire.

Death and desire, these are fitting states for the inaccessible virtual images of the mirror. We remember that, as contemporary physicists expressed it, these are truly specular and virtual, sealed up in the silver surface, forming behind the mirror, not as a real focus at the crossing of rays of light but as a form of *as if*, formed at the same distance away from it as the reflected person or object is in front of the mirror, the focus of the image is projected backwards into the mirror from the rays that return from its surface at the same angle as they have fallen upon it.[12] This image cannot be projected, only reflected again. Thus the virtual image is always inaccessible, always unreachable, always, in a sense, impossible.

Such shadows create a consuming desire without a content that leads to the consumption of desire itself. Simmel thought that his culture had begun to measure value by the quantum of desire rather than of productive labour.[13] We want what we cannot have.

Red and blue, the dominant colours of this section, are the colours at the extremes of the spectrum, and create chromatic aberration both in the eye and in other lens-based aids to vision because they pulsate at different rates. Because they move at different speeds, they are refracted at different angles. It is perhaps no coincidence that these dominate. However, it is more important to recognize that the generalized 'colours gay' of this section create an aura of visual delight at the same time as suggesting what the shadows suggest—appearance. Since Goethe, the idea of colour was being uncoupled from the idea of materiality. For colours reflect also; they are a form of mirror or screen. It was generally understood that colour is a property of surfaces that absorb the spectrum except for the part of the spectrum they reflect. Colour is an unstable appearance. Interestingly, these findings often related to red. A body placed in a light it is incompetent to transmit becomes black (such as red sealing wax placed in green light). There was great interest in 'subjective' colours. For instance red fatigue produces its complementary colour, green (if you stare at a red object long enough, after it is removed, the retina cannot accept red and produces its complementary colour.[14] Coloured shadows emerge for the same reason. The making strange of colour is one of the poem's projects.

There are other screens and mirrors in the poem. Lancelot's shield screens his body with a representation of erotic love, a red-cross knight kneeling to a lady, its light reflected—it 'sparkled on the yellow field' (l. 80)—on the cultivated fields around, punning on the visual field and the heraldic field. The river becomes a mirror as it reflects his inverted image. In section I, the river creates a waterscape screen-mirror. I will move now to the first 'beginning' of the poem.

2) Misalignment: Dialectics of Stereoscope and Kaleidoscope

Lustrous depth

From the beginning, critics noticed the strange, artifical lustre or aura of virtuality in a Tennysonian landscape. It is so with the poem's first section.

'On either side the river lie/Long fields of barley and of rye,/That clothe the wold and meet the sky;/And through the field the road runs by . . .' (ll. 1–4) *The* river, deictically summoned by diction, as if we are familiar with it before the poem begins, is the dividing line of a cut and riven landscape, doubly scored by the river and the road that 'runs by', that parallels the river. The fen landscape is given stark symmetry, the fields cut down the middle ('on either side'), split but doubling themselves. The poem makes us see the fields twice in four lines—'Long fields', 'through the field'. It puns on agrarian fields and on the field of vision and additionally on the *depth* of visual field. Rather as in the linguistic after-image of the lady, the fields flicker between flatness —'long fields'—and perspective depth—'and meet the sky'—reaching to the horizon.

Tennyson brilliantly brings landscape, labour (these are cultivated fields) and vision together. More than this, his landscape evokes the discrete eye movements that make it possible to register separate parts of visual field (river, fields, wold) and to encounter flatness and depth (sky, road). His prescience brings the split field of the flat stereoscopic view-card together with the uncanny depth and perspective of its converted, three-dimensional image, to bear on the 'field' of the text. The stereoscope appeared in 1838,[15] between the first (1832) and revised (1842) versions of 'The Lady of Shalott'. It was developed by Wheatstone as a serious physiological instrument—a 'philosophical' instrument —to explore the double nature of vision, whose binocular structure was already acknowledged and is a presence in the poem. It was well known that the outer world presented by each of our eyes is not precisely the same. Because of the separate alignments of the left and the right eyes, different pictures are presented to each. The stereoscope's double lens splits and reorganizes vision by enabling two plane representations of exactly the same scene or object configured for the left and right eye, respectively, to be recombined as a three-dimensional image. Two retinal images, in other words, are recombined to produce depth from flat surfaces: and, as Helmholtz claimed, 'with the same complete evidence of the senses with which we should look at the objects themselves'.[16] A preternatural solidity and an intensifying of depth—we see in, round, beyond and almost behind stereoscopic objects—is the hallmark of the stereoscope. Helmholtz claimed that landscapes, buildings and cities become so familiar through stereoscopic depth that, when visited, they seem to be always already known, in a way entirely unlike two-dimensional photographic images. Tennyson summons the experience of depth throughout this first section. The resolute solidity of the castle's 'Four grey walls, and four grey towers' (l. 15), which become a geometrical cube with a base, overlooking 'a space of flowers' (l. 16) as if seen from above; the tunnel effect of reapers 'In among the bearded barley' (l. 29); and the reverse convexity of 'uplands airy'(l. 34), a landscape exposed to the moon's distance, all suggest an acute awareness of surfaces configured as depth

The optical message, though, is not simply the disruption of an ordered, gradated 'prospect'. It is that vision is the result of a radical *misalignment* rather than correspondence, two incompatible images made to converge. Instances of *non-convergence* repeat themselves here: the aristocratic 'shallop' that 'flitteth silken-sail'd' (l. 22) remains 'unhail'd, as separate from 'the heavy barges trail'd/By slow horses' (ll. 20–21)—and presumably by slow people—as its archaic diction is incompatible with the language of labour. The two sets of reapers appear to hear different songs—one part of the everyday, one magical, as the rhymes 'cheerly' and 'fairy' suggest. In Part II it is clear that the Lady does not have the panoptical power attributed to her in Part I. All seem to live in different space-time relationships. Such non-convergences presage the ultimate misalignment, Lancelot's dazzling, meteoric flight through the mirror as pure image devoid of all but virtual contact with the Lady. Formal doublings and correspondences co-exist with non-convergent events. Lancelot's swerve out of the mirror's field, and his enigmatic refrain, ' "Tirra lirra," by the river' (l. 205), a kind of anagram of river/mirror, parallels in its pure non-semantic doubling without correspondence, the inversion by which his own doubled image flashes into the mirror—'From the bank and from the river' (l. 207). The mismatching extends to a stereoscopic signification of diction. In 1842, when Tennyson introduced 'And up and down the people go' to replace an excessively onomatopoetic cluster, the word 'people' could not but have had a massive political resonance. We have to see double, or two alignments of the fiduciary word 'people'. Are 'the people' to signify a unifying, cohesive element of the nation-state, a way the words could sometimes be used, as Linda Colley has suggested, or are these 'the people' in the more fractured sense of the working class, as chartists would claim themselves to be?[17] If the latter, in what sense do we receive 'up and down'?

Has the poem, despite its symmetries, withdrawn from correspondence to register a more troubling misalignment commensurate with the split world of modernity acknowledged by Hallam? It is necessary to turn aside briefly at this point to see how the stereoscope's active bringing into relationship of two misaligned fields intervenes crucially in an argument about vision that is latent in the text. Seeing double, misalignment, these facts of seeing dramatized epistemological issues that went to the very sources of the seer's agency. For Helmholtz, writing in 1868, the stereoscope decisively resolved two rival accounts of seeing, an active and a passive paradigm, in favour of the first. His essay was a summa of nineteenth-century physiology and psychology of visual experience, and condenses nineteenth-century optics in order to set up the resolution of an important conflict.[18]

The passive paradigm of vision is a theory of identity and correlation —Helmholtz terms it the 'Innate' theory—and is founded on an analogy of vision and picture. The active paradigm of vision—Helmholtz slightly misleadingly called it the 'Empirical' theory—is worked out in terms of the sign. The picture theory presupposes a unified visual experience; the sign theory presupposes the separate alignment of vision for each eye. The picture theory understands vision in terms of a *given* correlation between world and eye as optical apparatus. The eye transmits a coherent image because there are pre-given corresponding points in the receptive areas of the eye that match the picture offered in the external world. That is, any visual experience calls out matching propensities in the eye. It is a necessary corollary of the image/picture theory that the un-unified visual fields are harmonized into one *unified* image prior to interpretation.

The sign theory refuses a given correlation of the image and eye and replaces this with an active reading of *signs* that require interpretation and an inwardness with cultural meaning. The sign theory abandons the idea of pre-given correlation and a unified field and presupposes that the separate visual fields remain as a constant factor in perception. The 'single picture of the external world of which we are conscious in ordinary vision is not produced by any anatomical mechanism of sensation but by a mental act'.[19] Thus 'the meaning we assign to our experience depends upon experiment' and *not* on passive observation of external things.[20] Our eye movements bring about changes in the external world. Our *body* organizes seeing. Sight is an experiment with these rules for changing relations. Sight is a perpetual act of verification and the interpretation of signs that have no prior coherence. Helmholtz believed that the semiotic language of vision had parity with abstract verbal language and that sensory visual language could be propositional and work with universals. Only a long history of privileging abstract verbal language had prevented us from understanding the importance of the language of sight. Helmholtz's work is part of a long debate on the 'literacy' of visual culture.

For Helmholtz the stereoscope decisively establishes the sign-experiment theory because it could not *work* without the active bringing into relationship of two misaligned fields. Interestingly, it is to the factor of '*stereoscopic lustre*' that Helmholtz turns for conclusive evidence.[21] Icebergs and crystals, peculiarly difficult to interpret visually because they present a mass of incoherent surfaces, are best presented through a black and a white stereoscopic picture which come together as a shining, polished solid in the stereoscope. If the image resulted from a combination of black and white it would be a uniform grey. But as black and white throw off different reflections of different degrees of brightness from the separated pictures presented to each eye, the result of lustre proves that this is a re-ordering of the two images brought into relation and not a fusion of them.

'By the same means it is possible to produce in stereoscopic pictures the still more beautiful effect of the sheen of water or of leaves.'[22] This statement takes us back to the poem, to the lilies, to the sheen of the wave that runs forever, and to a series of questions: is the misaligned world calling out active hermeneutic energies—or not? Does repetition and doubling signify order or duplicity?

Symmetries

'And up and down the people go,/Gazing where the lilies blow/ . . . Willows whiten, aspens quiver,/Little breezes dusk and shiver/Thro' the wave that runs forever/By the island in the river . . .' (ll. 6–7, 10–13).

The sheen of water or leaves. Water is a kind of reflective screen here in a dusk-white scene—already the mirrored and mirroring world appears, incorporated in the lustre of water. The willows and aspens whiten and quiver in the wind and, doubled and redoubled, in the water. The breezes break up—'shiver'—the surface of the water, and also shudder, create a kind of convulsion, distributing images across propagated wave-forms through reflection and refraction. Consummately, the breezes 'dusk', and 'dusk thro'', the wave: the verbal energy makes their own energy available visually as their invisible power creates that darker sheen on the upside of the ripples they have set in action. The water is both reflecting the movement the breezes have made and being moved by those breezes themselves. A kaleidoscopic waterscape of multiple reflections appears. This shift to the mode of the kaleidoscope, with its multiple images, based on the reproduction of the same, appears to promise both pattern and newness, order and change. It is an instance of the way the poem creates a pull between a correspondent or a misaligned, stereoscopic world. Reordering the materials of vision through a process of correspondent reflections and symmetries, the kaleidoscope in a sense redresses the misalignment of the stereoscope—or seems to. The connection between it and the stereoscope is that for each the visual world can be made strange at any moment, becoming a heap of random angles and planes. The lens of the kaleidoscope regularizes these into non-signifying patterns, an internally coherent structure; the lenses of the stereoscope enable them to be turned into signs.

There are moments of indecision in the poem, when spatial markers become atopic—'Up and down', 'where', 'there below'. Nevertheless, 'The Lady of Shalott' is pulled towards kaleidoscopic symmetry and variation because it is structurally dependent on formal repetition. It seems to be attempting through the iconic presence of pattern to assert the necessity of an aligned world of transparent correspondences even when other elements in the poem produce a counter-movement.

According to David Brewster, the kaleidoscope was founded on symmetry:

> The objects, consisting of pieces of coloured glass, twisted glass of various curvatures, &c, are placed in a narrow cell between two circular pieces of glass, leaving them just room to move about, while this cell is turned round by the hand. The pictures thus presented to the eye are beyond all description splendid and beautiful; an endless variety of symmetrical combinations presenting themselves to view, and never again recurring with the same form and colour.[23]

Later he introduced a convex lens that produced an inverted image of a distant external object in combination with his coloured and twisted glass. This is not pure non-mimetic pattern, but arguably it resists the threatening possibilities of double vision by pulling the visual world into order.

Brewster solved two technical problems in constructing his kaleidoscope, and these solutions themselves introduce two further problems. First, mirrors placed at exactly sixty degrees will reflect an object reflected in the opposing mirror so as to form six parts of a circle, but one of these images is actually an overlapping double reflection. That is to say, symmetry is achieved at the expense of repressing the odd number, seven. It may be a coincidence that the non-refrain lines of the poem's stanza rhyme to a pattern of four and three—seven—not the Brewsterian six. Second, and more important, Brewster treats the object reflected by the first mirror, *and* the reflection of that reflection in the opposing mirror 'as new objects'.[24] Even though the image is a reflection of a reflection and by some readings a secondary image, he holds on to the idea of duplication in reflection as a recurrence of the new. The process of image formation is new even when the image is a reflection of a reflection. Literally at the heart of the kaleidoscope the intellectual problems of repetition reappear. In what sense may duplication be a deception? In what senses does repetition bring something new into the world? Or does it enclose us in anaphora?

3) Volcano

Solar Optics

'A bow-shot from her bower eves' (l. 73). Suddenly the poem moves from shadow to light. The traumatic velocity and violence of light arrives with this arrow-measure. Erotic artillery, yes. But also a poetics of light known through the darkness of the camera obscura is violently displaced in Part III by a calorific sublime of light, a large-scale cosmic upheaval of astronomical dimensions. Lancelot takes on the attributes of a phallic sungod around whom a whole solar system moves. His bridle resembles stars, his helmet is like a comet. The virtuosic incandescent diction—dazzling, flamed, sparkled, glitter'd, burned, burning, glow'd, burnish'd, flash'd—suggests the cataclysms of modern astronomy. The phenomenon of optical reversal was a familiar reference in optics. Extremes of light could reverse a black figure on a white horse to a white figure on a black horse, acting like a photographic negative.[25] The activation of scopic shock here has something of this effect and establishes the dialectical relationship between this section and the last. The image that possesses the Lady repeats the violence of the taboo, its psychic and somatic upheaval as coercive as the taboo that ordains the Lady's fixity. Taking into account the mirror's dysfunctional space—those things behind one seem to be coming towards one—and the oblique way in which Sir Lancelot enters the mirror—the greaves and lower body appear first in a montage of surfaces that appear to be composed of light—his arrival appears like a sinister eruption. Seeing and meaning are disarticulated. Lancelot's is a body of signs in place of the coherent pictures in the mirror prior to his appearance.

Much can be said about the solar research that was gradually usurping and secularizing theological meanings of the sun. Its comparatively recently discovered volcanic dangerousness made it a signifier of dissolution, danger and violence The red-cross knight, emblem of St George, patron saint of England, seems to be endangered, or else the emblem itself is being used as a screen image. Here, however, I stress the volcanic implications of Lancelot's image, since they draw out the primacy of the volcano in popular screen practice, one of the subtexts of the poem. I end by briefly pointing to volcano iconography.

Fire: Aesthetics and Pathology

The inseparability of light and matter is the essence of the volcano, signifying far-reaching violence and upheaval, social, psychic, and somatic. Lancelot's arrival, as it brings the alienated eye, sexuality and violence together, announces the dissolving certainty of structures in many contexts.

The popular aesthetic rapture in dissolving views that move volcanically from dark to light or light to dark, and whose consuming subject *is* the volcano, also puts value on the fiery igneous upheaval of light fused with matter as the central destructive experience of the dissolving view. Indeed, the dissolve of the volcano could be seen to *represent* the dissolving view, that practice in diorama and magic lantern entailing a fade from one state to another, and which depended on a moment of uncertainty as the views momentarily coalesced.[26] There is a long history of Vesuvius as the potent signifier of violent terrestrial upheaval, in diorama, magic lantern and combinations of them in the lumière presentations in public gardens.[27] Sir William Hamilton, a serious researcher of volcanism, exploited the resources of scholarship, painting and technology to produce moving pictures or pictures of motion through light and sound in the late 1790s.[28] By the 1840s Vesuvius had become a fascination of the cultural imaginary. Vesuvius was still active in the nineteenth century.[29] We remember that Adorno thought of fireworks as the essence of the aesthetic.

Mary Somerville drew on Hamilton's research when she described the random but lawbound violence of volcanic eruption.[30] It was not clear whether volcanoes emerged from fiery underground lakes or the igneous substrata of the earth. But their force was known as the product of weakness in the landmass, usually at the edge of the sea, where the weakest terrain was. They were both a product of geological or evolutionary law and appeared to violate it by their sudden eruptions. (The 'extinct' volcano is an example of this oxymoron.) They generated insecurity because they were not only subterranean, but their effects were at a remove, carrying destruction to different regions. Their unpredictable violence made them natural signifiers of catastrophe. But it was the openness of meaning that could be attributed to these spasms of energy that generated such intense responses. Displaced from industrial furnaces they could threaten industrial violence and its corollary in revolution. They could represent one's own repressed energies and the violent assault of the other. They tend to be representations *of* fire—the unsaid is the destruction of people, cities, civilizations. As products of the magic lantern they are curiously self-reflexive in their projection of flames. To create an image of fire, optical devices need to ignite a light source and establish a focus, the place where rays of light converge after being transmitted through a lens, ('focus' being the Latin word for 'hearth'). Technology ignites flames literally and representationally—it is as if the convulsion of energy redounds on the domestic hearth.

A move from teleology and myth to pathology is apparent as light and fire lose their theological prominence or, rather, as these are joined with the secular connections of light and danger. The derangement of the Lady's desire is a few decades away from *Memoirs of My Nervous Illness* (1903), the autobiography of Freud's patient, Schreber, whom he analysed in 1911.[31] Perhaps this document makes 'The Lady of Shalott' an uncanny memoir of the future in its gender anxieties and association of light and destructive phallic power. Schreber's sense that he was dominated by rays sent from an arbitrary God—the sun was sometimes the eye of God, sometimes a woman—that the rays penetrated his body, his nervous system, and spoke with him, directed his gaze and established taboos on looking, his sense that he was turning into a woman, with a woman's erotic zones of feeling, his paranoid response to parental and patriarchal power, with its metaphysic of domination, all suggest the grip of an imaginary that both overvalues and pathologizes light. The figuring of light as trauma is common to both texts. Interestingly, since we are thinking of the projection of images through light, this analysis contained Freud's first detailed account of 'projection', where others are a screen for our displaced feelings.[32] And Freud puzzled why this pathological projection was a variant of a perfectly normal, 'healthy' projection common to all, a phenomenon that has to happen in the everyday of ordinary intercourse as a necessary part of communicative action, developing a model of exchange between human beings less as reciprocal correspondence than as interaction across an asymmetrical field. Through light, both texts register a dissolve, misalignment, an anxiety of optics.

14

Photographed Tableaux and Motion-Picture Aesthetics
Alexander Black's Picture Plays

Kaveh Askari

Terry Ramsaye's chapter in *A Million and One Nights* (1926) on the writer, photographer and lanternist Alexander Black is, to date, the most enduring account of Black and his puzzling position in film history.[1] Ramsaye was struck by the likeness between the feature films of his own day and Black's picture plays, which debuted in New York in 1894.[2] The picture plays told stories with over 200 projected glass slides, they lasted about as long as a feature film, and they suggested movement through a system of dissolves. Black became famous exhibiting his picture plays across America, but he stopped touring several years before the production of the silent feature films with which Ramsaye allied his work.[3] It troubled Ramsaye that the picture play format did not fit neatly into a narrative of the progress of cinema. To him the picture play was like the duck-billed platypus, an anomaly that necessitated a revision in his evolutionary model of film's progress. For modern media historians who look at such linear evolutionary models as historical artefacts in their own right, Black's historical anomaly and messy intermediality are no longer troubling in the way they were to Ramsaye. In fact, it is precisely this aspect of Black's work that makes it so relevant for scholars concerned with how media practices converge and how these moments of convergence are shaped by discursive factors as much as by technical innovations.

The convergence of media practices that I address here could be described in the broadest sense as being between nineteenth-century pictorialist traditions such as the tableau vivant, pictorial staging in theatre, and illustration on the one hand and the new media of instantaneous photography and cinema on the other. The former pictorial traditions are generally understood to emphasize privileged moments, whereas cinema and instantaneous photography are frequently said to have introduced the contingency of fragmented or discontinuous instants into the visual culture.[4] Conceiving of these two analytic categories as aesthetically distinct has proven to be useful for media theory, but the task of multimedia historiography is to show how, in practice, these categories often overlap. Media producers exploited new creative possibilities in the period by selectively merging traditions associated with both of these aesthetic categories in their productions. In what follows I closely examine the development of Black's picture plays in order to show the overlap of the privileged moment of the tableau and the fragment of the film frame in a concrete way. I single out Black's picture plays as a case study because their focus on the convergence of instantaneous photography, pictorial culture, and cinema is thematic as well as practical.

As multimedia projects with a rich reception history and a unique theorist–practitioner like Black behind them, the picture plays can reveal a great deal about a wide range of multimedia phenomena in this period. However, as Black's work is still relatively unknown, these issues must be addressed by way of a comprehensive account of what made the picture plays unique with regard to the media that surrounded them. There are two immediately apparent historical connections that are, I believe, best approached through a more concentrated focus on the unique style and reception of the picture plays. First, Black's picture plays were not the only amusements that combined the tableau and photography. Black's work was part of an entire spectrum of popular and middlebrow magic-lantern performances to which it was often compared.[5] The picture plays were one particularly relevant success among others, but their aesthetic solution to the common concerns about how to represent motion pictorially was truly unique. While it is necessary to ask how and why other hybrid forms, a larger international tendency to which the picture plays belong, were so successful in this period, a closer look at the picture play's basic stylistic components will address this question more effectively. They present an opportunity for close examination because the performances are so thoroughly documented and, as it has only recently been discovered, the slides and scripts are so well preserved. I address this specific question of style in the next section when I examine how Black composed his still, serial pictures so they could be read as moving pictures.

The second deceptively immediate relation is between Black and cinema. Because of the picture play's unusual suggestion of motion, there is a tendency to describe it as simply an incomplete attempt at the kind of cinematic motion that Edison succeeded in creating. Because of the picture play's two-hour length and three-act structure there is a temptation to draw quick and superficial connections to the feature film. The connections to early and feature-length films can and should be made, but they need to be mediated more carefully through the reception of Black's work. Using the publicity materials and reviews of the picture plays in the following sections, I show how their success depended on an ambivalent relationship with early cinema. This ambivalent relationship would later become the reason for Black's rediscovery, when writers and filmmakers of the 1910s noticed affinities between Black's picture plays and the photoplays of this later generation. The reception history makes clear that the aesthetic of softened motion, which had distinguished Black's work from his early contemporaries using the magic lantern and the cinematograph, was suddenly useful to those who wanted to imagine an alternative history of cinema that downplayed the significance of the 'ungainly' cinema of attractions.

Still Pictures as Moving Pictures

The picture plays consisted of successively projected photographs of professional actors and artists' models posed as pictures. Black would read an accompanying narrative and dissolve from one slide to the next at regular intervals of about twenty seconds. The first picture play, *Miss Jerry*, debuted at the Carbon Studio Theatre on 9 October 1894. With subsequent performances of *Miss Jerry* and the advice of William Dean Howells, Black fine-tuned the picture-play format to a programme of around 250 slides (compared with fifteen slides in an average lantern story) lasting about an hour and a half. *Miss Jerry* would remain the most popular of his works, but Black went on to produce three more major works in this vein: *A Capital Courtship* (1896), *Miss America* (1897, the only nonfiction work of the four) and *The Girl and the Guardsman* (1899). Black exhibited these picture plays, along with shorter programmes and variants, to urban and rural communities across America for around ten years.

Black often described his picture plays as 'simply the art of the tableau vivant plus the science of photography'.[6] Much like Edison's allusion to 'what the phonograph does for the ear', the casual interpretations of Black's claim are potentially misleading. It would be wrong to take his description to mean that photography is an insignificant technical supplement—only an applied science used to record the tableaux. In this narrow sense of Black's formulation the evanescent tableau performance is given longevity and ease of distribution with the help of the photograph, but aesthetically it remains relatively unchanged. This assumption is inadequate based on Black's deep aesthetic engagement with instantaneous photography before he began making picture plays. Elsewhere I have shown that already in Black's early 'detective lectures' there was an inventive collaboration between the tableau and the photograph, an aesthetic collaboration that outstripped simple technical assistance.[7] The situation becomes more complicated only when Black begins staging performers for serial photographs. I want to focus on Black's unique approach to staging and sequencing because what set the picture plays apart from more common lantern practices also put them into the immediate vicinity of the cinema.

Black's tableaux depart fundamentally from the tableau traditions on which they feed. As I have already briefly noted, one commonality among the diverse traditions of theatrical tableaux, waxwork series, tableaux vivants, and shorter series of life-model lantern slides is that they share an affinity for privileged moments. These privileged moments ranged from climactic spectacular events to moments staged for the clearest pictorial communication of narrative and character information. A relatively small number of staged pictures, between five and twenty in these other traditions, calls for the economy of narration and dramatic effect of the privileged moment. With Black's plays of 250 pictures, the task shifts from creating effective privileged moments to creating continuity through these long sequences. This is a subtle but salient distinction between Black's work and other life-model lantern narratives. Reviewers remarked on the difference. A *Boston Herald* critic noted, 'Even when there is a conversation which requires the same scene for several minutes the views are constantly changing to show different expressions and postures.'[8] A scene from *A Capital Courtship* (1896) demonstrates the writer's point (see Fig. 33).[9] Nothing happens in the scene aside from a conversation.[10] There is discussion about a broken

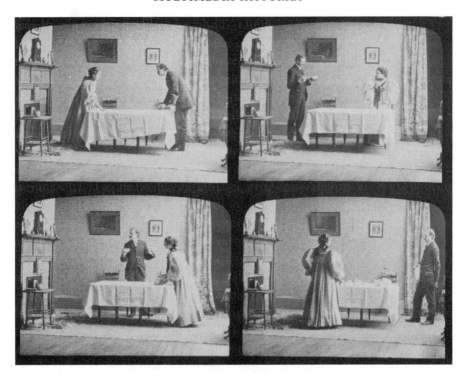

Fig. 33. Four lantern slides from *A Capital Courtship* (1896).
Courtesy of Alexander Black Collection, Princeton University
Rare Books and Manuscripts.

clock on the mantle towards which the characters gesture, but the only visual progression in the scene is in setting the table. This pictured activity does not move the events of the narrative forward, nor does it typify key character relations or situations. It might be called byplay were it actually performed by the actors and not deliberately composed as a set of pictures. Rather than emphasizing moments of intensified dramatic situations, the pictures form a regularly paced sequence, which integrates dramatic situations within a continuous flow of even and ordinary gestures. They are tableaux, but they are dynamic tableaux that give equal weight to the moments during which nothing in particular happens.

In sequences that do require tableaux of intense action, such as the only scene of violent confrontation in *Miss Jerry* (1894), the steadily paced pictures still do not yield to the climactic moment. The climax of this particular situation is pictured as the brandishing of a gun. The actors' postures are tensed as they struggle, and a chair has been thrown

"'I'VE BEEN JOLLYIN' THE GIRL A LITTLE,' HE SAID."

"'DON'T YOU SEE IT'S ONLY LITTLE JERRY?' SHOUTED PINK."

"SHE SURVEYED JERRY FROM HEAD TO FOOT."

"'STOP YOUR NOISE, PINK,' SAID MARY."

"'YOU DON'T LOOK LIKE A FOOL, EITHER.'"

"'BUT I WAS A LITTLE SCARED,' JERRY CONFESSED."

A SCENE FROM THE PICTURE PLAY "MISS JERRY."—[See Page 988.]

989

Fig. 34. 'Making the First Picture Play,' *Harper's Weekly*, 38
(20 October 1894), pp. 988–90.

to the floor. In a live performance this staged picture might have been
held static for a moment. In this scene, the moment of intensity does not
disrupt the steady unfolding of successive tableaux. The slide is shown
for the same amount of time as the others in the sequence, so it could be
read as a transitional moment like the others. The dissolve to the
following slide further suggests a continuous movement rather than an
interrupted series. The change happens as the narrator reads the words
'The Rose of the Rockies lowered a melodramatically huge revolver.'[11]
The script directs attention to the continuous movement represented by
the dissolve, connecting it to the remainder of the sequence, in which the
return to ordinary conversation is marked by the chair's return to its
upright place in the room.

The lowering of the revolver in this scene touches specifically on the representation of motion. It was not only the text that cued attention to the actors' movement during the slide changes. To say that the slides followed each other 'without friction', as one reviewer put it, implies something more than evenly paced sequences of pictures. The scenes were visually constructed for this frictionless effect. Each slide is carefully registered and the camera position is fixed so that the background and the elements of the decor remain in the same position throughout the scene. During the dissolves, the figures appear to move through a series of poses within this stationary *mise en scene*. Some audience members, like Seth Low, mayor of Brooklyn, actually believed that Black used some sort of cut-out animation device to make the figures move.[12] It was not a complete illusion of natural movement (if such a thing even exists), but it was a convincing representation of movement created with the dissolving view.

The dissolving view, a visual amusement in itself when it first appeared, was used to create effects of transformation. Lantern manuals from the turn of the century commonly featured anecdotes of comic and picturesque combinations of slides. They warned that the registration of slides could be accidental as well as intended. 'First of all there came a woman's peasant's dress. This was followed by a man whose lower extremities were clothed in tight-fitting white unmentionables. It so happened that one figure occupied on the screen exactly the same place as the other, so that when the lady was slowly dissolved into the gentleman, the astounding effect was produced of her clothes gradually melting from her form.'[13] Black claimed that the idea for the picture plays came from similar accidental combinations of dissolving images in his nonfiction lectures.[14] While he never used the dissolve to undress anyone, he did use it to place hats on women's heads and to make figures appear and disappear from scenes.[15] He used dissolves to make young people transform into old people and to make Victorian visual stereo-types transform into what he claimed were more accurate modern types. The sense of the dissolve as depicting transformation was important to his work.

Aside from these fantastical appearances and disappearances, the temporal continuity of the dissolve in itself appealed to audiences. It was most common for lanternists, Black included, to use the dissolving view to depict elapsed time rather than transformations in people's dress. Transformations in landscapes, changes between day and night or between seasons utilized to great advantage the dissolve effect and the saturated hand-colouring available with large glass slides. With the addition of smoke, snow or rain effects, the lantern could rival the diorama in its ability to depict a changing landscape.[16] Black used each of these effects to create atmosphere, but his main use for the dissolving view was its ability to depict passing time. Audiences could recognize the temporal dimension of this well-known effect—its suggestion of time extending from one picture into another. Unlike cinematic motion, in which one instantaneous photograph follows another in mechanical succession, the dissolving view represents change over an elapsed, indefinite time, which is under the complete control of the operator. Here is the integration of the celluloid progression of frames and the progression of serial tableaux that I pointed out in the introduction. Black's dissolves evoked transitions between film frames, but they were frames with temporal gaps insurmountable by the persistence of vision. His representation of movement is not the illusion of movement, but the idea of motion pictures laid bare and then corrected according to the ameliorative, softening function of the dissolve. His dissolves cross the gaps between the frames with a suggestion of passing time developed in dissolving landscape views.

The dissolve gave Black some control over the construction of passing time, but its gentle transformations would be ineffective if not combined with an innovative approach to staging. With landscapes as well as with dramatic scenes, the dissolve cannot give the effect of gradual transition if it simply joins one instant to another. In a transition from a daytime landscape to a night-time landscape each slide is meant to suggest, not an instant of day and an instant of night, but rather time passing in day and in night. The picture plays translated this type of temporality from painted landscapes to photographed bodies, encouraging spectators to suspend their disbelief and read each still image as a sort of living attitude. Poses of less decisive duration avoid the perception of grotesque and unbalanced attitudes.

In his picture-play poses Black actively erased any suggestion of instantaneous moments. He advises those who would produce amateur picture plays to '[a]void effects of action that will not bear the duration of twenty seconds . . . Prefer moments just before or just after action.'[17] The scene of a woman slapping a would-be seducer, for example, is shown in an approaching shot and then a shocked reaction shot, but the slap is not frozen mid-contact.[18] The effect of this is a series of photographs with a strange temporality. Neither a privileged moment nor an instant of action, each slide is designed to depict the elapsed time between the two adjacent slides in the series. Black's early nonfiction lectures showed bodies in postures that can be captured by the instantaneous photograph but which often could not be seen by the naked eye. The picture plays inverted this effect. They suggested movement the naked eye can readily see but which cannot actually be shown by the instantaneous photograph. They showed real people in faked time.

I have analysed Black's appropriation of the dissolving view and his unique approach to staging in order to highlight the specific aesthetic character of the picture plays' motion. The sense of passing time, while fluid and not altered by the magnifications of plot climaxes, is completely composed. The picture plays suggest natural movement, but by way of controlled manual techniques. What the cinematograph did relatively automatically, Black did by hand. He revised techniques of illustration, camera positioning, dissolving views and staging, and in doing so he created a suggestion of rather ordinary movement with a complicated aesthetic pedigree. He had been preoccupied with the aesthetics of motion since his early career, when he showed instantaneous photographs of runners and divers in action. He was deeply influenced by Eadweard Muyridge and Thomas Eakins, and he was well acquainted with the art-historical traditions of picturing motion. Black constructed the movement of his picture plays as a way to directly engage, in a multimedia performance, the relevance of these art-historical traditions for a consideration of cinema.

Cinema without the Cinematograph

The picture plays' unique suggestion of movement brought them into close vicinity to cinema. Cinematography had no technical association with the picture plays, but it featured prominently in their reception. In Black's own writings on his projects he stakes their novelty on their link to motion pictures. A reviewer notes,

> Mr. Black's picture play marks a distinct epoch in the development and use of the stereopticon. It retains a favorite means of entertainment, but it applies it in a totally new field . . . Here is an absolute novelty in a favorite amusement—a good story, with continuous illustrations; dramatic situations illustrated from real life; a sort of interrupted kinetoscope; a drama before an open camera.[19]

An 1895 review in the *Boston Herald* was likewise entitled 'Sort of Big Kinetoscope.'[20] Since the kinetoscope did not project images, this reviewer must have been referring to its illusion of motion. In numerous instances in his own writing, Black demonstrates current knowledge of the developments in Edison's laboratory. He was presumably in attendance when Edison staged his first public demonstration of the kinetoscope at the Brooklyn Institute of Arts and Sciences.[21] In 1896, Black wrote, 'Pending the perfection of the Vitascope, the cinematograph, and kindred devices, the ordinary camera, in partnership with the rapidly dissolving stereopticon, gives freest expression to the processes of the picture play . . . for a greater clearness and steadiness in pictorial result.'[22] The conceptual linkage with the cinema continued to grow with film's increasing popularity.

The invocation of cinema was a functional analogy. It was persistent and central to nearly every attempt to define the picture plays. This discussion is related to the birth of cinema in André Gaudreault's recent emphasis on the institutional definition of cinema in the early period. He supports the definition of cinema as 'a social, cultural, and artistic apparatus', as opposed to cinematography, the technological precondition for the later development of the medium. In Gaudreault's formulation it is imprecise to understand early cinema as a distinct medium in the years when it was chiefly understood as a technical aid to other practices such as lantern shows, magic shows and instantaneous photography.[23] Black's productions search for an institutional framework, a 'social, cultural, and artistic apparatus', based on an imagined possibility for the cinematograph without actually using a cinematograph. In other words, Black experimented with the creation of cinema by other means.

But the point of the reviewers' comparisons was just as much that the picture plays are not quite cinema. Their effectiveness in testing the boundaries of cinema, and hence their attraction, lay in that margin of difference. It is important to see the means of representing movement, analysed in the previous section, as an active choice. Black advocated his method as being better than cinema. In an interview he admitted, 'I have tried moving pictures, but they are too trying for the eyes, and I find dissolving views the best.'[24] He criticizes cinema's technological imperfections because of a preference for a different kind of aesthetic of motion. An 1894 article in *Harper's Weekly* contains the most pithy formulation of Black's method of representing movement: 'It was not wished to produce the illusion of actual action, as the Kinetoscope of Mr. Edison has since presented it, but of actual glimpses of action.'[25]

The picture plays erased the 'distressing glimpses' of suspended action and the moving pictures that 'try the eyes'—what early American film theorist Victor Freeburg would later term 'pictorial hysterics'.[26] The task remains to figure out the stakes of this aesthetic revision. One explanation is that Black's media experiments are retrofitted with nineteenth-century aesthetic ideas about pictorial representation. He avoids the visual discontinuity of instantaneous photography and mechanically reproduced motion that was essential to early cinema's popularity and would later become essential to modernist filmmakers. Exhibited in a period spanning the invention of motion-picture technology to the beginning of the nickelodeon era, the picture plays challenge the contingency of cinema with a new kind of movement assembled from traditions of nineteenth-century tableau culture, painting and related pictorial arts. The picture plays soften the distressing glimpses of the horse in motion and the kinds of mischievous grimaces noticed in the Lumiéres's still photographs with an aesthetic of motion that bears a mark of propriety from earlier in the nineteenth century.* This explanation makes sense in terms of Black's audiences. His first audiences in New York were painters suspicious of photography and its implications for the arts. His audiences during his national tours were Chautauqua (an institution that provided popular adult education), church and lyceum patrons suspicious in their own way of these new visual entertainments from the fairgrounds and vaudeville houses.

But even if the picture play was a form without a future, it was still not simply a reanimated artefact of the past. Black was hardly a traditionalist refusing to acknowledge the possibilities of the changes happening in his media environment. He was a pictorial innovator in journalism, a popularizer of instantaneous photography, and a modern showman. The success (albeit with rapid turnover) of hybrid forms like the picture plays raises the question, as Christine Gledhill puts it in relation to cinema's adoption of fragments from the Victorian stage, 'When did the nineteenth century end? . . . How far into the future are these fragments carried and how long does their significance remain the same?'[27] The picture plays present a similar puzzle. They carried on fragments from pictorialist traditions while directly challenging the limits of what cinema

*On mischievous grimaces and instantaneous photograph, see Tom Gunning, 'New Thresholds of Vision: Instantaneous Photography and the Early Cinema of Lumière,' in *Impossible Presence: Surface and Screen in the Photogenic Era*, edited by Terry Smith (Chicago: University of Chicago, 2001), pp. 71-100.

was and what it could become. The erasure of jerky movements and disjointed instantaneous poses may have appealed to the aesthetically conservative tastes of lyceum audiences, but, just as important, the very experiment in creating a series of frictionless tableaux as an answer to cinematography prompted these audiences to confront modern ideas about the representation of movement in new media.

The aesthetic of softened motion made the picture plays contemporary. It presented a viable collaboration among varied media and pictorial traditions at a time when people needed to make sense out of the wholesale appropriation of these traditions by new technologies. The fluidity of movement, the constructed duration of the postures, and the persistent comparison with cinematography ran against received notions about the illustrating and emphatic functions of the tableau. This prompted reviewers to make written and graphic comparisons to the evenly paced photograms of a film strip.[28] But this was a film strip that could never be resolved into the ungainly transitional postures found on an individual film frame. It was an aesthetic alternative. Far from being nostalgic in style, the picture plays staged precisely the kind of negotiation of media traditions that helped audiences consider the future of their media environment.

The picture-play format was not created to solidify into any kind of self-contained medium. It was not an underdeveloped form waiting for another technology or medium to complete it. Its novelty and its success depended on the uncertainty in its reception. It was most importantly, for its audiences, a media experiment, not quite one known medium and yet not quite another. It was partly for this reason that despite a handful of imitators and the increasing complexity of Black's subsequent productions, the picture play's popularity waned with the novelty of the first few productions.

A History Without an Invention

Black wrote in the 1890s about the picture play as a kind of imagined future for motion pictures, but after his touring shows tapered off with the coming of the nickelodeon this imagined future was largely forgotten. It was only when the terms 'picture play' and 'photoplay' had become names for the feature film that Black was recognized as an important figure in cinema history. The picture plays were once again relevant, this time for imagining the multimedia roots of a certain kind of cinema. Beginning in the mid 1910s, writers understood Black's first

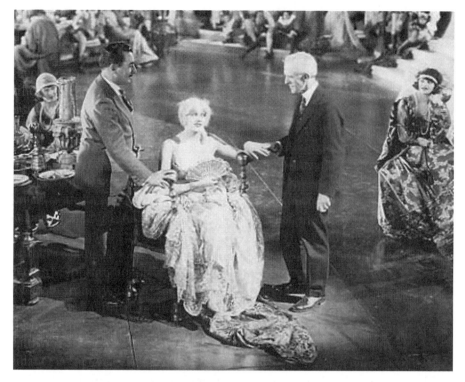

Fig. 35.   Alexander Black greets Barbara La Marr on
the set of *The Eternal City* (1923).
Black Family Collection.

screening of *Miss Jerry* within the same artistic horizon as the films made
a generation later. If Black's novel synthesis of pictorial practices allowed
spectators in 1896 to imagine possible futures for the kinetoscope and
the cinematograph, it also allowed spectators in 1917 to imagine an early
incarnation of the omnivorous feature film.

A 1915 article in the *Picture Play Weekly* uses, for the first time,
according to my research, a nickname that would stick with Black's
picture plays throughout the years of renewed interest in them. The
writer claims, 'The photo-play era began with Alexander Black ... but it
was a *slow movie* ... The real impetus to photo-play production did not
come until 1910.'[29] Adolf Zukor was among those who seized on this
term 'slow movie'. Zukor uses the term in his film *Alexander Black,
Grandfather of the Picture Play* (Paramount, 1918), and in a personal
letter to Black. He later reprinted part of the letter in *Moving Picture
World*:

Before you presented 'Miss Jerry' the screen had only still pictures. Then came your 'slow movie', in which you gave the effect of movement—long before the motion picture mechanism was perfected—making your audiences think the characters in your drama actually moved.[30]

The term 'slow movie' has a certain casual precision. It gets at the ambivalent relation to cinema in the picture play's aesthetic of motion. The picture play represents motion, like a movie, but with a slow progression of frames. It is not slow motion, a well-known effect, because it suggests a kind of natural pace. There is still a motion 'effect', however, because it is markedly distinct from attempts to record natural movement. While the picture play represents the ordinary passing of time, it possesses an elongated sense of transformation between scenes that is reminiscent of slow motion. This effect of motion, the picture play's most conspicuous characteristic in the 1890s, drew more interest in the 1910s than the more obvious connections to the feature film such as scene construction, feature length and narration.

Given this recurring tendency to see the picture plays as a kind of cinema but also as something else, a current historian might replace Terry Ramsaye's metaphor of evolutionary anomaly with a nonlinear metaphor. In the spirit of visual punning that was a hallmark of Black's nonfiction lectures, I would suggest replacing the duck-billed platypus with an amusement or puzzle dependent on a conceptual oscillation around a single image: the famous diagram of the bunny-duck. The picture plays generated continuing curiosity because they staged a conceptual oscillation between the tableau and the photogram, between living pictures and motion pictures, or between an allegiance to pictorial culture and an advocacy of the 'new' rhetoric of mechanically recorded bodies in motion. This ambivalence, fundamental to visual culture of the period, is implicit in Black's claim that he wanted to combine the art of the tableau vivant with the science of photography.

Black's media experiments presented viewers with a puzzle. The discussion that surrounded this puzzle in the 1890s and the 1910s amounted to a scattered, but functioning, form of media criticism. This cultural reception of experimental forms was an important venue for debates about pictorialism's encounter with the cinema. In the 1910s it was joined by the first American film theories though figures like Victor Freeburg and Vachel Lindsay, which relied heavily on notions of pictorial beauty and cross-media connections to establish a coherent film aesthetic. The picture play may never have become a mainstream practice, but the questions posed by this experimental form were not shelved alongside the slides for *Miss Jerry*. Instead of looking for the offspring of the picture plays, we might do better to ask how and why these questions find new consistency and rigour in the film theories of the 1910s.

15

DVDs, Video Games and the
Cinema of Interactions

Richard Grusin

On 16 May 2002, my son Sam and I attended one of the opening-day digital screenings of *Star Wars: Episode II—Attack of the Clones* at the Star Southfield Theatre, the only theatre in the Detroit metropolitan area (and one of only two in Michigan) equipped to project the film in the digital format in which George Lucas wanted us to see it. By now, most people have probably forgotten the hype that attended its release. The digital production, distribution and screening of *Attack of the Clones* was heralded in the popular media as a watershed in the history of film, 'a milestone of cinema technology' along the lines of *The Jazz Singer*.[1] Some industry executives claimed that because *Attack of the Clones* was produced entirely without the use of celluloid film it 'heralded the future of Hollywood and the death of actual "film" making.'[2]

Elsewhere I have discussed the significance of the digital production and screening of *Attack of the Clones* in relation to the early history of cinema.[3] Rather than considering the possibility of digital cinema as constituting a radical break or rupture with the cinema of the twentieth century, we need to understand how the emerging forms and practices of digital media provide us with a perspective from which the entire history of cinema up to this point can be seen as an extension of 'early cinema'. Borrowing from the idea that electronic textuality marks what has been called the late age of print, I argue that digital cinema marks us as inhabiting the late age of early cinema (or perhaps, phrased differently, the late age of celluloid film). In describing the current cinematic moment in this fashion, I do not mean to suggest that film will disappear, but that it will continue increasingly to be engaged with the social, technological and aesthetic forms and practices of digital media. This engagement will be marked not (as many digital enthusiasts contend) by the emergence of a distinctively new digital medium (and the concomitant abandonment of the technologically outmoded medium of celluloid film), but rather by the emergence of multiply networked, distributed forms of cinematic production and exhibition. Indeed I am convinced that we already find ourselves with a digital cinema—not as a distinctively new medium but as a hybrid network of media forms and practices, what I call a 'cinema of interactions'.

This phrase alludes to Tom Gunning's paradigmatic conception of a 'cinema of attractions', which rewrites one of the most powerful origin myths of early cinematic history—the received account of naive spectators who are thought to have mistaken the filmed image of a train for a real train and thus to have fled from the theatre so that they would not be run over.[4] Gunning reinterprets this narrative by suggesting that insofar as shock or surprise did attend upon the earliest exhibition of motion pictures, it was not because naive spectators mistook a filmed image for reality. Rather he argues that viewers of early cinema participated in an 'aesthetic of astonishment', produced by the contradiction between their conscious understanding that they were watching a moving picture in a theatre and their surprise or astonishment at perceiving an image that appeared to be, that affected them as if it were, real. Thus for Gunning the cinema of attractions produces an aesthetic of astonishment that results from the discontinuity between what spectators knew to be true and what they felt to be true. This aesthetic of astonishment involves a contradictory response to the ontological status of moving photographic images, a response which tries to incorporate two contradictory beliefs or states of mind—the knowledge that one is sitting in a public theatre watching an exhibition of a new motion-picture technology and the feeling that what one is seeing on screen looks real.

In characterizing our current historical moment as entailing a digital cinema of interactions, I want to suggest that at the onset of the twenty-first century, as motion pictures are increasingly moving away from a photographic ontology of the real towards a post-photographic digital ontology, cinema is defined not as the photographic mediation of an unmediated world that exists prior to and independent of its being filmed, but rather as the remediation of an already mediated world distributed among a network of other digital remediations. I introduce the concept of a cinema of interactions to challenge one of the most powerful myths of contemporary digital culture, paradigmatically articulated in William Gibson's *Neuromancer*—that digital media create an alternative reality or 'cyberspace', an immaterial simulacrum of the 'real' world inhabited by our bodies.[5] One of the most compelling cinematic remediations of this myth can be found in the first film of the *Matrix* trilogy, where the film's protagonist and its viewers soon discover that the cinematic world in which the film opens is not the 'real' world, but the world of the matrix—a massively multiuser computer program experienced by humans, whose immobile bodies inhabit a world ruled by artificially intelligent machines, which are using humans as batteries hooked up to generate power by which to rule the world. In setting forth the fantasy of humans inhabiting an illusory world, a shared, consensual hallucination created by a computer program, *The Matrix* (and the myth of cyberspace it participates in) fails to come to terms with the most interesting implications of digital media for contemporary cinema. What is truly significant about our current moment of digital media is not the Baudrillardian suggestion that reality doesn't exist, that the real is only a simulation, but something very different—the ways in which we customarily act in a fashion that suggests that digital media, computer programs, or video games, *are* real. The digital cinema of interactions entails what I think of as an aesthetic of the animate, in which spectators or users feel or act as if the inanimate is animate, in which we simultaneously know that the mediated or the programmed are inanimate even while we behave as if they were animate.

This cinema of interactions (and its concomitant aesthetic) is very much at play in *The Matrix Reloaded*, the long-awaited second film of the *Matrix* trilogy, which was released on 15 May 2003, one day short of a full year after the release of *Episode II* of *Star Wars*. As we had with *Attack of the Clones* last year, my son Sam and I saw *The Matrix Reloaded* in the first week both of its theatrical release in May and of its IMAX release in June. Screened in metro Detroit only at the Henry Ford IMAX Theatre in Dearborn, Michigan, *The Matrix Reloaded* was the third feature film to be digitally remastered for IMAX (following *Apollo 13* and *Attack of the Clones*). Due to improved remastering technology, however, it was the first to be done so without cuts. Compared with the digital production and screening of *Attack of the Clones*, the IMAX screening of *Matrix Reloaded* received little media hype, and it is not my intent in invoking the IMAX *Reloaded* to make hyperbolic claims about such digitally remastered projections as marking the future of Hollywood film (although Sam and I both agreed that the scenes in the underground world of Zion and the action sequences were much more impressive in IMAX than they were in 70mm). Rather I invoke the IMAX *Reloaded* because (along with its multiple remediations as a video game, an anime DVD and on the Web) it is one element of the distributed cinematic artefact created by the Wachowski brothers and their producer, Joel Silver.

In this essay I focus on the idea of digital cinema at the present historical moment, to look at the questions of convergence and hybridity in our contemporary digital cinema of interactions. Industry and media discussions of digital cinema have tended to focus on the digital production and screening of conventional films like *Attack of the Clones*, or on the threat posed by DVDs to theatrical movie-going, while academic discussions of interactive cinema often indulge in the desire for a radically new cinema along the lines of hypertext fiction and other new media art. I want to depart from both of these portrayals of digital cinema, to suggest that by looking at the relation between cinema and new media, we can see that we already find ourselves in a digital cinema of interactions. My argument has both a technocultural and an aesthetic dimension. I will first take up the social and economic distribution of cinema across a number of different digital media; I will then discuss some examples of how this cinema of interactions has manifested itself aesthetically and formally in some recent DVDs; and I will conclude with a brief discussion of the social, economic and aesthetic implications of Peter Greenaway's ambitious, hypermediated *Tulse Luper* project.

Over the past decade and more, film scholars have begun to find affinities between the viewing conditions or practices of contemporary film and media and those of early cinema, between what Miriam Hansen (among others) characterizes as 'preclassical and contemporary modes of film consumption'.[6] Such a characterization gets at some of what I am interested in elucidating about cinema at the current historical moment as a digital cinema of interactions. Like new digital media, cinema from its inception involved itself in refashioning or remediating earlier media. The construction of spectatorship relied upon such earlier technologies of representation as magic-lantern shows or panoramas. In depicting realistic and/or exotic subjects, such as war, travel, natural disasters or phantom rides, early cinema remediated such documentary and monstrative media as photography and stereography. And as early cinema began to employ rudimentary narratives, it engaged in the remediation of plays, novels and other familiar stories, for example, the Passion. The public presentation of early cinema, like the private and public presentation of new digital media, similarly remediated existing forms of entertainment. Hansen's reminder that early cinema remediated the format of early commercial entertainments such as vaudeville and travelling shows can also serve to alert us to the fact that, in contemporary culture, early digital media similarly borrow from and insert themselves into such commercial entertainments as sporting events, theme parks, movies and television.

Hansen avers that the principles that early cinema borrowed from these commercial entertainments 'preserved a perceptual continuum between the space/time of the theatre and the illusionist world on screen, as opposed to the classical segregation of screen and theatre space with its regime of absence and presence and its discipline of silence, spellbound passivity, and perceptual isolation'.[7] We can see an analogous perceptual continuum in today's digital cinema of interactions between the film screened in the theatre and its multiple remediations in DVDs, video games, trailers, websites and so forth. Just as the viewing conditions of early cinema did not enforce the separation of screen and spectator that emerged in so-called classical cinema, so early digital cinema breaks down the separation of the film-screened-in-theatre from its multiple remediations in videotape, DVD or television re-broadcasting. In today's cinema of interactions the photographic ontology of classical cinema gives way to a digital ontology in which the future, not the past, is the object of mediation—in which the photographic basis of film and its remediation of the past gives way to the premediation of the future more characteristic of video games and other digital mediation and networking.[8] This logic of premediation imagines an interactive spectator in a domestic or other social space rather than an immobilized spectator in the darkened dream-space of apparatus or gaze theory. The divide between screen and audience in Classical Hollywood cinema gives way to a continuum between the digital artefact and the viewer's/user's interaction. In the late age of early cinema we find ourselves at a historical moment when we can no longer consider the film screened in the theatre as the complete experience of the film. The conception of film as a distinctive medium is now giving way both conceptually and in practice to film as a distributed form of mediation, which breaks with classical cinema in several respects. In some cases it remediates elements of early cinema; in others it breaks with both early cinema and classical cinema. In our current cinema of interactions the experience of the film in the theatre is part of a more distributed aesthetic or cinematic experience. Our experience of almost any new film now inevitably includes the DVD (or often multiple editions of DVDs) complete with trailers, deleted scenes, storyboards, pop-up commentaries, hyperlinked mini-videos, director's and actor's commentaries, and so forth.

One of the most compelling examples of the way in which new digital media have participated in fundamental changes in mainstream contemporary cinema is the fact that the DVD release of a feature film is no longer seen as an afterthought, a second-order distribution phenomenon aimed at circulating the original film to a wider audience. Today the production, design and distribution of DVD versions of feature films are part of the original contractual (and thus artistic) intention of these films. Consequently it is now customarily the case that the conceptualization of the DVD precedes the commencement of production of the film itself; indeed in some cases production of the DVD begins even before the production of the film (as was reported to be true of Spielberg's *Minority Report* 2002). While such pre-production contractual considerations have for some time now been standard for other forms of post-release re-purposing (e.g., international, videotape and television rebroadcast rights or marketing and other commercial product tie-ins), I want to suggest that the remediation of theatrical releases in DVD and increasingly other digital formats marks a fundamental change in the aesthetic status of the cinematic artefact. This digital cinema of interactions is not a pure, new interactive medium but a distributed form of cinema, which demands that we rethink the cinema as object of study and analysis, to recognize that a film does not end after its closing credits, but rather continues beyond the theatre to the DVD, the video game, the soundtrack, the websites and so forth. Such a change is not simply a change in the technological basis of cinema, but rather a change that is distributed across practices of production, screening, exhibition, distribution, interaction, use and spectatorship. Recent industry and academic hype for digital cinema has focused on a notion of medium specificity that was overdependent on the technological base of the medium. While it is true that the distributed digital cinema of interactions manifests itself through new digital technologies, the 'new medium' or perhaps the new social logic of the medium, is a kind of hybrid alliance of digital technology, social use, aesthetic practice, cultures of spectatorship, and economic exchange. The *Matrix* franchise is an important example of this new hybrid medium—with the IMAX *Reloaded*, the *Animatrix* DVD (and its related web versions), the *Enter the Matrix* video game for X-Box, Game Cube, Play Station 2, and Windows PC, and now the new multiplayer online game. All of these artefacts simultaneously distribute *The Matrix* across different media practices and attempt to acquire for it a cinema audience that extends across any number of different media times and places, an audience not limited to the attendance of a feature film at a public screening in a suburban multiplex.

In this sense, then, distributed cinema is like other distributed media, is part of a logic of remediation in which media not only remediate each other but increasingly collaborate with other media technologies, practices and formations. At our current historical moment there is almost no sense of a medium that exists in itself, but rather only media that exist in relation to or in collaboration with other media. One might ask, if a medium only exists insofar as it is distributed across other media technologies, practices and social formations, then what exactly is 'television' or the 'internet' or 'film'? My answer would be that television or the internet or film should be understood as networks or systems of technologies, practices, and social formations that are generally stable for the most part, but that in the process of circulation and exchange tend to fluctuate or perhaps overlap at various nodes or crossings. In everyday usage we often tend to identify these media with their audiovisual manifestations on different screens (film, computer or TV), but we know that at the current historical moment these screens are not technologically limited to the display of particular media, but can each be used to display any of these three media—TV or the Internet can be projected on cinema screens by digital projectors, we can watch movies or surf the internet on a TV screen, computers let us watch TV and movies on our monitors with relative ease, and electronic games can be played on TV screens, computer monitors, handheld game systems, personal digital assistants (PDAs) and even mobile phones.

The digital cinema of interactions that we find ourselves in today exists not only in a socio-technical sense, but also in an aesthetic sense whereby there is the emergence of a visual style and narrative logic that bear more relationship to digital media like DVDs and video games than to those of photography, drama or fiction. It is not difficult to see how a digital medium like the DVD has come to function as a central element of a distributed, interactive cinema—indeed the formal features which are now commonplace in DVDs already function as a form of interactive cinema. For some time now, films on DVD have been broken into chapters so that viewers can interact with the film in a nonlinear fashion; indeed with the increased frequency of random buttons on recent models of DVD players, viewers even have the option of random-access cinema. The breaking of feature films into chapters is so customary that it comes as something of a surprise (albeit not entirely unexpected) when the DVD of David Lynch's *Mulholland Drive* (2001) is, like some of his earlier films, released without chapter breaks so that viewers will not be able to view the film in nonlinear fashion. Not only is the film not broken into chapters, but the DVD is designed so that if at any point in the film you use the remote to try to return to the previous chapter, you are instead sent back to the beginning of the film; and if you try to skip to the next chapter you are sent past the end of the film to the final graphical trademarks for Digital Video Compression Center and Macrovision Quality Control. Indeed Lynch consciously produces the *Mulholland Drive* DVD with as little interactivity as possible. The only bonus features on the DVD besides the theatrical trailer are brief bios of selected cast and a double-sided single-sheet case insert with 'David Lynch's 10 clues to unlocking this thriller.' The lack of interactive features calls attention to their ubiquity in contemporary DVDs. Director's and actors' commentaries that play over the feature's sound-track; videos on the making of the film or on historical or other background; alternate endings or deleted scenes—all of these are now DVD staples. In a more interactive vein are 'Easter eggs' that viewers must 'find' or earn by playing simple games designed into the DVD; storyboards of selected scenes that can be viewed with the soundtrack of the finished film; or hyperlinks that take the viewer to mini-videos related to a particular scene. I rehearse this partial list of DVD features not to celebrate the wonderfully enhanced content made possible by digital technology, but to think about the way in which these features can be understood as already constituting film as interactive.

If a director like Lynch calls attention to our digital cinema of interactions by purposefully stripping conventional interactive features from his DVDs, other directors release DVDs which push interactivity even further to insist upon the fact that the film is not confined to the form of its theatrical exhibition but is distributed across other media as well. In many cases these films were already experimental in their theatrical release. Take Christopher Nolan's *Memento* (2000), for example, which gained notoriety by presenting its story of a man with no short-term memory on the lookout for his wife's murderer in short scenes arranged in reverse chronological order (a device employed more recently in Gaspar Noe's troubling 2002 film *Irréversible*). Nolan uses the interactive features of the DVD in a number of interesting ways. The clever interactive design scheme visually remediates institutionalized psychiatric tests, which the DVD user must figure out how to negotiate to view the film or to access its extra features. In the director's commentary, Nolan's voice is played backwards at certain ambiguous moments of the film (although I have been told that some of these also play forwards on repeated viewings, but do so in contradictory ways). Perhaps most interesting is the 'hidden' feature that allows the film's scenes to be reordered chronologically. Viewing the film in this fashion provides a very different cinematic experience from the one audiences enjoyed in the theatre and is certain to alter the sense of the film's meaning in quite significant ways.

Another unconventional film in which the interactivity of the DVD provides a fundamentally different cinematic experience from that of the theatre is Mike Figgis's *Time Code*, a 97-minute film which was shot simultaneously by four digital video cameras in real time in one single cut. Figgis shot the film fifteen times before he got a take he wanted to keep (the dialogue and action were improvised around certain basic elements of the story line). To produce the film, he divided the screen into quadrants, each presenting one of the four films from the final take. Although there are no visual cuts in the film, the sound editing serves to influence the viewer's focus of attention by alternately raising or lowering the volume in one of the quadrants at particular moments of the film. In the DVD of the film, the viewer can watch the film as Figgis released it theatrically. But there are other interactive options that can be used to create a very different cinematic experience. The DVD allows viewers to listen to a single quadrant in its entirety or to edit the film's sound themselves by moving at will from one quadrant to the next. Figgis also includes the full-length version of the first take; presumably future DVDs could be released to include the remaining thirteen. In a project like this it is even more difficult than with *Memento* to make a clear-cut distinction between the theatrical release and the interactive versions available on DVD. Furthermore, from its very conceptualization a film like *Time Code* is already understood to be more than its theatrical release, to be distributed not only across the four quadrants of the screen but across the seemingly infinite interactive versions available via the DVD. Indeed, rather than seeing the DVD as a second-order phenomenon in relation to the theatrical release, it would in some strong sense be more accurate to consider the theatrical release as the second-order phenomenon in its attempt to reproduce or remediate the inter-activity of the DVD, with the viewer's shifting attention substituting for the digital shifting made possible by the same digital technology employed in the DVD.

Just as films like *Memento* and *Time Code* remediate the interactivity of DVDs and other digital media, so other films are engaged in a process of mutual remediation with video games. For some time now video games (both PC- and platform-based) have been remediating cinema in a variety of ways. Perhaps the least interesting aspect of this remediation involves the design and release of games based on successful films. More interesting are games like the 'Grand Theft Auto' series, which has been marketed like a film, including cinema-style promotional billboards and the release of CD soundtracks for each game. *Tom Clancy's Splinter Cell* remediates film (and of course fiction) in a different way; the game includes 'extras' like those on a DVD, including an 'interview' which operates on the premise that the game's main character (a digitally animated fictional creation) is in fact an actor cast in the role of the main character. But for my purposes perhaps the most interesting remediation of film by video games is the way in which the semiotics of video game screen space have become increasingly conventionalized in their in-corporation of 'cut scenes' or 'cinematics', letter-boxed narrative segments introducing a game's various levels of play (whereby it looks as if widescreen cinema has been transferred to videogame format). It is now customary in almost every game (even animated games with no connection to previously released films) to employ a semiotic distinction between the full-screen visual space of the video game and the wide-screen (letter-boxed) visual space of the cinematics, where the space of play is the full-screen space of the TV monitor, but the space of spectatorship is the wide-screen space of the letter-boxed film. Just as letter-boxing has begun to acquire a certain symbolic cachè on television, with sophisticated shows like 'The Sopranos' or 'Six-Feet Under' or network shows like 'ER' or 'The West Wing' being presented in letter-boxed format, or letter-boxed sequences being edited into commercials for luxury or high-tech commodities, so it is often used in video games to indicate the quality of a game's graphics (even though, in most cases, the cinematics are generated by a different digital technology than the game's graphics, often even by digital video or film).

Of major film directors, Peter Greenaway, in his hyper-ambitious

Tulse Luper project, most explicitly and wholeheartedly addresses the question of the future of cinematic aesthetics in an age of premediation. The first film of a projected trilogy, *The Tulse Luper Suitcases: The Moab Story*, premiered at Cannes in May 2003. Although it premiered as an autonomous cinematic artefact, Greenaway also considers the three parts of the trilogy as 'one very long film' divided into three sections for pragmatic reasons. In interviews supporting the film's premiere, Greenaway articulates his vision of what I have been calling a digital cinema of interactions, detailing how the *Tulse Luper* films participate in a complex, multimedia project.[9] He imagines this project, first, as distributed across three different films—the trilogy format already in practice in *Star Wars*, *Lord of the Rings* and *The Matrix*. But as he suggests in one of his interviews, the multipart structure is also a further formalization or conventionalization of the phenomenon of sequels that has become more widespread in the past few decades, but which has also been part of the cinematic phenomenon of repetition and sequence from film's inception. In addition to this basic sense in which the film as aesthetic object extends beyond the experience of viewing it in the theatre, Greenaway imagines that the film will be remediated in DVDs and websites, in books and on television, and 'in lots of different versions and perspectives'. Motivated by the fact that the film audience has been distributed across many other digital media, Greenaway is aiming not just 'at cinema audiences but all the new audiences that are cropping up as we all know in all different guises all over the world', after what he describes as 'essentially the digital revolution'.[10]

Not only does Greenaway imagine the *Tulse Luper* project to be distributed across any number of different new media forms and practices, but he also conceives of a cinema of interactions as demanding new aesthetic and narrative logics. He says in one of his Cannes interviews:

> Anybody who immediately sees the film might feel that to describe it even as a piece of cinema might be a little strange. It's not a window on the wall cut and paste movie. It's many, many multi-layered, it's fragmented into all sorts of moving frames which are superimposed over one another. We also very, very deliberately use calligraphy and text on the screen, so all those advertising techniques which you're aware of in commercials and video clips—[were] trying to use all the different many, many tropes out there that are very,

very apparent to anybody who looks at any moving image material whatever in the year 2003.[11]

In the *Tulse Luper* films, the cinematic narrative is interrupted by nonlinear elements such as links (remediated as suitcases), which will allow us to interact with the film through one of ninety-two DVDs that will be released, one for each of the ninety-two suitcases that appear in the films. Other elements of this hybrid cinematic project will be presented on the internet, including the daily release of contemporary remediations of the *1001 Tales of Arabian Nights*, one of which is planned to be released each day. So not only do the films interact with DVDs and websites, but the viewer interacts with the film/DVD/Internet hybrid as well. These ninety-two supplementary DVDs and the accompanying websites would be used to provide additional elements of the *Tulse Luper* story, not unlike what the Wachowski brothers have been trying to do by distributing *The Matrix* not only across three films but also across the DVDs, *The Animatrix* and its soundtrack, the *Enter the Matrix* game, and on the internet.

Regardless of the way in which Greenaway's hyper-ambitious project finally materializes (it's hard to imagine, for example, the development and commercial release of ninety-two DVDs, and from evidence available on the Web, his momentum seems already to have stalled), it articulates three key elements of our current digital cinema of interactions. First, he imagines the project as a distributed artefact, the most basic sense in which the film as aesthetic object extends beyond the experience of viewing it in the theatre. Next, he imagines the aesthetic artefact as interactive, interrupted by nonlinear elements or links (remediated as suitcases), which will allow viewers of the film to interact with it through DVDs or on the internet. Finally he imagines that these different media formats will interact as they remediate the form and content of one another across different media formats. Among the most pressing challenges posed by this new digital cinema of interactions, as Greenaway himself recognizes, is how to assemble and motivate an interactive network of creative people, producers and audiences. The new cinema of interactions involves not the creation of a distinctly new medium, but the remediation of a number of older, existing media —the redeployment not only of human agents but also of nonhuman agents such as media technologies, forms and practices, and social, economic and commercial networks. And although Greenaway does not specify this challenge himself, the emergence of projects like *Tulse Luper*

Suitcases also challenges critics and historians of film and new media to find new ways to make sense of this kind of digital or cinematic *gesamtkunstwerk*, to create new forms of knowledge suitable to the changing conditions of moving-image technologies brought about by the changes in media technologies, forms and practices that have accompanied what has come to be called the digital revolution.

16

From 'Nip/Tuck' to Cut/Paste
Remediating Cosmetic Surgery

James Lyons

A common feature of the present era of media convergence is the ubiquity of dedicated websites launched by entertainment conglomerates to accompany the broadcast of their new television shows. The content of these websites ranges from basic programme descriptions and broadcast schedules to the type of original material (e.g. character backstory, additional plotlines or even fictitious weblogs) constituting what Henry Jenkins terms the sort of complex, multilayered 'transmedia storytelling' developed across the various media incarnations of a programme franchise.[1] In this essay I examine one specific instance of a website dedicated to its network show, namely FX Network's 'Nip/Tuck', an hour-long drama series that has attracted extensive press coverage for its provocative and stylistic portrayal of the lives of two Miami plastic surgeons. The show's graphic depiction of surgical operations and penchant for *outré* storylines revealing the social and sexual proclivities of the central protagonists, friends, families and patients has helped establish a lucrative niche audience for the FX network, consolidating its recent move into original programming, and enhancing its reputation in the 'boutique TV' market forged by HBO. As this essay will illustrate, the 'Nip/Tuck' website follows the lead established by the TV show in offering edgy and thought-provoking content, in particular through two online cosmetic surgery 'games' designed to be played by visitors to the site. However, my interest lies less with the implications of the site's content for the transmedia convergence of storytelling, and more with the way that it may be situated within a genealogy of screen apparatuses stretching back to the nineteenth century which have displayed the surfaces of the body for the purpose of surgical augmentation and enhancement. My argument concerns the way in which the 'Nip/Tuck' website extends and exposes the 'clinical gaze' established by these preceding screen apparatuses, and, through its games, acts as a critical space for considering the ethical and theoretical issues raised by the burgeoning extension of online cosmetic-surgery advertising.

It is no coincidence that the development of plastic surgery for aesthetic purposes (cosmetic surgery) emerged at the same historical moment that also saw the cinema come into being. While medical historians cite important nineteenth-century advances in anaesthesia and antisepsis as vital to the formation of modern surgery, Elizabeth Haiken points out that conventional medical history lacks an explanation for the peculiarities of cosmetic surgery; in particular the way that it diverges from other medical practices in terms of etiology (causes), nosology (classification) and symptomology (effects).[2] Above all, as Haiken notes, what is required is a mode of analysis that can explain both the desire and the justification for operating on the body of the physically healthy individual. One key frame of reference is the way in which 'surveillant looking and physiological analysis' became 'broadly practiced techniques of everyday public culture' in the nineteenth century, and provided the context for the emergence of instruments and technologies shaped by these new regimes of visibility, including both the cinematic apparatus and the range of needles and knives developed specifically for cosmetic surgical procedures.[3]

The cutting and suturing of celluloid and skin have remained closely aligned ever since, as Hollywood provided models of physical 'perfection' (achieved by means of cinematic technique and concealed surgical enhancement) influential in shaping standards of beauty by which individuals self-scrutinize, and opt in increasing numbers for elective cosmetic surgery. In addition, new digital medical-imaging technologies continue the practice of 'screening the body' for surgical and clinical procedures, in the process supplanting and extending the historic role of cinema in medical science. For instance, a computer tomography scan (CT or CAT scan) may be used as a diagnostic imaging procedure to produce cross-sectional images of the body prior to cosmetic surgery. Moreover, a preliminary consultation with a cosmetic surgeon may well involve the use of computer-enhanced imaging in order to generate 'before' and 'after' views of the patient's face as a result of various possible cosmetic surgical procedures: after using a video camera to capture front-view and profile images, computer software allows a digital image of the face on screen to be morphed in order to erase wrinkles, remove bags from under the eyes, sculpt the neck or chin line, narrow or reshape the nose, etc. Such effects are also available, with the promise of extra physiognomic accuracy, with a new generation of laser surface scanners. Yet such algorithmic approximations can present only digital visualizations of the generalized hypothetical response of real skin, flesh and bone to the individualized trauma of surgical procedure. Surgeons typically praise such advances for their capacity to aid patient reassurance about the likely outcome of a surgical procedure (one Beverly Hills practitioner stating, 'The patient is much more comfortable having a solid visual image of the outcome'[4]), and for allowing the patient to share what the doctor 'sees' ('While I can visualize the end product of my work, the prospective patient cannot'[5]). However, this ostensibly democratic decentring and desubjectivizing digital visual projection of what Mary Anne Doane terms the 'clinical eye' actually serves to diffuse further an epistemology of the body as mediated through representational apparatus, as a series of surfaces to be observed, evaluated and refashioned.[6]

It is no surprise that much of the critical literature on cosmetic surgery draws on the work of Michel Foucault, extending his analysis of the birth of the clinic, the institutional authority of the medicalized gaze, and the hierarchies of power and knowledge contained therein in order to address the ways in which the notion of the *elective* cosmetic surgical procedure 'performs a seductive role in facilitating the ideological camouflage of the absence of choice' enshrined in the 'technological beauty imperative'.[7] Feminist writers in particular have sought to interrogate the extent to which the practice of cosmetic surgery reproduces gendered discourses of physical attractiveness that serve to 'discipline the unruly female body [and] reconstruct it in keeping with culturally determined ideals of feminine beauty'.[8] However, given the inexorable enmeshing of body and technology in contemporary culture, the impulse to fall back on what Anne Balsamo calls 'romantic conceptions of the "natural" body' may not be an adequate or even viable response to the burgeoning market for women's cosmetic surgical procedures.[9] Instead, feminist strategies that seek to reappropriate the technologies of body enhancement in ways that destabilize ideologies of feminine beauty, for instance Kathryn Pauly Morgan's call for 'performative form[s] of revolt' as enacted by Parisian body artist Orlan,

represent attempts to purposefully subvert fantasies of corporeal transformation.[10] As Jay David Bolter and Richard Grusin point out, such
activities can be understood as 'radical' remediations of the body. They
call attention to the body as a medium and challenge the conventions
that govern its normative visual codes.[11]

In situating cosmetic surgery within a genealogy of cultural remediation, Bolter and Grusin support and extend a number of earlier
attempts to come to terms with the practice's oscillation between modes
of 'despecularization' and 'respecularization'. Their notion of the 'double
logic of remediation' encapsulates what they see as our culture's desire to
'multiply its media and to erase all traces of mediation: ideally, it wants
to erase its media in the very act of multiplying them.'[12] Thus the
individual whose body has been remediated through cosmetic surgery
most typically desires to expunge all evidence of the procedures that
have been undertaken. This wish for what Bolter and Grusin term
'transparent immediacy' is in keeping with what Sander Gilman argues
has historically been the overriding goal of aesthetic procedures, namely
to produce (in)visibility. As Gilman points out, 'aesthetic procedures are
intended to move an individual from being visible in one cohort to being
a member of another cohort or collective, which is *so* visible that its
visibility has been defined as normal.'[13] However, it is possible to argue
that with the diminishing social stigma of elective cosmetic procedures,
the wish to deny the act of mediation and body refashioning may become
less compelling, and the willingness to parade a perceptibly 'hypermediated' body will meet with greater sanction, particularly if, as
Kathryn Morgan argues, the normalization of cosmetic surgery leads to
an 'inversion of the domains of the deviant and the pathological'.[14]

Evidence for a series of noteworthy shifts in the cultural discourse on
cosmetic surgery that attests to changing ideologies of beauty technology
lies in the proliferation of 'extreme' make-over shows on US and UK
television in recent years. Such programming suggests the increasing
assimilation of potentially traumatic elective surgical procedures into the
panoply of prosaic, normative beauty treatments to be contemplated in
search of a more youthful and attractive appearance. However, such
representations of cosmetic surgery, as implied by the adjective 'extreme',
also function as a site for the articulation of a series of imbricated
residual and emergent meanings associated with the practice. In addition
to the increasing preponderance of docusoaps, one television show that
has garnered much critical attention in this respect is 'Nip/Tuck', which
debuted on the US basic cable network FX in 2003 and has been sold to

TV stations worldwide, including Sky TV and Channel 4 in the UK. The series' uneasy mix of comedy, pathos and gothic horror has predictably divided critical opinion, with some deriding the high-sheen melodrama's moments of social commentary as superficial attempts to mask its essential depthlessness. The show has also come under attack from the Parents Television Council, a conservative pressure group, which launched a major campaign to compel advertisers to drop the show, with a number of corporations (e.g., Cingular Wireless and Gateway Inc.) doing just that. In addition, 'Nip/Tuck' has found itself on the receiving end of criticism from the American Society of Plastic Surgeons (ASPS) and the American Society for Aesthetic Plastic Surgery (ASAPS), both of which have denounced the show for sensationalizing their profession. For instance, in July 2003 the ASPS issued a press release announcing that it had 'serious concerns about the show's inappropriate representation of the practice of medicine and specialty of plastic surgery' and that the organization took 'great offense at the spurious depiction of its medical specialty, which is . . . sensational, bordering on the absurd'.[15] The ASAPS followed suit in December 2003, responding to the nomination of 'Nip/Tuck' for a Golden Globe by stating that its members disapproved strongly of what they saw as the show's deployment of 'violence, sex and graphically unrealistic portrayals of plastic surgery to boost ratings'.[16]

The disapprobation of both the ASPS and ASAPS demonstrates an inevitable concern over notions of professional integrity and propriety, and one can imagine similar missives being proffered by other professional bodies as a consequence of seemingly egregious and damning depictions of lawyers or (heaven forefend) academics. However, given the fact that the practice of cosmetic surgery is so heavily invested in shaping and controlling the facets of its own mediation—indeed, uses the projection of fantasies of body transformation through the technologies of mediation as a primary means of giving the prospective patient a 'solid visual image of the outcome'—institutional anxiety over the circulation of 'unauthorized' and 'spurious' imagery is particularly fraught, and has indeed marked the profession throughout its history.[17]

Yet if 'Nip/Tuck' the TV show represents a provocative intervention into the cultural discourse on cosmetic surgery, an arguably more intriguing and theoretically suggestive locus of mediation is the programme's official website, a sub site of the FX network's homepage. The primary purpose of the 'Nip/Tuck' website is akin to that of 'official' homepages for other network television shows, namely to provide an authorized range of complementary and supplementary content to augment and enhance the experience of the TV show, rather than in any sense replace or displace it. Cast and crew biographies, synopses of broadcast episodes, and brief clips of upcoming instalments all serve to reinforce a sense of the website as a subsidiary textual interface that requires the experience of the televised show to facilitate a requisitely knowledgeable engagement. However, even as digital technology ensures that the convergence of TV and the Web continues apace, the nature of the engagement with the 'Nip/Tuck' website remains distinct qualitatively from that of the transmitted TV show, most specifically in the accessing of hypertext through an interactive browser. Particularly intriguing is the way in which the essential terminology and metaphors of hypertext interactivity can be said to evoke the language and logic of cosmetic surgery. Manipulation through cutting, pasting, pulling, clicking, dragging, pointing, moving and layering echoes the phraseology of surgical procedure. Moreover, as Bolter and Grusin point out, 'replacement is the operative strategy of the whole windowed style',

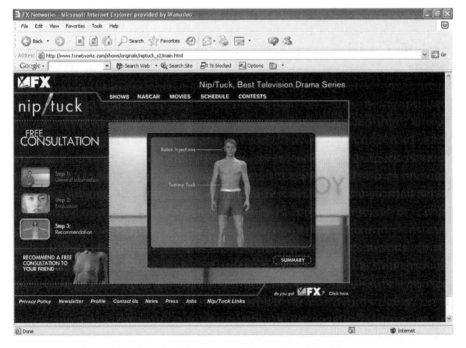

Fig. 36. 'Free Consultation' game, 'Nip/Tuck' website, http://fxnetworks.com/shows/originals/niptuck_s2/main.html.

employing terminology that enables the user to manipulate 'devices for replacing the current visual space with another'.[18]

This embedded structure of language and logic, facilitating the aptly termed 'operative strategy' of hypertext, provides the basis for the 'Nip/ Tuck' website's more provocative and playful approaches towards the notion of 'replacement'. In addition to the aforementioned sections of content, the site also includes two 'games', entitled 'Free Consultation' and 'Interactive Surgery Tool', both accessible via links on the front page. 'Free Consultation' offers the user 'a simple 3 step process that helps you to determine what types of plastic surgery might be suited for you'.[19] The user is asked, 'Please tell us a bit about yourself so that we may better assist you', and is required to enter name, age and sex into a form. The user is then asked, 'What areas of your face to do you think need improvement (check all that apply)?', and the choice of forehead wrinkles, droopy eyebrows, tired puffy eyes, sagging cheeks, dispro- portionate nose and thin lips is provided.

This selection of surgical procedures, which largely reflects the ASPS's statistical data on the most popular facial cosmetic operations, is then followed by a list of the most common cosmetic procedures for the rest of the body, which differs depending on which sex has been entered: men can choose from 'belly bulge; large butt; flat butt; flabby thighs; and tiny calves', while women have the added options of 'sagging, too small breasts' and 'sagging, too large breasts'. Depending on what has been specified by the user, step three, entitled 'Evaluation', will generate a digital avatar onto which the details of the selected surgical procedures are graphically depicted with use of Macromedia Shockwave software. For instance, the selection of 'calf implants' will result in the avatar's calf being morphed to generate an image of the body part transforming in physical appearance from 'before' to 'after', which is visualized as if the calf were being inflated from within, in other words neatly bypassing the crucial intermediary stage of operative surgery. Similarly, selected breasts will inflate, sagging cheeks will tauten, and wrinkles will vanish as if by digital magic wand. Once this is accomplished, the final page, entitled 'Summary', provides a cost breakdown of the selected procedures and concludes the process with the upbeat message: 'Thanks for coming in for your free consultation. We'll follow up in a few days with more information and an appointment to meet the doctors. Have a great day and remember, the truth is only skin deep.'[20]

After being asked to scrutinize one's face and body for areas of 'improvement', the performative mode of the final section is intended clearly to resituate the user in an imaginary frame of role-play that recognizes explicitly the interaction with the 'Consultation' game as a supposedly pleasurable engagement with a fictional programme, culminating in the fantasy of 'meeting' the doctors. Yet the parting hope that the user will 'have a great day' seems risible given the activity that has preceded it, while the concluding maxim that 'the truth is only skin deep' repeats the televised show's tag line, rephrasing the customary adage 'beauty is only skin-deep' to ambiguous effect. The original phrase, suggesting that physical beauty is not a reliable guide to an individual's other qualities, operates with reference to the dualistic Western surface/depth model of the body, whereby the 'essence' of who we are truthfully is 'underneath' the skin, manifested through personality, character, wit or morality. With 'truth' replacing 'beauty', the modified phrase could suggest the superficiality of truth, and by implication the unreliability of truth as a guide to the essence of the individual. On the other hand, the phrase can also taken to suggest that truth is that which is visible. This interpretation, following Foucault's notion that 'truth, which by right of nature, is made for the eye', supports the ocularcentrism enshrined in the dominance of the clinical gaze in structuring medical knowledge.[21] In the context of cosmetic surgery, this reading of the phrase might imply that *all* is surface, and is in keeping with Anne Balsamo's suggestion that the 'technological gaze' of the surgeon is used to reinforce a sense that the patient's 'interior story has no truth of its own', in the process dispensing with a 'surface/depth model of the material body'.[22] Here, the truth *is* visible beauty, manifested through the layers of the dermis and epidermis, stretched over the surface of the body, and detached archly from its capacity to connote fidelity to an original.

While the 'Consultation' game can be seen to support and reinforce the notion of the body as surface to be screened and evaluated through representational apparatus, and indeed retains the normatively gendered categories of body enhancement, augmentation and replacement mobilized by the ASPS and ASAPS and circulated through popular culture, it also contains some noteworthy quirks. For instance, despite the user's entering widely varying ages into the game, the software still generates the same avatar, which, like a department store mannequin, represents an ostensibly 'universal' but actually very specific approximation of an idealized, youthful face and body for men or women (the avatar is also Caucasian in appearance by default). The game willingly accepts a request by 'Methuselah', aged 969, for botox injections and tummy tuck, priced at a total of $6,000, while it rather less humorously also permits and generates a price for a hypothetical 14-year-old girl to undergo cosmetic breast surgery. The fact that the 'Free Consultation' is 'free' in the sense of imposing no limits or injunctions against registering a desire for absurd, unsound or even unethical cosmetic surgical procedures could be seen as troubling, and it is clear that the game circumvents the potential difficulties this could pose *visually*, by ensuring that the digital avatar remains the same irrespective of what information is entered. Thus whatever 'deviant' desires for surgical enhancement are entered into the game, the body of the idealized digital avatar maintains its uniformity, which has the effect of weakening any projections of subjectivity onto the screened fantasy of desired procedures, while at the same time reinforcing a sense of what constitutes an apposite paradigm for surgical enhancement.

Those users seeking a more personalized visual interaction with the website have the option to play instead the 'Interactive Surgery Tool' game, accessible from the same section of the site. The game's opening window depicts Dr Christian Troy, one of the 'Nip/Tuck' cosmetic surgeons, over which image is superimposed the following text:

> Welcome. What don't you like about yourself. Your nose? Your eyes? Your lips?
> We can fix any feature that's troubling you. All you need is a photo and a dream.
> Simply UPLOAD a photo of yourself into the INTERACTIVE SURGERY TOOL or use one of our MODEL FACES.
> Then CLICK your choice of nose, eyes or lips and design a new you.
> If you're ready to transform yourself, let's get STARTED.

The opening line, which asks the user to self-scrutinize, repeats the phrase employed in the consultation-room scene that begins many of the televised show's episodes, in the process invoking the diagnostic logic that has become customary in cosmetic surgical consultations, namely that the prospective patient, rather than the doctor, decides what is 'wrong'. As Haiken points out, cosmetic surgery 'lies at the nexus of medicine and consumer culture', and it is here that the utterance of consumer desire, couched in terms of visible 'like' and 'dislike', replaces the assessment of symptoms of illness or malady.[23] Here, the user is once again presented with a choice between some of the most frequently requested aesthetic procedures, and an opportunity to experiment visually with the hypothetical results of desired operations. If the user requests to employ one of the models, a front-on photograph of a physiognomically symmetrical and normatively attractive Caucasian male or female in their 20s or early 30s is provided, with no opportunity to vary the choice of model. While the overwhelming majority of cosmetic surgery is in fact performed on white patients, the decision to provide either male or female models is at odds with the fact that over 85 per cent of patients are female, and the pictorial age of the subjects is decidedly below the statistical average for aesthetic operations as provided by the ASPS's procedural data.[24] The decision to produce photographic models at variance with the norms of surgical statistical data is an intriguing one, and a reasonable conclusion would be that the game has generated a visual correlative for the show's core demographic, rather than the national cosmetic surgical cohort.

Also apparent here is the way in which the 'Interactive Surgery Tool' serves to remediate bona fide websites that advertise the services of cosmetic surgeons, and frequently include carefully selected front-on photographs of patients 'before' and 'after' surgical procedures (e.g. http://www.plasticsurgery4u.com/procedure_folder/face_lift.html). The objective of such websites is to advertise the skills of the surgeon, and thus the onus is on the visual archive of previous patients to provide impressive transformations from ostensibly unappealing 'before' to comparatively alluring 'after'. In contrast, the 'Nip/Tuck' website's 'Interactive Surgery Tool' offers two pre-operative countenances that would be handsome additions to any genuine surgeon's online gallery of procedural accomplishments. Moreover, an interaction with the game's simulation of potential operative choices continues this reversal of the logic of aesthetic enhancement. Once the user has selected either the male or female face, the next page provides a selection of eyebrows, eyes, noses and mouths for the user to consider, and the instructions to 'mix and match the features you think would look best on you. CLICK and DRAG to their location so you see how they might look.' The selection is divided into male and female subsections, and each contains three features from which to choose. All the facial-feature selections provided by the game represent normatively attractive and desirable physiognomic choices: lips are full, eyes are clear and wrinkle-free, and noses are straight and proportional. All betray their origins on the faces of youthful, white and dermatologically unblemished subjects. Yet once the process of clicking and dragging begins, it is clear that it is impossible to do anything other than create a quite perplexing visage: differences in

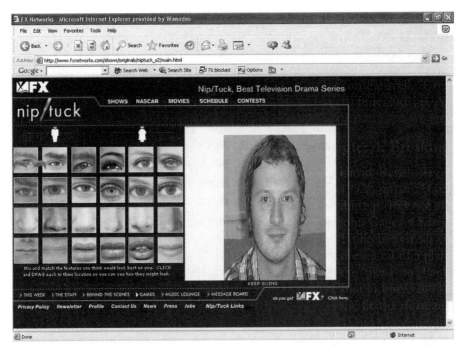

Fig. 37. 'Interactive Surgery Tool', author's photograph, 'Nip/Tuck' website, http://fxnetworks.com/shows/originals/niptuck_s2/main/html.

skin tone, proportion and size mean that rather than generating a smooth synthesis of idealized features, the 'surgically enhanced' photograph can never escape its identity as a maladroit amalgam of different individuals' facial parts. The fact that the game also allows the user to select freely from male and female features means that the enhanced face can take on an even more aesthetically challenging and radically hypermediated appearance.

These possibilities are multiplied infinitely by the opportunity for the user to substitute his or her photograph for those provided by the site. Uploading portraits with myriad potential variations in race, age and physiognomic proportion, but having to restrict their enhancement to the specific facial options provided by the game, creates irreconcilable visual tensions and incongruities. Yet whatever enhancements are undertaken by the game, the result is the same standardized parting message: 'Congratulations on a whole new you! Is it all you dreamed it would be? Click to LAUNCH or DOWNLOAD your new and improved image.' Given the inevitability of the sorts of aesthetically

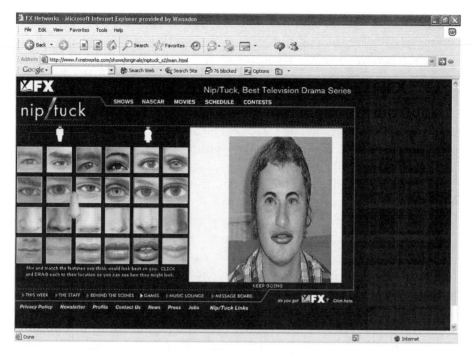

Fig. 38. 'Interactive Surgery Tool', author's cosmetically
'enhanced' photograph, 'Nip/Tuck' website,
http://www.fxnetworks.com/shows/originals/niptuck_s2/main.html.

aberrant transformations engendered by the parameters of the game, this final statement underlines the way that the application caricatures visually and verbally the ethos of elective cosmetic surgery. That the 'after' resulting from the use of the 'Interactive Surgery Tool' parodies the type of imagery mobilized by actual surgeons' websites serves to undermine the ideology of surgical enhancement and physical 'improvement' that they work to perpetuate. Since there is no way that manipulation of the 'Surgery Tool' will possibly generate an image of 'transparent immediacy' that can act to reproduce the (in)visibility essential in sustaining discourses of cosmetic surgery, the result is instead a series of extreme and hypermediated countenances that expose the cultural biases and dispositions inherent in the typology of idealized facial characteristics propagated by the cosmetic industry. Such remediations are as 'graphically unrealistic' as the depictions of surgical procedure that have brought about criticism of the 'Nip/Tuck' TV show from the ASPS and the ASAPS, yet their significance is decidedly more telling. In particular, the fact that the Interactive Surgery Tool allows users to 'visualize the end product' of *their* work is a consequence of the game's function to redirect control of the computer-enhanced imaging process away from the surgical consultant and place it in the hands of each and every user. While on the one hand that gesture could be seen simply to further disseminate the evaluative impulse that supports and sustains elective surgery, the fact that the end result is an inevitably parodic and 'radically remediated' visualization can serve only to destabilize culturally determined ideals of beauty, imply the folly of 'invisible' enhancement and adumbrate the subversive pleasures of non-normative augmentation.

Clearly, the capacity of the games on the 'Nip/Tuck' website to overturn the dominant modes of analytic visualization culturally reproduced through professional and popular discourses of cosmetic surgery is modest, to say the least. Yet the impulse of the Interactive Surgery Tool in particular to 'counter-mediate' the function of actual cosmetic-surgery websites is an acknowledgement of the fact that the World Wide Web is, like previous screen-entertainment apparatuses, evolving as a 'cultural technology for the discipline and management of the human body'.[25] The proliferation of advertising for cosmetic surgery online extends and evolves the classificatory, diagnostic and regulatory techniques of previous means of surveillant viewing, with the opportunity for modes of interactivity that enhance the self-scrutinizing experience through the manipulation of digital-imaging software. Moreover, the notion that the 'operative strategy' of hypertext is 'replacement' may serve to further diffuse and normalize a telos of changeable surfaces and layers in ways that pre-existing forms of media could not. Yet the idea that an acute critique of the social and libidinal impetus for normative surgical enhancement emerges from a website that is the property of the FX network, a subsidiary of Fox TV, and consequently part of Rupert Murdoch's News Corporation is striking, and underlines the fact that even the most inured corporate profile shouldn't be taken at face value.

Notes

Foreword

1. Walter Benjamin, 'Theses on the Philosophy of History', in *Illuminations*, ed. Hannah Arendt, trans. Harry Zohn (London: Fontana, 1973), pp. 253–64.

Introduction

1. See Jay David Bolter and Richard Grusin, *Remediation: Understanding New Media* (Cambridge, MA: MIT Press, 2000); Lev Manovich, *The Language of New Media* (Cambridge, MA: MIT Press, 2001); Martin Lister, et al. *New Media: A Critical Introduction* (London: Routledge, 2003); William Boddy, *New Media and Popular Imagination: Launching Radio, Television, and Digital Media in the United States* (Oxford University Press, 2004); Lauren Rabinovitz and Abraham Gell (eds), *Memory Bytes: History, Technology, and Digital Culture* (Durham, NC: Duke University Press, 2004); Wendy Hui Kyong Chun and Thomas W. Keenan (eds), *New Media, Old Media: A History and Theory Reader* (London: Routledge, 2005).
2. Bolter and Grusin, *Remediation* p. 14.
3. See Bolter and Grusin, *Remediation* pp. 3–84 ; Henry Jenkins, 'Convergence? I Diverge', *Technology Review* (June 2001), p. 91.
4. Mark Poster, 'Underdetermination', *New Media and Society*, 1:1 (1999), pp. 12–17 (p. 12).
5. Henry Jenkins, 'The Cultural Logic of Media Convergence', *International Journal of Cultural Studies*, 7:1 (2004), pp. 33–44 (p. 34).
6. Jenkins, 'Convergence? I Diverge', p. 91.
7. Recent work includes Laurent Mannoni, *The Great Art of Light and Shadow: An Archaeology of the Cinema*, trans. Richard Crangle (Exeter: University of Exeter Press, 2000); Stephen Herbert (ed.), *A History of*

Pre-Cinema, 3 vols (London: Routledge, 2000); Simon During, *Modern Enchantments: The Cultural Power of Secular Magic* (Cambridge, MA: Harvard University Press, 2002); Lisa Gitelman and Geoffrey B. Pingree (eds), *New Media 1740–1915* (Cambridge, MA: MIT Press, 2003); Laurent Mannoni, Werner Nekes and Marina Warner, *Eyes, Lies, and Illusions* (London: Hayward Galley and Lund Humphries, 2004); Jonathan Crary, *Suspensions of Perception: Attention, Spectacle, and Modern Culture* (Cambridge, MA: MIT Press, 2001); Simon Popple and Vanessa Toulmin (eds), *Visual Delights 2: Exhibition and Reception* (Eastleigh: John Libbey, 2005); David Robinson, Stephen Herbert and Richard Crangle (eds), *Encyclopaedia of the Magic Lantern* (London: Magic Lantern Society, 2001).

8. Roger Fidler uses the term 'mediamorphosis' to name the process of media transformation. Roger Fidler *Mediamorphosis: Understanding New Media* (London: Sage, 1999).

Chapter 1: Toys, Instruments, Machines: Why the Hardware Matters

1. Hollis Frampton, 'For a Metahistory of Film', in *Circles of Confusion: Film, Photography, Video, Texts 1968–1980* (Rochester, NY: Visual Studies Workshop Press, 1983), p. 112.

2. One of the many virtues of Yuri Tsivian's study of the cultural reception of early cinema in Russia is his treatment of 'the reception of interference', covering film damage, breakdown, extraneous noise and the like, revealing that this was as much a part of the experience as supposedly seamless illusion: see Tsivian, *Early Cinema in Russia and its Cultural Reception* (London: Routledge, 1994), ch. 4.

3. On early conceptions of the phonograph, see Ian Christie, 'Early Phonograph Culture and Moving Pictures', in Richard Abel and Rick Altman (eds), *The Sounds of Early Cinema*, (Bloomington: Indiana University Press, 2001), pp. 3–12; and on electricity as a spectacle, see Carolyn Marvin, *When Old Technologies Were New* (Oxford: Oxford University Press, 1988).

4. 'The Cinematograph', *The Times*, 22 February 1896, p. 15.

5. 'The Month: Science and Arts', *Chambers's Journal*, 25 April 1896.

6. 'Lantern Mems', *The Lantern Record, Supplement to the British Journal of Photography*, 1 May 1896, p. 33.

7. After the original launch of the phonograph in 1878, Edison relaunched this as the 'Perfected Phonograph' in 1888, stimulated by the appearance of a rival sound recording system, the graphophone. See Paul Israel, *Edison: A Life of Invention* (New York: John Wiley, 1998), pp. 288–302. He would subsequently appropriate other inventions by claiming to have 'perfected' these, as in the case of x-rays (see Israel, *Edison*, p. 309) and the projector acquired from Thomas Armat and renamed the Edison Vitascope, publicly

hailed in the *New York Herald* (4 April 1896), as 'the Kinetoscope perfected'; quoted in Terry Ramsaye, *A Million and One Nights* (1926) (New York: Simon and Schuster, 1986), p. 227.

8. The phrase appears in a report on Edison's Vitascope by Joseph MacMahon, in the *Sidney Bulletin* of 12 September 1896, quoted by Deac Rossell in his introductory notes to the invaluable 'Chronology of Cinema 1889–1896', *Film History*, 7:2 (Summer 1995), p. 118.

9. 'Edison's Vitascope Cheered', *New York Times*, 24 April 1896, p. 5; quoted in Charles Musser, *Before the Nickelodeon: Edwin S. Porter and the Edison Manufacturing Company* (Berkeley: University of California Press, 1991), p. 61.

10. 'Instrument', *Oxford English Dictionary* (1910), vol. 5.

11. *Webster's Revised Unabridged Dictionary* (1913).

12. 'Toy', II. 6, *Oxford English Dictionary* (1910), vol. 10.

13. See Jim Endersby, 'Classifying Sciences: Systematics and Status in mid-Victorian Natural History', in Martin Daunton (ed.), *The Organisation of Knowledge in Victorian Britain* (Oxford: British Academy/Oxford University Press, 2005), pp. 61–85.

14. *Oxford English Dictionary* (1910).

15. John Baptista Porta (Giambattista della Porta), *Natural Magick* (London: Thomas Young and Samuel Speed, 1658), First Book, Chapter 2, 'What is the nature of Magick?' This is the first English edition of della Porta's *Magiae Naturalis*, originally published in Naples 1558. For biographical and bibliographic clarification, see Louise Clubb, *Giambattista della Porta, Dramatist* (Princeton: Princeton University Press, 1965), ch. 1.

16. See, for instance, Frances Yates' essay 'The Hermetic Tradition in Renaissance Science' (1967), in Frances A. Yates, *Ideas and Ideals in the North European Renaissance: Collected Essays*, vol. 3 (London: Routledge, 1984), pp. 227–46.

17. Anon., 'A True Description and Direction of what is Most Worthy to be Seen in all Italy', in W. Oldys (ed.), *The Harleian Miscellany* (London, R. Dutton, 1810), vol. 5, p. 31. Quoted in Vaughan Hart, *Art and Magic in the Court of the Stuarts* (London: Routledge, 1994), p. 93.

18. On these automata, see Shelby T. McCloy, *French Inventions of the Eighteenth Century* (Lexington: University of Kentucky Press, 1952), p. 108. On automata, see Silvio A. Bedini, 'The Role of Automata in the History of Technology', *Technology and Culture*, 5:1 (1964), pp. 24–42; also Bedini, *Patrons, Artisans and Instruments of Science, 1600–1750* (Aldershot: Ashgate, 1999). See also Dan North's essay in this book.

19. Derek J. de Solla Price, 'Automata and the Origins of Mechanism and Mechanistic Philosophy', *Technology and Culture*, 5:1 (1964), pp. 9–23.

20. Daniel Tiffany, *Toy Medium: Materialism and Modern Lyric* (Berkeley: University of California Press, 2000), p. 44.

21. Roget's paper was read to the Royal Society of London in December 1824 and published in the *Philosophical Transactions*, 115 (1825), pp. 131–40; Faraday's paper to the Royal Institution was given on 10 December 1830 and published as 'On a peculiar class of optical deceptions', in the *Journal of the Royal Institution*, 1 (1831), pp. 205–23. For a discussion of these, and of the intervening contribution of Joseph Plateau, see Laurent Mannoni, *The Great Art of Light and Shadow*, trans. Richard Crangle (Exeter: University of Exeter Press, 2000), pp. 199–220.

22. Charles Wheatstone, 'Description of the kaleidophone or phonic kaleidoscope: a new philosophical toy, for the illustration of several interesting and amusing acoustical and optical phenomena', *Quarterly Journal of Science, Literature and Art*, 23 (1827), p. 344.

23. David Brewster, *A Treatise on the Kaleidoscope* (London and Edinburgh: Archibald Constable and Co., 1819), p. 1.

24. Ibid., p. 133.

25. Nicholas Jardine notes that 'there are . . . remarkable continuities over several centuries in the traditions of practices and competences associated with microscopes, telescopes and surveying instruments'. See Jardine, *The Scenes of Inquiry: On the Reality of Questions in the Sciences* (Oxford: Clarendon Press, 1991), p. 166.

26. Jonathan Crary, *Techniques of the Observer: On Vision and Modernity in the Nineteenth Century* (Cambridge, MA: MIT Press, 1992), p. 116.

27. Carpet making was an important industry in Kilmarnock, Dundee, Glasgow and other Scottish towns and cities in the eighteenth century, before Joseph Marie Jacquard's invention of the mechanical loom in 1801, controlled by punched cards, ushered in a new vogue for complex patterns.

28. Lecture by Helen Weston on the image of the lantern in eighteenth-century France at the *Lantern Projections* symposium, British Academy, February 2001; and a paper, 'Magic Lanterns in Revolutionary France: Where Street and Salon Intersect', *Association of Art Historians Annual Conference, 2004*.

29. Karl Marx and Friedrich Engels, *The German Ideology* (1846), quoted in Crary, *Techniques of the Observer*, p. 114.

30. Charles Baudelaire, 'The Painter of Modern Life' (1859–60), in, P.E. Charvet (ed. and trans.), *Baudelaire: Selected Writings on Art and Artists*, (Harmondsworth: Penguin, 1972), p. 400; also quoted, in a different translation, by Crary, p. 113.

31. The concept of 'mentalité' was central to the work of the *Annales* historians of cultural and material history in France. For a brief account and guide to further reading, see Peter Burke, *What Is Cultural History?* (Cambridge: Polity, 2004), p. 4.

32. Charles Baudelaire, 'Morale du joujou' ['Moral of the toy'] (1853), in Baudelaire, *Œuvres Complèts* (Paris: Gallimard, 1961), pp. 527–28.

33. Crary writes that the phenakistoscope and stereoscope 'eventually disappeared' (*Techniques of the Observer*, p. 132), apparently ignoring the persistence and constant reinvention of such devices which continues today. Most museum and art gallery shops sell versions of the stereoscope and kinetoscope. I have before me a 'Naturescope', manufactured by Werkhaus Gmbh in Germany in 2001.

34. André Gide, *If I Die: An Autobiography* (*Si le grain meurt*, 1926), trans. Dorothy Bussy (New York: Random House, 1935), pp. 6–7.

35. On optical aspects of Proust's *A la recherche du temps perdu* (1913–27) and James Joyce's *Ulysses* (1922), both set at the turn of the century, see, most recently, Sarah Danius, *The Senses of Modernism: Technology, Perception and Aesthetics* (Ithaca, NY: Cornell University Press, 2002).

36. Dolf Sternberger, *Panorama of the Nineteenth Century* (1955), trans. Joachin Neugroschel (New York: Urizen Books, 1977), pp. 131–63. Sternberger's focus is on the German interior, but see also research undertaken under the auspices of the AHRB Centre for the Study of the Domestic Interior at http://www.rca.ac.uk/csdi/.

37. Robert-Houdin was the stage name of Jean Eugène Robert (1805–71), the son of a watchmaker and one of the pioneers of modern technologically assisted magic. His 'light and heavy chest' trick, used to trounce the Algerian Marabout folk magicians, relied on a concealed electromagnet. For an effective fictionalized account of this episode, see Brian Moore's novel *The Magician's Wife* (London: Flamingo, 1998).

38. The monologue was first published in Browning's collection *Dramatis Personae* in 1864, which followed the death of his wife Elizabeth Barrett Browning, who had been a believer in spiritualism.

39. E. Jentsch's work on the uncanny was Freud's starting point for a psycho-analytic interpretation of the sources of this feeling. See Sigmund Freud, 'The Uncanny', in James Strachey (ed. and trans.), *Standard Edition of the Complete Psychological Works of Sigmund Freud* (London: Hogarth Press, 1955) vol. 17, pp. 217–56 (p. 217).

40. Price, 'Automata', p. 15.

41. See introduction to Paul's catalogue, *Apparatus for the Elementary Electrical Laboratory*, (London and New York, 1914) Section S.

42. R.W. Paul, contribution to 'Before 1910: Kinematograph Experiences', *Proceedings of the British Kinematograph Society*, 38 (1936), p. 6.

43. Jules Carpentier (1851–1921), who began his engineering career in railways, also manufactured the first Branly radio-wave detector tubes in 1900. For a brief account of his career and relationship with Louis Lumière, see Auguste and Louis Lumière, *Letters: Inventing the Cinema*, trans. Pierre Hodgson, with annotation by Jacques Rittaud-Hutinet (London: Faber, 1995), p. 26.

44. André Bazin, 'The Myth of Total Cinema' (1946), in A. Bazin, *What Is*

Cinema?, ed. and trans. Hugh Gray (Berkeley: University of California Press, 1967), pp. 17–22 (p.17). Bazin's essay was actually a review of the first volume of Georges Sadoul's *Histoire générale du cinéma*, which countered Sadoul's 'Marxist views' by proposing a 'paradoxical' reversal of 'the order of historical causality, which goes from the ideological infrastructure to the ideological superstructure' (p. 17). Apart from caricaturing Marxist thought, Bazin's essay misrepresents many cinema pioneers and completely ignores the continuum of illusory arts.

45. Christian Metz, 'On the Impression of Reality in the Cinema', in C. Metz, *Film Language: A Semiotics of the Cinema*, trans. Michael Taylor (New York: Oxford University Press, 1974), p. 4.

46. Laurent Mannoni, 'The Art of Deception', in *Eyes, Lies and Illusions*, eds. Laurent Mannoni, Werner Nekes and Marina Warner (London: Hayward Gallery and Lund Humphries, 2004), pp. 41–52.

Chapter 2: 'The suppleness of everyday life': CGI, the Lumières, and Perception after Photography

1. See Dai Vaughn, 'Let There Be Lumière', in Thomas Elsaesser and Adam Barker (eds), *Early Cinema: Space, Frame, Narrative*, 2nd edn (London: BFI, 1994), p. 64.

2. Mary Ann Doane, *The Emergence of Cinematic Time: Modernity, Contingency, the Archive* (Cambridge, MA: Harvard University Press, 2002), p. 177.

3. For recent discussions see William J. Mitchell, *The Re-Configured Eye: Visual Truth in the Post-Photographic Era* (Cambridge, MA: MIT Press, 1994), and Lev Manovich, *The Language of New Media* (Cambridge, MA: MIT Press, 2001).

4. A second 'conceit' of the Hell's Angels sequence in *The Aviator* is that the process repeats that used to 'place' DiCaprio on the prow of the ship in *Titanic* (James Cameron, Fox/Paramount, 1997).

5. Audrey Doyle, 'Move for Move', *Computer Graphics World*, 24:9 September 2001, pp. 44–50 (p. 44).

6. Audrey Doyle, 'Dune Bugs', *Computer Graphics World*, 24:5 May 2001, pp. 48–51 (p. 51).

7. Doyle, 'Dune Bugs', p. 51.

8. Walter Benjamin, 'A Short History of Photography' (1931), *Screen*, 13:2 (1972), pp. 5–27 (p. 7).

9. Henri Bergson, *Creative Evolution* (1907), trans. Arthur Mitchell (London: Macmillan, 1911).

10. Leo Charney, 'In a Moment: Film and the Philosophy of Modernity', in Leo Charney and Vanesa R. Schwartz (eds), *Cinema and the Invention*

of Modern Life, (London: University of California Press, 1995), pp. 279–96.

11. Henri Bergson, *Matter and Memory* (1896), trans. Nancy Margaret Paul and W. Scott Palmer (1911; 1996 5th edn) (New York: Zone, 1996). See also Walter Benjamin, 'Some Motifs on Baudelaire' (1939) in *Illuminations*, ed. by Hannah Arendt, trans. by Harry Zohn (London: Fontana, 1973), pp. 157–202.

12. Bergson, *Creative Evolution*, p. 323.

13. Ibid., p. 321.

14. Ibid.

15. Ibid., p. 288.

16. Ibid., p. 322.

17. Tom Gunning, 'The Cinema of Attractions: Early Film, its Spectator and the Avant-Garde' (1986), in Thomas Elsaesser and Adam Barker (eds), *Early Cinema: Space, Frame, Narrative*, 2nd edn (London: BFI, 1994), pp. 56–62 (p. 57).

18. Gunning, 'The Cinema of Attractions', p. 58.

19. Jacques Aumont, 'Lumière Revisited', *Film History*, 8:1 (1996), pp. 416–30.

20. Doane, *The Emergence of Cinematic Time*, p. 144.

21. See Gilles Deleuze, *Cinema 1: The Movement-Image* (1983), trans. Hugh Tomlinson and Barbara Habberjam, 2nd edn (London: Athlone, 1997), and *Cinema 2: The Time-Image* (1985), trans. Hugh Tomlinson and Robert Galeta, 2nd edn (London: Athlone, 1994).

22. Paul Douglass, 'Bergson and Cinema: Friends or Foes?', in John Mullarkey (ed.), *The New Bergson* (Manchester: Manchester University Press, 1999), pp. 209–27 (p. 211).

23. Miriam Hansen, 'Benjamin, Cinema and Experience: "The Blue Flower in the Land of Technology"', *New German Critique*, 40 (1987), pp. 179–224 (p. 216)

24. Sean Cubitt, *The Cinema Effect* (Cambridge, MA: MIT Press, 2004), p. 23.

25. Bergson, *Creative Evolution*, p. 321.

Chapter 3: 'Wouldn't you rather be at home?'
Electronic Media and the Anti-Urban Impulse

1. Erik Davis, 'TV's Fascinating, Frightening Future', *The Utne Reader*, 48 (July/August 1990), pp. 86–87.

2. For a discussion of the shared contexts of early cinema and electronic media, see William Boddy, *New Media and Popular Imagination: Launching Radio, Television, and Digital Media in the United States* (Oxford: Oxford University Press, 2004), esp. ch. 1, 'Cinema and Wireless in Turn of the Century Popular Imagination'.

3. Mary Barnett Gilson, 'The Relation of Home Conditions to Industrial Efficiency', *Annals of the American Academy of Political and Social Science*, 65 (May 1916), pp. 277-89 (p. 283). Gilson was the employment and service superintendent in the Clothcraft Shops of the Joseph & Feiss Company.

4. Hugo Gernsback, letter to *New York Times*, 29 March 1912; quoted in Susan J. Douglas, *Inventing American Broadcasting, 1899–1922* (Baltimore: Johns Hopkins University Press, 1987), pp. 199–200.

5. Tom Gunning, talk at Deutches Haus, Columbia University, 19 April 2002.

6. Quoted in Carolyn Marvin, *When Old Technologies Were New: Thinking About Electric Communication in the Late Nineteenth Century* (New York: Oxford University Press, 1988), p. 200.

7. Marvin, 'When Old Technologies Were New', p. 200.

8. Raymond Williams, *Television: Technology and Cultural Form* (London: Routledge, 1993); William Boddy, 'The Rhetoric and Economic Roots of the American Broadcasting Industry', *Cinetracts*, 2 (1979), pp. 37–54.

9. Bertold Brecht, 'Radio as a Means of Communication', in . John Hanhardt (ed.), *Video Culture* (Rochester, NY: Visual Studies Workshop Press, 1990), p. 53.

10. See David Nye, *American Technological Sublime* (Cambridge, MA: MIT Press, 1994), esp. ch. 5, 'The Factory: From the Pastoral Mill to the Industrial Sublime'.

11. Quoted in Ithiel de Sola Poole, *Forecasting the Telephone: A Retrospective Technology Assessment of the Telephone* (Norwood, NJ: Ablex, 1983), pp. 48–49.

12. 'Removing the Last Objection to Living in the Country', *Country Life*, February 1922, p. 63. Randall Patnode argues that radio was promoted by the US popular press in the 1920s as a modernizing technology aimed at rural residents; see Patnode, '"What These People Need is Radio": New Technology, the Press, and Otherness in 1920s America', *Technology and Culture*, 44:2 (2003), pp. 285–305. For more general discussions of early radio audiences, see Susan Smulyan, *Selling Radio, The Commercialization of American Radio, 1920–1934* (Washington, DC: Smithsonian Institution Press, 1994); Susan Douglas, *Listening In: Radio and the American Imagination, from Amos 'n' Andy and Edward R. Murrow to Wolfman Jack and Howard Stern* (New York: Times Books, 1999).

13. *Get Ready Now to Sell Television: A Guidebook for Merchants Who Recognize an Extraordinary Opportunity* (New York: Caldwell-Clements, Inc., 1944), p. 94. The book was prepared by the staff of *Radio and TV Retailing* journal.

14. Lee DeForest, *Television Today and Tomorrow* (London: Hutchinson, 1945), pp. 19–20.

15. Ibid., p. 167.

16. Ibid., p. 171.
17. Bill Gates, *The Road Ahead* (New York: Penguin, 1995), pp. 135–36.
18. Ibid., p. 155.
19. Ibid.
20. Gates, *The Road* Ahead, p. 156.
21. Ibid., p. 221.
22. Ibid., p. 269.
23. Ibid.
24. George Gilder, 'Breaking the Box', *National Review*, 15 August 1994, pp. 37–8, 40, 42–3 (p. 40).
25. Ibid., p. 37.
26. Ibid., p. 38.
27. Ibid.
28. Gilder, 'Breaking the Box', p. 42.
29. Larry Armstrong, 'Cars, Beer, and Web Browsers', *Business Week*, 12 May 1997, p. 113. AOL executive Robert Pittman explained to *Business Week* in 1997: 'Every company is seeing the same thing we are . . . the group of early adopters is 100 percent penetrated, so everyone is now going after the mass market. To do that, they have to use TV, the mass-market tool.'
30. Bruce Horovitz, 'Competing for PC Buyers: PC Sellers Targeting Home Users', *USA Today*, 28 November 1994, p. 1B.
31. Armstrong, 'Cars, Beer, and Web Browsers', p. 113.
32. On Packard Bell's industry position and marketing strategies, see Gerry Khermouch, 'Packard Bell Becomes Contrarian with Launch of Sub-Brand: Spectria', *Brandweek*, 20 June 1994, p. 9; Gerry Khermouch, 'Packard Bell Axes Q4 Brand Ad Plans', *Brandweek*, 26 September 1994, p. 9
33. On Packard Bell's market share and competitive problems, see 'Packard Bell Readies First TV Ads', *Home Furnishing News*, 22 July 1996, p. 64; John Tylee, 'M&C Saatchi Lands First US Business', *Campaign*, 10 May 1996. In November 1999, Packard Bell announced plans to close by the end of the year, terminating 1,600 US jobs; 'Diary', *Cleveland Plain Dealer*, 5 June 1996, p. 1C.
34. Quoted in Shelly Garcia, 'Packard Ad Brings Message Home', *Adweek*, 21 October 1996, p. 5.
35. Armstrong, 'Cars, Beer, and Web Browsers', p. 113.
36. Bradley Johnson, 'Intel's Chip Launches New Era in Marketing', *Advertising Age's Business Marketing*, 11 November 1996, p. A4; John Tylee, 'TV Spectacular Fronts Packard Bell Euro Blitz', *Campaign*, 8 November 1996.
37. Tylee, 'TV Spectacular'.
38. 'Best Spots—Creative', *Adweek*, 18 November 1996, pp. 33–36 (p. 34).
39. Jeremy Pemberton, 'Private View', *Campaign*, 6 December 1996, np.

40. Ibid.
41. 'Morning Briefing', *St Louis Post-Dispatch*, 4 November 1999, p. C2.
42. Eric Sorensen, 'Wyo. Town in Spotlight Not So Wired After All: Microsoft Ads Tout Network to Nowhere', *Denver Post*, 1 March 1999, p. C5.
43. Ron Fanscell, 'Town is No Stranger to Fate's Shifting Winds', *Denver Post*, 10 June 2001, p. A1.

Chapter 4: Breaking the Time Barrier with John Cage

1. David Revill, *The Roaring Silence: John Cage A Life* (New York: Arcade, 1992), pp. 165–66.
2. Ibid., p. 163; see also John Cage, *Silence* (London: Marion Boyars, 1968).
3. John Cage, *A Year from Monday* (London: Marion Boyars, 1968), p. 98.
4. To be honest no contemporary accounts of the first performance mention the sound of a plane, only of rain and the audience itself. I owe the idea of the plane to Paul Morley's brilliant book *Words and Music* (London: Bloomsbury, 2003), in which in the middle of a long footnote describing the first performance of *4' 33"* he asks a series of questions, one of which is '[D]id Cage organise that plane passing overhead?' (p. 277). The idea of a plane becoming part of the performance was too neat to resist, given the theme of this essay. I am also grateful to Perry Sloan, whose website *AirTimes, A Source for Airline History* (http://www.airtimes.com) is an excellent resource and fascinating in its own right. According to Sloan it would have been possible for a scheduled upstate New York or Montreal flight to pass in the Hudson Valley and Woodstock area on the way either to or from the New York or Newark airports at that time, as well as unscheduled civil or pleasure aircraft. However he also pointed out that there is no way to reconstruct today the specific departure and arrival times or flight paths of scheduled flights from those days. While flight details would be recorded by tracking computers today, air traffic control was far less sophisticated fifty years ago. Except in the immediate vicinity of airport terminal areas, it was pretty much free flight, and a national radar system wasn't developed until after a collision of airliners over the Grand Canyon in 1956.
5. Margot A. Henriksen, *Dr. Strangelove's America* (Berkeley: University of California Press, 1997), p. 91.
6. Ibid.
7. Ibid. p. 96.
8. Ibid., pp. 95–96.
9. Ibid., p. 193ff.
10. Ibid., pp. 125–26.
11. Ibid., p. 108.
12. For a comprehensive history of the GOC and other civil-defence measures,

see Kenneth Schaffel, *The Emerging Shield: The Air Force and the Evolution of Continental Air Defense, 1945–1960* (Washington, DC: Office of Air Force History, United States Air Force, 1991).

13. Cage, *Silence*, p. 103.
14. Revill, *The Roaring Silence* pp. 20–21.
15. Ibid., pp. 63–65. The afore mentioned 'untitled event' at Asheville in 1952, described by some at the time as a 'multimedia happening' was a musical composition for three speakers, piano, dancer, gramophone, radios, film and slide projectors, and paintings. The score called for alternating action and silence.
16. Ibid., pp. 81–82.
17. For a comprehensive account of the history of the radar, see Robert Buderi, *The Invention that Changed the World* (London: Abacus, 1998).
18. Claude Shannon, 'A Mathematical Theory of Communication', *The Bell System Technical Journal*, 27 (July and October 1948), pp. 379–423, 623–56.
19. Ibid., *passim*.
20. Ibid., pp. 14–15.
21. Ibid., p. 10.
22. Jeremy Campbell, *Grammatical Man: Information, Entropy, Language, and Life* (New York: Simon and Schuster, 1982), pp. 51–52.
23. Catherine N. Hayles, *Chaos Bound: Orderly Disorder in Contemporary Literature and Science* (Ithaca: Cornell University Press, 1990), p. 51.
24. Gunther Stent, *The Coming of the Golden Age: A View of the End of Progress* (New York: Natural History Press, 1969) p. 100.
25. Ibid., pp. 100–01.
26. Ibid., p. 101.
27. Ibid., p. 102.
28. Ibid., p. 104.
29. Ibid.
30. Ibid., p. 98.
31. Ibid., p. 104.
32. Ibid., p. 105.
33. Leonard Meyer, *Music, the Arts, and Ideas: Patterns and Predictions in Twentieth-Century Culture* (Chicago: University of Chicago Press, 1994), p. 72.
34. For a detailed account of Jünger's concept of breaking the time barrier, see Charlie Gere, 'Breaking the Time Barrier', *Culture and Organization*, 10:1 (2004), pp. 53–60.
35. Marshall McLuhan (ed), *The McLuhan Dew-Line Newsletter* (New York, Human Development Corporation, 1964).
36. Marshall McLuhan, *Understanding Media: The Extensions of Man* (New York: McGraw-Hill, 1964) p. xi.

37. Reinhold Martin, *The Organizational Complex: Architecture, Media, and Corporate Space* (Cambridge, MA: MIT Press, 2003), pp. 187–88.
38. For an account of SAGE's contribution to modern computing see Paul N. Edwards, *The Closed World: Computers and the Politics of Discourse in Cold War America* (Cambridge, MA: MIT Press, 1996).

Chapter 5: From the Album Page to the Computer Screen: Collecting Photographs at Home

1. See, for example, John Tagg, *The Burden of Representation* (London: Macmillan Education, 1988).
2. Walter Benjamin, 'The Work of Art in the Age of Mechanical Reproduction', ed. Hannah Arendt, trans. Harry Zohn, *Illuminations* (London: Fontana, 1973), pp. 219–53 (p. 221).
3. Linda Williams, 'Corporealized Observers: Visual Pornographies and the "Carnal Density of Vision"', in Patrice Petro (ed.), *Fugitive Images* (Bloomington: Indiana University Press, 1995), pp. 3–41 (p. 17).
4. Elizabeth Edwards, 'Photographs as Objects of Memory', in Marius Kwint, Christopher Breward and Jeremy Aynsley (eds), *Material Memories* (Oxford: Berg, 1999), pp. 221–36 (p. 226).
5. Geoffrey Batchen, 'Vernacular Photographies', *Each Wild Idea: Writing, Photography, History* (Cambridge, MA: MIT Press, 2001), pp. 56–80 (p. 61).
6. Ibid., p. 61; see also Roland Barthes, *Camera Lucida* (1980), tr. Richard Howard (London: Fontana, 1984).
7. Hubertus van Amelunxen, 'The Terror of the Body in Digital Space', in Hubertus van Amelunxen, Stefan Ilghaut and Florian Rötzer (eds), *Photography after Photography: Memory and Representation in the Digital Age* (Amsterdam: G+B Arts, 1996), pp. 115–23 (p. 123).
8. Victor Burgin, 'The Image in Pieces: Digital Photography and the Location of Cultural Experience', in Amelunxen et al. (eds), *Photography after Photography*, pp. 26–35 (p. 29).
9. Laura U. Marks, 'How Electrons Remember', in L.U. Marks, *Touch: Sensuous Theory and Multisensory Media* (Minneapolis: University of Minnesota Press, 2002), pp. 161–75 (p. 161).
10. Mary Warner Marien, *Photography: A Cultural History* (London: Lawrence King, 2002), p. 486.
11. See for example Karen Chichester's 'Heritage Album Class' on: www.creativescrapbooking.com/topics/heritageAlbum.html, September 2004.
12. Don Slater, 'Domestic Photography and Digital Culture', in Martin Lister (ed.), *The Photographic Image in Digital Culture* (London: Routledge, 1995), pp. 129–46.

13. Lev Manovich, 'The Paradoxes of Digital Photography', in Amelunxen et al. (eds), *Photography after Photography*, pp. 57–65 (p. 58).
14. Sarah Kember, 'The Shadow of the Object: Photography and Realism', *Textual Practice*, 10:1 (1996), pp. 145–63 (p. 145).
15. See, for example, Martha Rosler, *Decoys + Disruptions: Selected Writings 1975–2001* (Cambridge, MA: MIT Press, 2006); Allan Sekula, *Fish Story* (NY: D.A.P Distributed Art Publisher, Inc., 1995); John Tagg, *Grounds of Dispute: Art History, Cultural Politics and The Discursive Field*, (Minnesota: University of Minnesota Press, 1992).
16. Patrizia Di Bello, 'The Female Collector: Women's Photographic Albums in the Nineteenth Century', *Living Pictures*, 1:2 (December 2001), pp. 2–20.
17. See Françoise Heilbrun and Michael Pantazzi, *Album de collages de l'Angleterre Victorienne* (Paris: Éditions du Regard, 1997).
18. Helmut Gernsheim, *Lewis Carroll: Photographer* (New York: Dover, 1969), p. 79.
19. Charles Sander Peirce, 'Logic As Semiotic: The Theory of Signs' (1893–1910), in Justus Buchler (ed.), *Philosophical Writings of Peirce*, (New York: Dover, 1955), pp. 98–119; Rosalind Krauss, 'Notes on the Index', *The Originality of the Avant-Garde and Other Modernist Myths* (Cambridge, MA, and London: MIT Press, 1986), pp.196–220.
20. Barthes, *Camera Lucida*, p. 80.
21. David Brewster, 'Photogenic Drawing, or Drawing by the Agency of Light', *Edinburgh Review*, 76 (January 1843), pp. 309-44 (p. 330–31).
22. Diana Cooper and Norman Battershill, *Victorian Sentimental Jewellery* (Newton Abbot, Devon: David and Charles, 1972).
23. Bill Jay, *Cyanide & Spirits: An Inside-Out View of Early Photography* (Munich: Nazraeli Press, 1991), pp. 79–100.
24. Elizabeth Barrett Browning, 'Letter 320, [Thursday] Dec. 7.1843', *The Letters of Elizabeth Barrett Browning to Mary Russell Mitford 1836–1854*, eds. Meredith Raymond and Mary Sullivan (Waco: Armstrong Browning Library of Baylor University, 1983), p. 357.
25. Elizabeth Eastlake, 'Photography', *Quarterly Review*, 101 (April 1857), pp. 442–68; reprinted in Beaumont Newhall (ed.), *Photography: Essays and Images* (New York: Museum of Modern Art, 1980), p. 94.
26. Christian Metz, 'Photography and Fetish', *October*, 34 (1985), pp. 81–91 (p. 84).
27. Tagg, *The Burden of Representation*, p. 4.
28. Laura U. Marks, 'Immanence Online', in L.U. Marks *Touch*, p. 190.
29. Lindsay Smith, *The Politics of Focus: Women, Children, and Nineteenth-Century Photography* (Manchester: Manchester University Press, 1998), pp. 52–73.

30. Ibid., p. 70.
31. Sean Cubitt, *Digital Aesthetics* (London: Sage, 1998), p. 88.

Chapter 6: The Return of Curiosity: The World Wide Web as Curiosity Museum

1. Michel Foucault, 'The Masked Philosopher', in Trans. John Johnston *Foucault Live, Interviews 1966–84* (New York: Semiotext[e], 1996), pp. 198–99.
2. See Barbara M. Benedict, *Curiosity: A Cultural History of Early Modern Inquiry* (Chicago and London: University of Chicago Press, 2001); Lorraine Daston and Katharine Park, *Wonders and the Order of Nature 1150–1750* (New York: Zone Books, 1998).
3. Charlie Gere, 'Museums, Contact Zones and the Internet', in David Bearman and Jennifer Trant (eds), *Museum Interactive Multimedia 1997: Cultural Heritage Systems Design and Interface* (Pittsburgh: Archives & Museum Informatics, 1997), pp. 59–68; Charlie Gere, 'Hypermedia and Emblematics', in Tanya Szraijber (ed.), *Computing and Visual Culture: Representation and Interpretation. Fourteenth Annual CHArt Conference* (London: CHArt, 1999), pp. 45–62; Wolfgang Ernst, 'Archi(ve)textures of Museology', in Susan A. Crane (ed.), *Museums and Memory* (Stanford: Stanford University Press, 2000), pp. 17–34; Anna Munster, *Wundernet* (1998), online artwork at http://wundernet.cofa.unsw.edu.au; Steve Dietz 'The Online Museum-Archive-Library of Wonder-Curiosity-Art', paper given at the symposium *Excavating the Archive: New Technologies of Memory* at the Parsons School of Design, New York, 3 June 2000, published online at http://gallery9.walkerart.org.
4. Michel Foucault, *Language, Counter-Memory, Practice: Selected Essays and Interviews*, edited and with an introduction by Donald F. Bouchard (Ithaca: Cornell University Press, 1977), p. 142.
5. Geoffrey Batchen, *Each Wild Idea: Writing, Photography, History* (Cambridge, MA.: MIT Press, 2001); Jonathan Crary, *Techniques of the Observer: On Vision and Modernity in the Nineteenth Century* (Cambridge, MA: MIT Press, 1992).
6. Walter Benjamin, 'Theses on the Philosophy of History' (1940) in Hannah Arendt (ed.), *Illuminations* (London: Fontana 1973), pp. 245–55 (p. 254).
7. Susan Buck-Morss, *The Dialectics of Seeing: Walter Benjamin and the Arcades Project* (Cambridge, MA: MIT Press, 1989), pp. 92–95; Walter Benjamin, 'On Some Motifs in Baudelaire' (1939) in Hannah Arendt (ed.), *Illuminations* (London: Fontana 1973), pp. 152–90, (pp. 171–73).
8. Georg Simmel, 'The Berlin Trade Exhibition' (1896), in Ben Highmore (ed.), *The Everyday Life Reader* (London and New York: Routledge, 2002), pp. 297–300 (p. 299).

9. Wolfgang Ernst, 'Archival Phantasms. Between Imaginary Museum and Archive: Cyberspace', posted to *Nettime*, 21 Dec 2000, www.nettime.org/Lists-Archives/nettime-l-0012/msg00115.html.
10. Eilean Hooper-Greenhill, *Museums and the Shaping of Knowledge* (London: Routledge, 1992), pp. 105–26.
11. Thomas A. King, 'Performing Akimbo: Queer Pride and Epistemological Prejudice', in Moe Meyer (ed.), *The Politics and Poetics of Camp* (London and New York: Routledge, 1994), pp. 23–50.
12. Marek Walczak and Martin Wattenberg, *Wonderwalker: A Global Online Wunderkammer* (2000), http://wonderwalker.walkerart.org.
13. Shiralee Saul, *Information Tsunami Wunderkammer* (1998), http://www.labyrinth.net.au/~saul/wunder/digframe.html.
14. Tony Kemplen, *Encyclopaedia Mundi* (2003). Details available at www.kemplen.co.uk/Encyclopaediamundi.htm.
15. Quoted in Rebecca Shatwell, 'Unaccompanied Yield: Tony Kemplen in Conversation with Rebecca Shatwell', in *Philosophy Pathways*, 55 (6 April 2003), http://www.shef.ac.uk/~ptpdlp/newsletter/issue55.html.
16. See Walter Benjamin, 'The Work of Art in the Age of its Technological Reproducibility, Second Version', trans. Edmund Jephcott and Harry Zohn, in *Selected Writings 1935–1938*, vol. 3, Howard Eiland and Michael W. Jennings (eds), (Cambridge, MA, and London: Harvard University Press. 2002), pp. 101–33.
17. Walter Benjamin, 'The Paris of the Second Empire in Baudelaire', in W. Benjamin, *Charles Baudelaire: A Lyric Poet in the Era of High Capitalism* (London: Verso, 1983), pp. 9-10.
18. See Buck-Morss, *The Dialectics of Seeing*, pp. 159–201; John McCole, *Walter Benjamin and the Antinomies of Tradition* (Ithaca, NY: Cornell University Press, 1993); Peter Bürger, *Theory of the Avant-Garde* (Manchester: Manchester University Press, 1984), p. 68.
19. McCole, *Walter Benjamin*, p. 137.
20. Buck-Morss, *The Dialectics of Seeing*, pp. 165–68.
21. Ibid., pp. 168, 172.
22. See Andrew Herman and Thomas Swiss (eds), *The World Wide Web and Contemporary Cultural Theory* (New York: Routledge, 2000); Mark Poster, 'Cyberdemocracy: The Internet and the Public Sphere', in David Trend (ed.), *Reading Digital Culture* (London: Blackwell, 2001), pp. 259–71.
23. Buck-Morss, *Dialectics*, pp. 177–81.
24. Ibid., pp. 172–75.
25. Ibid., pp. 179–82.
26. Benjamin cited in ibid., p. 182.
27. Rosamond Wolff Purcell and Stephen Jay Gould, *Finders Keepers: Eight Collectors* (New York: W.W. Norton & Company, 1992), p. 32.

28. Ibid., p. 145.
29. Benjamin, 'On Some Motifs in Baudelaire', pp. 182–84.
30. Ibid., p. 184.
31. Ibid., pp. 185–87.
32. Baudelaire cited in ibid., p. 186.
33. Ibid., p. 185.
34. Friedrich Kittler, *Gramophone, Film, Typewriter*, trans. Geoffrey Winthrop-Young and Michael Wutz (Stanford: Stanford University Press, 1999), p. 13.
35. McCole, *Walter Benjamin*, p. 136; Buck-Morss, *The Dialectics of Seeing*, p. 161.
36. Benjamin cited in McCole, *Walter Benjamin*, p. 144.
37. Benjamin cited in ibid., p. 146.
38. Purcell and Gould, *Finders Keepers*, p. 18.

Chapter 7: From Android to Synthespian: The Performance of Artificial Life

1. Julius Wiedemann, *Digital Beauties* (London: Taschen, 2001), p. 244. For more information, see the official Yuki Terai website: http://www.teraiyuki.net.
2. Quoted in S.A. Mathieson, 'Let Me Be Your Fantasy', *The Guardian: Online*, 26 April 2001, pp. 2–3.
3. Roman Paska, 'The Inanimate Incarnate', in Michel Feher, Ramona Naddaff and Nadia Tazi (eds), *Fragments for a History of the Human Body: Part One* (New York: Zone, 1989), pp. 410–14.
4. Richard Dyer, *Stars* (London: British Film Institute, 1998), p. 1.
5. See Dan North, 'Virtual Actors, Spectacle and Special Effects: Kung Fu Meets "All That CGI Bullshit"', in Stacy Gillis (ed.), *The 'Matrix' Trilogy: Cyberpunk Reloaded*, (London: Wallflower Press, 2005), pp. 48–61.
6. Quoted in Paul Baylis, 'Weekend Beat: In Quest of the "Holy Grail" of the Truly Lifelike Digital Actor', *The Asahi Shimbun*, 7 June 2003, http://www.asahi.com/english/weekend/K2003060700271.html. Accessed 12 Aug. 2003.
7. Kelly Tyler, 'Virtual Humans', *Nova Online*, November 2000, http://www.pbs.org/wgbh/nova/specialfx2/humans.html. Accessed 19 Dec. 2003.
8. Quoted in 'Virtual stunt artists audition for the part', *CNN.com*, 22 February 2002, http://www-2.cs.cmu.edu/afs/cs.cmu.edu/user/christos/www/petros-cnn.htm. Accessed 19 Dec. 2003
9. Clark Elliott, 'Hunting for the Holy Grail with "Emotionally Intelligent" Virtual Actors', 28 February 1997, http://condor.depaul.edu/~elliott/papers/intelligence/. Accessed 19 Dec. 2003.

10. As cited in P.J. Huffstutter, 'Having Desired Effect on *Matrix*', *Chicago Tribune*, 20 May 2003, http://www.chicagotribune.com/technology/local/chi0305200029may20.0,6725932.story. Accessed 12 Aug. 2003.

11. Martin Lister, et al., *New Media: A Critical Introduction* (London: Routledge, 2003), p. 293.

12. The word originates as an acronym based on a line from *The Wizard of Oz*—'Pay no attention to that man behind the curtain.'

13. Richard S. Wallace, 'The Lying Game', *Wired* 5:8, August 1997, http://www.wired.com/wired/archive/5.08/idees_fortes.html. Accessed 11 April 2005

14. Quoted in Etienne Benson, 'Science Historian Examines the Eighteenth-Century Quest for Artificial Life', *Stanford Report*, 19 October 2001, http://news-service.stanford.edu/news/october24/riskinprofile-1024.html. Accessed 11 April 2005.

15. They have also been recorded by Talia Films for a video, *The Jaquet-Droz Androids* (Philippe Sayous, 2001).

16. See, for example, Max von Boehm's account of automaton history, incorporating many unsubstantiated accounts, including the claim that in the mid-sixteenth century Giovanni Torriani created an automaton which could walk through Toledo to fetch bread from the archbishop's palace; Max von Boehm, *Puppets and Automata* (New York: Dover Publications, 1972) p. 10. This text is a reprint of vol. 2 of Boehm's *Dolls and Puppets* (Munich: F. Bruckmann, 1929).

17. For a description of the Jaquet-Droz androids' performance, see Gaby Wood, *Living Dolls: A Magical History of the Quest for Mechanical Life* (London: Faber & Faber, 2002), pp. 13–14.

18. The Jaquet-Droz harmonium player is perhaps the inspiration for Olympia in E.T.A. Hoffmann's *The Sandman*, in which an automaton musician is successfully passed off by her creator as his real daughter.

19. Alfred Chapuis and Edmond Droz, *Automata: A Historical and Technological Study* (London: B.T. Batsford, 1958), pp. 280–82.

20. 'On Automatons. Communicated to the Editor', *The Scientific Gazette; or, Library of Mechanical Philosophy, Chemistry, and Discovery July to December, MDCCCXXV* (London: James Robins & Co., 1826), pp. 157–58.

21. David Brewster, *Letters on Natural Magic* (1832; London: William Tegg, 1861), p. 286.

22. Voltaire, from 'Registre Contenant le Journal des Conférences de L'Académie de Lyon', quoted in A. Doyon and L. Liaigre, *Jacques Vaucanson, Mécanicien de Génie* (Paris, 1966), p. 148. Reprinted in Jean-Claude Beaune, 'The Classical Age of Automata: An Impressionistic Survey from the Sixteenth to the Nineteenth Century', in Feher, Naddaff and Tazi (eds), pp. 430–80.

23. George A. Jenness, *Maskelyne and Cooke: Egyptian Hall, London, 1873–1904* (Enfield, Middlesex: George A. Jenness, 1967), p. 35.
24. Jim Steinmeyer, *Hiding the Elephant: How Magicians Invented the Impossible* (London: William Heinemann, 2004), pp. 103–05.
25. Tom Standage, *The Mechanical Turk: The True Story of the Chess-Playing Machine that Fooled the World* (London: Penguin, 2002), pp. 193–221.
26. Thomas Huxley, 'On the Hypothesis that Animals Are Automata, and Its History' 199–250 in *Thomas Huxley: Collected Essays I: Method and Results* (London: Macmillan, 1893), pp. 199–200.
27. Patricia S. Warrick, *The Cybernetic Imagination in Science Fiction* (Cambridge, MA, and London: The MIT Press, 1980), p. 33.
28. Alan Turing, 'Computing Machinery and Intelligence', *MIND (the Journal of the Mind Association)* 59:236 (Winter 1950), pp. 433–60.
29. P.J.R. Millican and A. Clark (eds), *Machines and Thought: The Legacy of Alan Turing, Vol. 1.* (Oxford: Clarendon Press, 1996), p. 1.
30. Robert M. French, 'Subcognition and the Turing Test', in Millican and Clark (eds), *Machines and Thought* (Oxford: Clarendon Press, 1996), pp. 11–26.
31. Henry Jenkins, 'Celluloid Heroes Evolve', *Technology Review*, 4 April 2003, p. 1.
32. Beaune, 'The Classical Age of Automata', p. 431.
33. John Cohen, *Human Robots in Myth and Science* (London: George Allen & Unwin, 1966), pp. 137–39.
34. Brooks Landon, 'Synthespians, Virtual Humans and Hypermedia: Emerging Contours of Post-SF Film', in Veronica Hollinger and Joan Gordon (eds), *Edging into the Future: Science Fiction and Contemporary Cultural Transformation* (Philadelphia: University of Pennsylvania Press, 2002), pp. 57–72.

Chapter 8: As Seen on TV: Kinaesthetic Crossover and the Animation of Social Dance Pedagogy

1. 'Countdown', Australian Broadcasting Corporation, 30 April 1978.
2. Victor Silvester, *Modern Ballroom Dancing: History and Practice* (London: Stanley Paul, 1977), p. 18.
3. Ibid., p. 40.
4. An Expert, *The Modern Ballroom Dance Instructor* (London: Geographia, c.1926).
5. Ann Hutchinson Guest, *Dance Notation: The Process of Recording Movement on Paper* (London: Dance Books, 1984), pp. 62–67.
6. Irene Castle and Vernon Castle, *Modern Dancing* (New York: World Syndicate Co., c.1914).

7. Jim Dawson, *The Twist: The Story of the Song and Dance that Changed the World* (Boston and London: Faber and Faber, 1995).

8. Bob More and Margaret More, *Everybody Dance! It's Nice 'N' Easy* (London: C. Arthur Pearson Ltd., 1962), p. 28.

9. *Twist* (Dir. Ron Mann, Sphinx Productions, Canada, 1992).

10. Chubby Checker, interviewed in *Twist*.

11. Ibid.

12. Hank Ballard, interviewed in *Twist*.

13. Marshall Stearns and Jean Stearns, *Jazz Dance: The Story of American Vernacular Dance* (New York: Da Capo Press, 1994), p. 3.

14. Maxine Powell, in 'Dancing in the Street: A Rock And Roll History' (Dir. David Espar, British Broadcasting Corporation, 1996), episode 1, 'Whole Lotta Shakin'. Broadcast 15 June 1996.

15. Cholly Atkins, interviewed in 'Dancing in the Street'.

16. Ballard, interviewed in *Twist*.

17. Peter Buckman, *Let's Dance: Social, Ballroom and Folk Dancing* (New York and London: Paddington Press, 1978), p. 215.

18. More and More, *Everybody Dance!* p. 28.

19. Dick Blake, *Discotheque Dances* (Cleveland and New York: The World Publishing Company, 1965).

20. Silvester, *Modern Ballroom Dancing*, p. 49.

21. Ibid., p. 249.

22. Jennifer Meloney, *You Can Disco* (New York: Exeter Books, 1979), p. ii.

23. Jack Villari and Kathleen Sims Villari, *The Official Guide to Disco Dance Steps* (Sydney: Methuen of Australia, 1979), pp. i, iii.

Chapter 9: Depth, Colour, Movement: Embodied Vision and the Stereoscope

1. See Charles Wheatstone, 'To the Editor of The Times', *The Times*, 31 October 1856, p. 10.

2. Jonathan Crary, *Techniques of the Observer: On Vision and Modernity in the Nineteenth Century* (Cambridge, MA: MIT Press, 1992). Laura Burd Schiavo, 'From Phantom Image to Perfect Vision: Physiological Optics, Commercial Photography, and the Popularization of the Stereoscope', in Lisa Gitelman and Geoffrey B. Pingree (eds), *New Media 1740–1915*, (Cambridge, MA: MIT Press, 2003), pp. 113–38.

3. David Bewster, 'Binocular Vision and the Stereoscope', *North British Review*, 17 (1852), pp. 165–204 (p. 201).

4. Charles Wheatstone, 'Contributions to the Physiology of Vision. – Part the First. On some remarkable, and hitherto unobserved, Phenomena of Binocular Vision', *Philosophical Transactions of the Royal Society of London*, 128 (1838), pp. 371–94 (p. 371).

5. Wheatstone, p. 376.
6. 'A Word on the Stereoscope', *Leisure Hour*, 3 (1858), pp. 346–49 (p. 346).
7. *Stereoscopic Magazine*, 1 (July 1858), p. 8.
8. See Robert J. Silverman, 'The Stereoscope and Photographic Depiction in the Nineteenth Century', *Technology and Culture*, 34:5 (1993), pp. 729–56.
9. David Brewster, The Stereoscope. Its History, Theory and Construction. With its Application to the Fine and Useful Arts (London: John Murray, 1856) p. 157.
10. 'The Stereoscope, Pseudoscope, and Solid Daguerreotypes', *Illustrated London News*, 24 January 1852, pp. 78–79 (p. 78).
11. 'A Word on the Stereoscope', p. 349.
12. See Richard Amer, no. 2832 (29 November 1856), John Owning, no. 2914 (9 December 1856).
13. John Tyndall, 'Reports on the Progress of the Physical Sciences', *London, Edinburgh and Dublin Philosophical Magazine*, 4th series, 3 (October 1852), pp. 271–76.
14. 'Notice of a Chromatic Stereoscope', *Edinburgh New Philosophical Journal*, 48 (October 1849–April 1850), p. 150.
15. David Brewster to William Henry Fox Talbot, 22 September 1849, The Correspondence of William Henry Fox Talbot, http://www.foxtalbot.arts.gla.ac.uk.
16. Brewster, The Stereoscope, p. 129.
17. 'Notes of Recently Published Stereographs', *Liverpool and Manchester Photographic Journal*, 1 December 1859, p. 297.
18. *Catalogue of the Binocular Pictures of the London Stereoscopic Company*, included at the end of David Brewster's book, *The Stereoscope. Its History, Theory and Construction, With its Application to the Fine and Useful Arts* (London: John Murray, 1856), p. 14.
19. 'The Patent Mirror Stereoscope', *Liverpool and Manchester Photographic Journal*, 15 November 1859, p. 284.
20. 'London Stereoscopic Company', *The Times*, 31 March 1859, p. 8.
21. Mark Gosser, *Selected Attempts at Stereoscopic Moving Pictures and their Relationship to the Development of Moving-Picture Technology 1852–1903* (New York: Arno Press, 1977), p. 85.
22. *Humphrey's Journal*, 4 (15 July 1852), p. 111.
23. M.J. Plateau, 'Troisiéme note sur de nouvelles applications curieuses de la persistance des impressions de la rétine', *Bulletin de l'Academie Royale des Sciences de Belgique*, 16 (7 July 1849), pp. 37–39. See also Gosser, pp. 80–85.
24. 'Photographic Wheel of Life', *Photographic News*, 14 November 1878, p. 541.
25. See Antoine Claudet, 'On Moving Photographic Figures, illustrating some Phenomena of Vision connected with the combination of the Stereoscope

with the Phenakistoscope', *London, Edinburgh and Dublin Philosophical Journal*, 30 (October 1865), pp. 271–76.

26. Antoine Claudet, *Improvements in Stereoscopes*, patent no. 711 (23 March 1853) p. 6.
27. 'The Stereo-Phantasmascope', *British Journal of Photography*, 12 (15 September 1865) p. 473.
28. Claudet, *Improvements in Stereoscopes*, p. 6.
29. William Henry Wills and Henry Morley, 'Photography', *Household Words*, 7 (19 March 1853), pp. 54–61 (p. 60).
30. William Thomas Shaw, 'Description of a New Optical Instrument called the Stereotrope', *Proceedings of the Royal Society of London*, 11 (1860–62), pp. 70–73. See also 'Soiree of the Photographic Society', *Photographic News*, 12 April 1861, p. 169.
31. Thomas Sutton, editorial, *Photographic Notes*, 15 March 1861, pp. 82–83
32. A.D. Jundzill, 24 May 1856, no. 1245; Phillipe Benoist, 23 Aug 1856, no. 1965.
33. William Newton, 7 April 1854, no. 822; Pierre Czugajwiz, 9 January 1860, no. 58; Peter Hubert Devisgnes, 27 February 1860, no. 537; Henry Du Mont, 8 June 1861, no. 1457; Gaetano Bonelli and Henry Cook, 19 August 1863, no. 2063.
34. Thomas Sutton, editorial, *Photographic Notes*, 1 December 1860, pp. 318–19 (p. 318). See also Thomas Sutton, editorial, *Photographic Notes*, 1 January 1861, pp. 1–2.
35. Sutton, 1 January 1861, p. 2; Thomas Sutton, editorial, *Photographic Notes*, 15 March 1861, pp. 82–83.
36. Coleman Sellers, US Patent 31,357, p. 1.
37. Thomas Sutton, 'On a New Application of the Stereoscope', *Photographic Notes*, (1 January 1856), pp. 5–6.
38. Thomas Sutton, editorial, *Photographic Notes*, 15 August 1858, pp. 184–85 (p. 184).
39. Joseph D'Almeida, 'Nouvel appareil stéréoscopiques; par M.J. Ch. D'Almeida', *Comptes Rendus des séances de L'Academie des Sciences*, 47 (12 July 1858), pp. 61–63.
40. *Patents for Inventions. Abridgement of Specifications Relating to Photography* (London: George E. Eyre and William Spottiswoode, 1861), p. 132.
41. Thomas Rose, letter, *Photographic News*, 4 (18 May 1860), p. 33.
42. Jay David Bolter and Richard Grusin, *Remediation: Understanding New Media* (Cambridge, MA: MIT Press, 2001), p. 9.

Chapter 10: Penny Gaffs and Picture Theatres: Popular Perceptions of Britain's First Cinemas

1. W.A. Williamson, 'The Cinematograph: A Fantasy and a Forecast', *The Pictures*, 2:55 (2 November 1912), p. 15; emphasis in original.

2. André Gaudreault, 'Méliès the Magician: The Magical Magic of the Magic Image', presented at the Conference 'Visual Delights III: Magic, Illusion and Popular Culture Before 1914', University of Sheffield, 15–17 July 2002.

3. 'Photoplay Gossip', *The Pictures*, 2:31 (18 May 1912), p. 22.

4. H.D. Rawnsley, 'The Child and the Cinematograph Show. And the Picture Post-Card Evil', *Hibbert Journal*, 11 (1913), pp. 1–24 (pp. 3–4).

5. 'Terrible', *The Pictures*, 4:95 (2 August 1913), p. 21.

6. Shelley Stamp, *Movie-Struck Girls: Women and Motion Picture Culture After the Nickelodeon* (Princeton.: Princeton University Press, 2000), p. 18.

7. 'Not so much of it!', *The Pictures*, 4:86 (24 May 1913), p. 24.

8. Alec Braid, 'Ultus and the Grey Lady', *Pictures and the Picturegoer*, 11:137 (30 September 1916), pp. 5–7 (p. 5).

9. I use the term 'institution-cinema' to denote the impossibility of separating production and exhibition practices from film discourse.

10. Harry Furniss, *Our Lady Cinema: How and Why I Went into the Photo-Play World and What I Found There* (Bristol: J.W. Arrowsmith, London: Simpkin, Marshall, Hamilton, Kent & Co., 1914), p. 143.

11. Charles F. Ingram, 'Film Gossip', *Illustrated Films Monthly*, 1:5 (January 1914), pp. 274-75 (p. 275).

12. Advertisement, *The Top-Line Indicator* 1:8 (18 December 1912), p. 4.

13. Valentia Steer, *The Romance of the Cinema* (London: Pearson, 1913), p. 14.

14. See Andrew Shail '"A Distinct Advance in Society": Early Cinema's "Proletarian Public Sphere" and Isolated Spectatorship in the UK, 1911–1918', *Journal of British Cinema and Television*, 6 (November 2006).

15. James Ewing Ritchie, *Here and There in London* (London: W. Tweedie, 1859), p. 116.

16. Henry Mayhew, *London Labour and the London Poor* (London: Griffin, Bohn and Co., 1861), p. 223.

17. Ibid.

18. For accounts of the penny theatre (albeit often from the standpoint of moral panic) see James Grant, *Sketches in London* (London: W.S. Orr, 1838) ch. 5, where he estimates the number of penny theatres in London at eighty (p. 162); James Greenwood, *The Seven Curses of London* (London: S. Rivers, 1869), ch. 4; James Greenwood, *The Wilds of London* (London: Chatto & Windus, 1874), pp. 12–20. The institution is discussed in John Springhall, *Youth, Popular Culture and Moral Panics* (London: Macmillan, 1998), ch. 1.

19. Montagu Williams, *Round London: Down East and Up West* (London: Macmillan & Co., 1892), p. 7. I am grateful to David Schmid for pointing out this source.
20. Williams, *Round London*, p. 8.
21. Ibid., p. 10.
22. Ibid., p. 7.
23. Ibid., p. 12. The latter was the subject of both popular folk song and many penny-theatre dramas.
24. Arthur St John Adcock, 'Sideshow London', in George R. Sims (ed.), *Living London*, 3 vols (London: Cassell, 1902), vol. 2, pp. 281–85 (p. 283).
25. Ibid., p. 283.
26. 'The Electric Mind', *Kinematograph and Lantern Weekly* 8.192 (12 January 1911), p. 602.
27. 'Motion Picture News', *The Pictures*, 3:76 (date unspecified, early 1913), p. 22.
28. Tyne and Wear Archives, Newcastle upon Tyne, 963/B1666.
29. Letter, 'Picture Notes', *The Pictures*, 1:16 (3 February 1912), p. 16.
30. 'Motion Picture News', *The Pictures*, 3:70 (date unspecified), p. 23.
31. H. Chance Newton, 'Music-Hall London', in Sims (ed.), *Living London*, 3 vols, (London: Cassell, 1902), vol. 2, pp. 222–28 (p. 225).
32. Quoted in *The Top-Line Indicator* 1:6 (4 December 1912), p. 2; emphasis added.
33. 'Picture Pars', *Rinking World and Picture Theatre News*, 1:11 (12 February 1910), p. 15.
34. 'Picture Theatre Finance', *Rinking World and Picture Theatre News*, 1:5 (1 January 1910), p. 18.
35. 'Picture Pars', *Rinking World and Picture Theatre News*, 1.18 (2 April 1910), pp. 17–19 (p. 17).
36. Adcock, 'Sideshow London', p. 281.
37. Simon Popple and Joe Kember, *Early Cinema: From Factory Gate to Dream Factory* (London: Wallflower, 2004), p. 79.
38. Charles Urban, *The Cinematograph in Science, Education and Matters of State* (London: Charles Urban Trading Co., 1907), p. 56.
39. Jon Burrows, 'Penny Pleasures: Film Exhibition in London during the Nickelodeon Era, 1906–1914', *Film History*, 16:1 (2004), pp. 60–91; 'Penny Pleasures II: Indecency, Anarchy and Junk Films in London's Nickelodeons, 1906–1914', *Film History*, 16:2 (2004), pp. 172–97.
40. It was remarked in February 1910 that '[i]n no other part of London are the Picture Palaces so close together as we find them near Camberwell Gate'. 'Picture Pars', *Rinking World and Picture Theatre News*, 1:11 (12 February 1910), p. 15.
41. Rowland Talbot, 'The Photo-Play Writer', *Illustrated Film Monthly*, 2:7 (March 1914), p. 60.

42. H.R. Parsons, 'Progress', *Pictures and the Picturegoer*, 14.219 (20–27 April 1918), p. 402.
43. Patrick Glynn, 'Have Picture Theatres Come to Stay?', *The Pictures*, 2:48 (14 September 1912), p. 21.
44. 'Moving Pictures or Book?', *The Pictures*, 3:49 (21 September 1912) p. 6.
45. Rawnsley, The Child and The Cinematography Show, pp. 3–4.
46. Ibid., p. 6.
47. Furniss, *Our Lady Cinema*, p. 143.
48. Ibid., pp. 143–44.
49. Ibid., p. 144.
50. Ibid.
51. Ibid., p. 15.
52. Evan Strong, 'Musings', *Illustrated Films Monthly*, 1:3 (November 1913), pp. 117–19 (p. 117).
53. 'Cinema News', *The Pictures* 1:6 (25 November 1911), p. 21.
54. 'Picture News from Far and Near', *The Pictures*, 1:8 (9 December 1911), p. 21.
55. 'Photoplay Gossip', *The Pictures*, 1:16 (3 February 1912), p. 15.
56. Williamson, p. 15.
57. Burrows, 'Penny Pleasures II', pp. 194–95.
58. Furniss, *Our Lady Cinema*, p. 15.
59. C. Tallentine Ashton, 'The Girl Who Wants To Be a Picture Actress', *The Pictures*, 4:90 (28 June 1913), p. 3.
60. Ingram, 'Film Gossip', p. 275.
61. 'Our Screen', *The Pictures*, 5:114 (13 December 1913), p. 24.
62. 'Aeroplanes in a Romaine Fielding Film', *The Pictures* 5:121 (31 Jan 1914), p. 8.
63. *Pictures and the Picturegoer* 6:13 (16 May 1914), p. 290.
64. 'The Cinematographing of the Melancholy Dane', *Dress and Vanity Fair* 1:1 (September 1913), p. 28.
65. See Thomas Elsaesser, 'The Institution Cinema: Industry, Commodity, Audiences', in T. Elsaesser (ed.), *Early Cinema: Space, Frame, Narrative* (London: BFI, 1990), pp. 153–73 (p. 156).
66. James Donald and Stephanie Hemelryk Donald, in Christine Gledhill and Linda Williams (eds), 'The Publicness of Cinema', *Reinventing Film Studies* (London: Arnold, 2000), pp. 114–29 (p. 114).
67. André Bazin, 'In Defense of Mixed Cinema', in Hugh Gray (ed.), *What is Cinema?* (London: California UP, 1967), pp. 53–75 (p. 57); Christian Metz, *Essais Sur la Signification au Cinema* (1968), trans. Michael Taylor (Oxford: Oxford UP, 1974), p. 58.
68. *The Pictures*, 2:28 (27 April 1912), p. 1.

Chapter 11: From Museum to Interactive Television: Organizing the Navigable Space of Natural-History Display

1. BBC News Online, 15 November 2001.
2. Karen Scott and Anne White, 'Unnatural history? Deconstructing the *Walking with Dinosaurs* Phenomenon' *Media, Culture and Society*, 25:3 (2003), pp. 315–32.
3. Quoted in Helen Wheatley, 'The Limits of Television? Natural History Programming and the Transformation of Public Service Broadcasting', *European Journal of Cultural Studies*, 7:3 (2004), pp. 325–39 (p. 330).
4. Alison Griffiths, *Wondrous Difference: Cinema, Anthropology and Turn-of-the-Century Visual Culture* (New York: Columbia University Press, 2002), p. 47.
5. Tony Bennett, *The Birth of the Museum: History, Theory, Politics* (London New York: Routledge, 1995).
6. Anne Friedberg, *Window Shopping: Cinema and the Postmodern* (Berkeley: University of California Press, 1993), pp. 2–3.
7. Quoted in Alison Griffths, '"Journeys for Those Who Can Not Travel": Promenade Cinema and the Museum Life Group', *Wide Angle*, 18:3 (1996), p. 53.
8. Bennett, The Birth of the Museum, p. 6.
9. John Caldwell, 'Second-Shift Media Aesthetics: Programming, Interactivity and User Flows', in John Caldwell and Anee Everett (eds), *New Media: Theories and Practices of Digitextuality*, (London and New York: Routledge, 2003), pp. 127–44 (p. 135).
10 Ibid., p. 136.
11. Griffiths, *Wondrous Difference*, p. 84.
12. Indeed, programmes such as 'Built for the Kill' (2004) are premised entirely on the display of these spectacular moments, as its press release promised: 'With over 2400 edits in each programme, *Built for the Kill* deconstructs the minutes and seconds leading up to a kill, revealing these acts of predation in a whole new light.'
13. Scott and White, 'Unnatural History?' pp. 315–32.
14. Griffiths, 'Journeys' p. 71.
15. Tom Gunning, 'The Cinema of Attractions: Early film, its spectator and the avant-garde', *Wide Angle* 8:3–4 (1986), p. 65.
16. Griffiths, 'Journeys', p. 61.
17. Donna Haraway, *Primate Visions: Gender, Race and Nature in the World of Modern Science* (London and New York: Verso, 1992), p. 29.
18. Griffiths, Journeys, p. 71.
19. See D. Bouse, *Wildlife Films* (Pennsylvania: University of Pennsylvania Press, 2000)
20. Quoted in Haraway, *Primate Visions*, p. 45; emphasis added.

21. See Alison Griffiths, 'Animated Geography: Early Cinema at the American Museum of Natural History', in J. Fullerton (ed.), *Celebrating 1895: The Centenary of Cinema*, (London and Sydney: John Libbey, 1998).
22. Friedberg, *Window Shopping*, pp. 2–3.
23. See William Boddy, *New Media and Popular Imagination: Launching Radio, Television, and Digital Media in the United States* (Oxford: Oxford University Press, 2004); Jason Jacobs, *The Intimate Screen: Early British Television Drama* (Oxford and New York: Oxford University Press, 2000).
24. Jacobs, *The Intimate Screen*, p. 25.
25. Wheatley, 'The Limits of Television?' pp. 328–29.
26. Janet Murray, *Hamlet on the Holodeck: The Future of Narrative in Cyberspace* (Cambridge, MA: MIT Press, 1997), p. 89; emphasis added.
27. Jeremy Butler, 'VR in the ER: *ER*'s Use of E-Media', *Screen*, 42:4 (Winter 2001), p. 325.
28. As Patrick Dalzell (BBC's senior executive producer of sport) argues, the load time of interactive applications can be up to thirty seconds, which in an age of instantaneous communications is like a slow death and won't be tolerated by viewers. The anxiety of the 'blue screen of death' load time was reflected and addressed by the Barwise Report (2005) on the BBC's new digital television services, which asked the BBC to invest the requisite funds to halve this waiting time.
29. Discussing why and how he became interested in developing cyberspace, William Gibson recalls watching youths at a video arcade: 'These kids clearly believed in the space these games projected. Everyone who works with computers seems to develop an intuitive faith that there's some kind of actual space behind the screen' (quoted in Karen Lury, *British Youth television: Cynicism and Enchantment*, (Oxford: Clarendon Press, 2001) Of course, the rhetoric of the 'Walking with Beasts' introductory sequence attempts to reinforce the sense of a space behind the screen by encouraging the viewer to 'delve deeper' and 'explore' the interactive spaces of the programme by 'pressing the red button'.
30. Dan Harries, 'Watching the Internet', in D. Harries (ed.), *The New Media Book* (London: BFI, 2002), pp. 171–82.
31. This fear of confusion can perhaps be more appropriately thought of as the worry of 'What have I just missed?!'

Chapter 12: Imaginary Spaces: User Participation in Networked Narrative Environments

1. This essay is based on a research publication for which I invited fellow artists and theorists to discuss and define their own versions of a networked narrative model: Andrea Zapp (ed.), *Networked Narrative Environments as Imaginary Spaces of Being* (Manchester: Manchester

Metropolitan University/Liverpool: Foundation for Art and Creative Technology (FACT), 2004).

2. Margaret Morse, 'Nature Morte: Landscape and Narrative in Virtual Environments', in Mary Anne Moser and Douglas MacLeod (eds), *Immersed in Technology: Art and Virtual Environments* (Cambridge, MA. MIT Press, 1996), p. 203.

3. Götz Grossklaus, 'Medium und Zeit. Zum Verschwinden des zeitlichen Intervalls', in Sven Drühl and Birgit Richard (eds), *Dauer— Simultaneität—Echtzeit*, (Kunstforum International, Bd 151: Ruppichteroth, 2000), p. 210.

4. Jonah Brucker-Cohen, 'Report from ISEA (International Symposium on Electronic Art) 2002', taken from 'NOEMA' website: http://www.noemalab.com/sections/ideas/ideas_articles/pdf/brucker_cohen_isea.pdf, Date accessed 7 August 2003.

5. For further information on these earlier works in relation to a discussion about character, role-play and mimesis, see Andrea Zapp, 'net.drama:// myth/mimesis/mind_mapping', in Martin Rieser and Andrea Zapp (eds), *New Screen Media: Cinema/Art/Narrative*, (London: BFI, 2002), pp. 77–89.

6. The premiere took place in October 2002 at the Chapman Gallery in Salford, Manchester, and was linked to the Cornerhouse, Manchester, and the Folly Gallery, Lancaster. It was supported by the Leverhulme Trust London, the Arts Council England/North West, and the University of Salford.

7. Peter Weibel, 'Narrated Theory: Multiple Projection and Multiple Narration (Past and Future)', in Rieser and Zapp (eds), *New Screen Media* p. 49.

8. Noted in Thomas J. Campanella, 'Eden by Wire: Webcameras and the Telepresent Landscape', in Ken Goldberg (ed.), *The Robot in the Garden: Telerobotics and Telepistemology in the Age of the Internet*, (Cambridge, MA: MIT Press, 2001), p. 27.

9. Jacob Lillemose, June 2004, www.vaerk.dk. The model house project was commissioned for the internet art show 'VAERK 04', which took place in the Knabstrup Kulturfabrik, Denmark, June to September 2004.

10. Michel Foucault, *Dits et Ecrits: Selections, Vol. 1* (New York: New Press, 1997). Quoted in Lev Manovich, 'Spatial Computerisation and Film Language', in Rieser and Zapp (eds), *New Screen Media* p. 72.

11. Lev Manovich, 'To Lie and to Act: Potemkin's Villages, Cinema and Telepresence', in Goldberg (ed.), *The Robot in the Garden*, p. 175.

12. Slavoj Žižek, 'Die Virtualisierung des Herrn', in ed. Brigitte Felderer (ed.), *Wunschmaschine Welterfindung. Eine Geschichte der Technikvisionen seit dem*

18 Jahrhundert (Wien and New York: Springer Verlag, 1996), pp. 109–10. Author's translation.

13. Söke Dinkla, 'The Art of Narrative—Towards the Floating Work of Art', in Rieser and Zapp (eds), *New Screen Media*, pp. 37–38.

14. Quoted in Žižek, 'Die Virtualisierung des Herrn', p. 110. Author's translation.

Chapter 13: The Lady of Shalott: Optical Elegy

1. References are to the revised (1842) version of Tennyson's poem. See Christopher Ricks, *The Poems of Tennyson*, 2nd edn., 3 vols (London: Longman, 1987).

2. *The Pictures: An Illustrated Magazine of Fiction for Lovers of Moving Pictures*, 1 (21 October 1911), p. 1. Thanks to Andrew Shail for this reference.

3. An excellent account of the early history of the camera obscura and magic lantern and their subsequent role as optical toys is given in *A History of Pre-Cinema*, ed. Stephen Herbert, 3 vols (London and New York: Routledge, 2000), vol. 1. See also, for a penetrating account of the cultural meaning of the magic lantern, Simon During, *Modern Enchantments: The Cultural Power of Secular Magic* (Cambridge, MA., and London: Harvard University Press, 2002), pp. 283–85.

4. Martin Meisel, *Realisations* (Princeton: Princeton University Press, 1983), pp. 27, 61.

5. Mary Somerville (whose work Tennyson knew) exemplifies this referential structure among innumerable examples, offering the scientific experiment in two forms, *On the Connexion of the Physical Sciences* (1834), 9th edn (London: John Murray, 1858), p. 162.

6. Arthur Hallam, 'On Some of the Characteristics of Modern Poetry', *Englishman's Magazine*, 1 (August 1831), pp. 616–28. See Isobel Armstrong, *Victorian Scrutinies* (London: Athlone Press, 1972), p. 87.

7. Arthur Hallam, 'Essay on the Philosophical Writings of Cicero', in T.H.Vail Motter (ed.), *The Writings of Arthur Hallam* (New York: Modern Language Association of America, 1943) pp.142–81 (p. 167).

8. Immanuel Kant, 'What does it mean to orient oneself in thinking?', in *The Cambridge Edition of the Works of Immanuel Kant. Religion and Rational Theology*, trans. and ed. Allen Wood and George di Giovanni (Cambridge: Cambridge University Press, 1996), pp.1–18.

9. Hermann von Helmholtz, 'The Recent Progress of the Theory of Vision', in David Cahan (ed.), *Science and Culture: Popular and Philosophical Essays* (Chicago: University of Chicago Press, 1995) pp. 127–203 (p. 163).

10. Lindsay Smith, *Victorian Photography, Painting and Poetry: The Enigma of*

Visibility in Ruskin, Morris and the Pre-Raphaelites (Cambridge: Cambridge University Press, 1995), pp. 198–202.

11. John Herschel, 'Light', *Encyclopedia Metropolitana* (London, 1845) vol. 9, pp. 341–586 (p. 394). Herschel's influential entry was composed in 1827 and reprinted in several reissues of the *Encyclopedia*. Paragraphs 335–7 state that 'the "perfect polish" of the looking-glass ensures that the image appears "like a real object behind the reflector".'

12. John Tyndall, *Notes on a Course of Nine Lectures on Light*, 2nd edn (London: Longmans, Green, and Co., 1870), p. 22.

13. For this reading of exchange, see Georg Simmel, *The Philosophy of Money*, second enlarged edition (1907), trans. Tom Bottomore and David Frisby (London: Routledge, 1990), pp. 67–94.

14. Popular dissemination of optical information on colour is represented by F. Marion's *The Wonders of Optics*, trans. Charles W. Quin (New York: Charles Scribner and Co., 1870). The chapter on colour is particularly preoccupied with red and red blindness (pp. 44–53). See also pp. 84–106, which sum up generally known accounts of colour in the century. See David Brewster, *A Treatise on Optics* (1831) (Philadelphia: Blanchard and Lea, 1854), pp. 254–61, for stress on red. Goethe, of course, repudiated Newton's account of colour, but was intensely interested in after-images.

15. See David Brewster, *The Stereoscope. Its History, Theory and Construction, With its Application to the Fine and Useful Arts* (London: John Murray, 1856).

16. Helmholtz, 'The Recent Progress' p. 182.

17. Linda Colley, *Britons: Forging the Nation 1707–1837* (New Haven: Yale University Press, 1992), p. 349.

18. Helmholtz in 'The Recent Progress of the Theory of Vision' both summed up and revised existing knowledge of optics. He took the accepted principles and reframed them by formulating them in terms of the interpretation of signs. For instance, his reading of colour presupposes a qualitative difference in the sensations of light (p. 152): we do not see unmediated red but register through the nerves different wave-lengths of light that we learn to interpret as red. He accepted the objective existence of Newton's spectrum but believed that we understood it indirectly. Thus he stands halfway between objective accounts of colour such as we find in Brewster and subjective (anti-Newtonian) accounts such as we find in Schopenhauer. See Arthur Schopenhauer, *On Vision and Colours*, trans. E.F.J. Payne, ed. David E. Cartwright (Oxford and Berg Publishers Inc., 1994).

19. Helmholtz, 'The Recent Progress' p. 192.

20. Ibid., p. 195.

21. Ibid., p. 188.

22. Ibid.

23. Brewster, *Optics*, p. 263. This is a condensed account of the kaleidoscope from earlier writings: see *A Treatise on New Philosophical Instruments* (Edinburgh: W. Blackwood; London: John Murray, 1813).

24. Brewster, *Optics*, p. 262.

25. See Helmholtz, 'The Recent Progress' p. 164: Marion, *The Wonder of Optics* p. 40.

26. On the dissolving view see 'Dissolving Views', *The Mirror of Literature, Amusement, and Instruction*, 1 (12 February 1842), p. 98. 'The original picture fades insensibly from the sight, and another as stealthily takes its place.' Reprinted in Herbert *A History of Pre-Cinema*, vol. 2, p. 234. This effect was created in a number of ways but commonly by two lanterns, one of whose lights was dimmed as the other produced the second superimposed image.

27. Kevin Salatino, *Incendiary Art: The Representation of Fireworks in Early Modern Europe* (Los Angeles: Getty Research Institute for the History of Art and the Humanities, 1997), pp. 54–86.

28. See Bent Sorenson, 'Sir William Hamilton's Vesuvian Apparatus', *Apollo*, 159 (May 2004), pp. 50–57.

29. Vesuvius was active from 1750 to 1820. Goethe (*Italian Journey, 1786–1788*) and Dickens (*Pictures from Italy*, 1846), took considerable risks to climb to the Vesuvius crater. An indicator of the fascination with Vesuvius is the appearance of Vesuvius lantern slides three years in succession (1829–31) in Negretti and Zambra's slide catalogue for *c.*1890. No other scene appears so frequently.

30. Somerville, *On the Connexion of the Physical Sciences* pp. 232–37.

31. Daniel Paul Schreber, *Memoirs of My Nervous Illness*, ed. and trans. Ida Macalpine and Richard A. Hunter (London: W. Dawson, 1955).

32. Sigmund Freud, *Standard Edition of the Complete Psychological Works*, trans. James Strachey and Anna Freud (London: Hogarth Press and the Institute of Psychoanalysis, 1958) vol. 12, p. 66.

Chapter 14: Photographed Tableaux and Motion-Picture Aesthetics: Alexander Black's Picture Plays

1. Terry Ramsaye, *A Million and One Nights: A History of the Motion Picture* (New York: Simon and Schuster, 1926), pp. 91–103.

2. For a contemporary discussion of this likeness see Burnes Saint Patrick Hollyman, 'Alexander Black's Picture Plays, 1893-1894,' in John L. Fell (ed.), *Film before Griffith* (Berkeley: University of California Press, 1983), pp. 236–43.

3. The last year of travelling exhibition in Black's ledger at the New York Public Library is 1904. A programme exists for another picture play

entitled *Zalia*, but I have found no record of when and where it was performed.

4. See Mary Ann Doane, *The Emergence of Cinematic Time: Modernity, Contingency, the Archive* (Cambridge, MA: Harvard University Press, 2002).

5. Black's work was often compared to such famous illustrated poems as 'Little Jim'. See 'On Black's Picture Plays', *Photogram*, 3:36 (1896), pp. 287–88. His audiences would have known the life model sets, in which actors were posed for serial photographs by companies like Bamforth in the UK and Scott and Van Altena in the US. These practices became particularly viable in the form of the illustrated song, which developed alongside the picture plays and became a staple of nickelodeon shows. Black was occasionally compared to illustrated song pioneer Charles K. Harris. Black even claimed credit for the invention of the illustrated song. See 'An Interview with Alexander Black', *Kalamazoo Telegraph* (1901), Undated clipping, Billy Rose Theatre Collection, New York Public Library. While 'invention' is too strongly put, 'influence' is not. Edward van Altena saw Black's New York shows before he became one of the largest producers of illustrated songs. In a private letter written in 1959 van Altena claims to remember two of Black's 1890s performances well; from the private Marnan Collection of Illustrated Song Slides and Sheet Music, Minneapolis. Not entirely comfortable with his works being grouped with these popular amusements, Black tried to align it with the activities of artistic and literary circles. There were others at this time who, like Black, had careers in loftier circles and sought these kinds of audiences. The most notable of these was probably Hubert von Herkomer, whose staged pictorial music shows outside London helped him make the transition from painting to film making. See Ian Christie, 'Before the Avant Gardes: Artists and Cinema, 1910–14,' in Leonardo Quaresima and Laura Vichi (eds), *The Tenth Muse* (Udine: Forum, 2001), p. 374.

6. Alexander Black, 'Photography in Fiction: "Miss Jerry," the First Picture Play', *Scribner's Magazine*, 18:3 (1895), p. 348.

7. I examine the history of Black's early photography and his relationship with Eadweard Muybridge and Thomas Eakins in Kaveh Askari, 'From "the Horse in Motion" to "Man in Motion": Alexander Black's Detective Lectures', *Early Popular Visual Culture*, 3:1 (May 2005), pp. 59–76.

8. 'Sort of Big Kinetoscope', *Boston Herald*, undated clipping (1896?) from Alexander Black Clippings File, St Lawrence University Library Special Collections.

9. Box I, Slides 17–20, Alexander Black Collection, Princeton University Special Collections.

10. Script from the Alexander Black Collection, New York Public Library Rare Books and Manuscripts.

11. This is slide-change number 102 in the script held at the Alexander Black Collection, St Lawrence University Special Collections.

12. Alexander Black, *Time and Chance: Adventures with People and Print* (New York: Farrar & Rinehart Inc., 1937), p. 137.

13. Thomas Craddock Hepworth, *The Book of the Lantern* (London: Hazell, Watson, and Viney, 1899), p. 282.

14. Black, *Time and Chance*, p. 129.

15. Slides 113–15 in Alexander Black Collection, Princeton University Special Collections.

16. See Lewis Wright, *Optical Projection* (New York: Longmans, Green, and Co., 1891), pp. 143–44.

17. Alexander Black, 'How to Give a Picture Play', *Ladies Home Journal*, 15:11 (1898).

18. Alexander Black, *A Capital Courtship* (New York: Scribner, 1897). Illustration facing p. 24.

19. Programme from the Billy Rose Theatre Collection of the New York Public Library.

20. 'Sort of Big Kinetoscope,' *Boston Herald*. Undated clipping from Alexander Black Clippings File, St Lawrence University Library Special Collections.

21. Charles Musser and Carol Nelson, *High-Class Moving Pictures: Lyman H. Howe and the Forgotten Era of Traveling Exhibition, 1880–1920* (Princeton: Princeton University Press, 1991), p. 166.

22. Alexander Black, 'The Camera and the Comedy', *Scribner's Magazine*, 20 (1896) pp. 606–10 (p. 607).

23. Andre Gaudreault, 'The Diversity of Cinematographic Connections in the Intermedial Context of the Turn of the 20th Century', in Simon Popple and Vanessa Toulmin (eds), *Visual Delights: Essays on the Popular and Projected Image in the 19th Century* (Trowbridge: Flicks Books, 2000), pp. 8–15.

24. 'An Interview with Alexander Black', *Kalamazoo Telegraph* (1901).

25. 'Making the First Picture Play', *Harper's Weekly*, 38 (1894), p. 988.

26. Victor Oscar Freeburg, *Pictorial Beauty on the Screen* (New York: Macmillan, 1923), p. 36.

27. Christine Gledhill, 'Introduction', *Nineteenth-Century Theatre*, 25:2 (1997), pp. 85–91.

28. For a graphic comparison to the film strip see Black, 'The Camera and the Comedy'. The illustrations are presented in a single vertical row on each page to invite comparison to celluloid.

29. Alexander Black File, Billy Rose Theatre Collection, New York Public Library, clipping from *The Picture Play Weekly*, 2 October 1915, pp. 25–28 (my italics).

30. Letter from Zukor to Black dated 8 October 1919. Black family collection.

Chapter 15: DVDs, Video Games and the Cinema of Interactions

1. Brian McKernan, untitled, *Digital Cinema Magazine* http://www. uemedia.com/CPC/digitalcinemamag/index.shtml; accessed 16 May 2002.
2. Jon Healey and P.J. Huffstutter, 'Digitally Mastered: "Star Wars" breaks new ground in fully digital movie making', *LA Times*, 11 May 2002, http://www.latimes.com/entertainment/movies/la-051102digital.story.
3. Richard Grusin, 'Remediation in the Late Age of Early Cinema', in André Gaudreault, Catherine Russell and Pierre Véronneau (eds), *Early Cinema: Technology and Apparatus*, (Montreal: Payot Lausanne, 2004), pp. 343–60.
4. See, for example, Tom Gunning, 'An Aesthetic of Astonishment', Linda Williams (ed.), *Viewing Positions: Ways of Seeing Film* (New Brunswick, NJ: Rutgers University Press, 1995), pp. 114–33.
5. William Gibson, *Neuromancer* (New York: ACE/Berkley Publishing Group, 1984).
6. Miriam Hansen, 'Early Cinema, Late Cinema: Transformations of the Public Sphere', in Williams (ed.), *Viewing Positions*, p. 139.
7. Ibid., pp. 138–9.
8. For a fuller discussion of the concept of premediation, see Richard Grusin, 'Premediation', *Criticism*, 46:1 (Winter 2004), pp. 17–39.
9. Peter Greenaway, Interviewed at Cannes, 'Interview/Photo Call: The Tulse Luper Suitcases—Part 1. The Moab Story', http://www. festival-cannes.com/films/fiche_film.php?langue=6002 &partie=video&id_film=4086413&cmedia=4912; accessed 20 June 2005; 'Press Conference: The Tulse Luper Suitcases—Part 1. The Moab Story', http://www.festival-cannes.com/films/fiche_film.php?langue=6002& partie=video&id_film=4086413&cmedia=4914; accessed 20 June 2005.
10. Greenaway, 'Interview'.
11. Ibid.

Chapter 16: From 'Nip/Tuck' to Cut/Paste: Remediating Cosmetic Surgery

1. Henry Jenkins, 'Transmedia Storytelling', in *Technology Review*, 15 January 2003, http://www.technologyreview.com/articles/03/01/wo_jenkins011503. asp?p=1. Accessed 6 November 2005.
2. Lois N. Magner, 'The Art and Science of Surgery', in Lois N. Magner, *A History of Medicine* (New York and Basel: Marcel Dekker, Inc., 1992), pp. 279–94; Elizabeth Haiken, *Venus Envy: A History of Cosmetic Surgery* (Baltimore: Johns Hopkins University Press, 1997), p. 6.

3. Lisa Cartwright, *Screening the Body: Tracing Medicine's Visual Culture* (Minneapolis: University of Minnesota Press, 1995), p. xi.
4. Quote from Dr. Robert Kotler, http://www.robertkotlermd.com. Accessed 2 June 2005.
5. Ibid.
6. Mary Anne Doane, 'The Clinical Eye: Medical Discourses in the "Woman's Film" of the 1940s', in Susan Rubin Suleiman (ed.), *The Female Body in Western Culture* (Cambridge, MA, and London: Harvard University Press, 1986), pp. 152–74.
7. Kathryn Pauly Morgan, 'Women and the Knife: Cosmetic Surgery and the Colonization of Women's Bodies', *Hypatia*, 6:3 (Fall 1991), pp. 38, 41.
8. Anne Balsamo, *Technologies of the Gendered Body: Reading Cyborg Women* (Durham, NC, and London: Duke University Press, 1996), p. 58.
9. Ibid., p. 78.
10. Morgan, 'Women and the Knife', p. 46.
11. Jay David Bolter and Richard Grusin, *Remediation: Understanding New Media* (Cambridge, MA: MIT Press, 2000), p. 239.
12. Ibid., p. 5.
13. Sander L. Gilman, *Creating Beauty to Cure the Soul* (Durham, NC, and London: Duke University Press, 1998), p. 4.
14. Morgan, 'Women and the Knife', p. 28.
15. 'F/X "Nip/Tuck" Misrepresents the Specialty of Plastic Surgery', *ASPS* website, http://www.plasticsurgery.org, published 14 July 2003. Accessed 2 April 2005.
16. 'American Society for Aesthetic Plastic Surgery Gives Thumbs Down to "Nip/Tuck" Golden Globe Nomination', *ASAPS* website, http://www.surgery.org, published 18 December 2003. Accessed 2 April 2005.
17. For more information, see Haiken, *Venus Envy*, and Gilman, *Creating Beauty*.
18. Bolter and Grusin, *Remediation*, pp. 43–44.
19. *Nip/Tuck* website, http://www.fxnetworks.com/shows/originals/niptuck _s2/main.html.
20. Ibid.
21. Michel Foucault, *The Birth of the Clinic* (London: Routledge, 1989), pp. 165–66.
22. Balsamo, *Technologies of the Gendered Body*, pp. 57–58.
23. Haiken, *Venus Envy*, p. 12.
24. '2003 cosmetic surgery gender distribution (male)'; '2003 cosmetic surgery gender distribution (female)'; '2003 Quick Facts: Cosmetic and Reconstructive Plastic Surgery', *ASPS* website, www.plasticsurgery.org, accessed 1 March 2005.
25. Cartwright, *Screening the Body*, p. 3.

Index